Trans Technologies

Trans Technologies

Oliver L. Haimson

The MIT Press
Cambridge, Massachusetts
London, England

The MIT Press
Massachusetts Institute of Technology
77 Massachusetts Avenue, Cambridge, MA 02139
mitpress.mit.edu

The MIT Press would like to thank the anonymous peer reviewers who provided comments on drafts of this book. The generous work of academic experts is essential for establishing the authority and quality of our publications. We acknowledge with gratitude the contributions of these otherwise uncredited readers.

This book was set in Stone Serif and Stone Sans by Westchester Publishing Services. Printed and bound in the United States of America.

Library of Congress Cataloging-in-Publication Data

Names: Haimson, Oliver L., author.
Title: Trans technologies / Oliver L. Haimson.
Description: Cambridge, Massachusetts : The MIT Press, [2025] | Includes
    bibliographical references and index.
Identifiers: LCCN 2024022814 (print) | LCCN 2024022815 (ebook) |
    ISBN 9780262551861 (paperback) | ISBN 9780262382564 (epub) |
    ISBN 9780262382571 (epub)
Subjects: LCSH: Transgender people.
Classification: LCC HQ77.9 .H34 2025 (print) | LCC HQ77.9 (ebook) |
    DDC 306.76/8—dc23/eng/20240730
LC record available at https://lccn.loc.gov/2024022814
LC ebook record available at https://lccn.loc.gov/2024022815

10 9 8 7 6 5 4 3 2 1

EU product safety and compliance information contact is: mitp-eu-gpsr@mit.edu

For the independent, community-based, and nonprofit bookstores, and especially for Redbud Books, which seems to be carrying out the dream we started with Boxcar Books.

Contents

Key Terms

Trans technology (practical definition): Technology that addresses the unique needs and challenges faced by trans people and communities

Trans technology (theoretical definition): Technology that embraces change and/or transition, fosters the creation of new trans worlds, and opens up new possibilities for what technology means and what it can do

Technological trans care: Trans people (and sometimes cisgender allies) creating innovative technological mechanisms to help address the needs and challenges that they and their communities face

Technological separatism: An approach in which marginalized groups create new technologies specifically for that group

Technological inclusionism: An approach in which marginalized groups attempt to fit into, and potentially improve, existing technological systems

Trans capitalism: The strategic commodification and monetization of trans identities, such as through targeted marketing and the development of profit-driven or investment-backed trans technologies

Trans technology studies: An academic subfield at the intersection of trans studies and human-computer interaction which examines both the material and theoretical implications of trans people's relationships with technology, with a focus on building theory *and* documenting and improving trans people's lives

Introduction

Solace, a gender transition resource app created in 2019[1] by a transgender[2] woman in the US, is an example of what in this book I call a "trans technology"—a technology (a tool that extends the boundaries of what people can do) that helps address some of the needs or challenges faced by trans people and communities. Solace (see figure I.1) enables its users to create a gender transition to-do list and then provides resources to accomplish those goals. The app gained substantial attention and notoriety when its leadership announced in 2021 that they had received venture capital funding. Solace's influx of funding shifted the app to a for-profit model, monetizing the user base via premium fees and a subtle form of advertising that prioritized information from strategic partners. This new version of the app stood in stark contrast to the realities faced by many trans people, who struggle to access basic resources like housing and health care.[3] The app also stood in contrast to trans people's historically strong sense of community and reliance on mutual aid: Solace encourages its users to transition in isolation, for it

---

1. Solace seems to have been quietly sunsetted by its creator as I was finalizing this manuscript in 2024. Although it is still available in the Apple and Google app stores at the time of this writing, Solace's website and social media presence have disappeared, and the app was last updated in 2022.

2. In this book, by "transgender" I mean anyone whose current gender is different than their gender assigned at birth. This definition explicitly includes nonbinary trans people. I use "trans" as an abbreviation for transgender from here forward. I note that language changes rapidly, especially that related to gender, and many of the terms used in this book will seem outdated to readers in the future.

3. For instance, 30 percent of US trans people have been homeless, and roughly one-fourth refrain from seeing a health care provider because of the cost or fear of mistreatment (James et al. 2024); these numbers are typically higher for trans people of color (James et al. 2016).

Figure I.1
"Made for the individual." Solace gender transition and resource app. Screenshot from the Apple App Store by the author, 2023.

does not include social or community elements.[4] Yet at its peak Solace had tens of thousands of users, and it was clearly important for a large group of trans people—perhaps isolated people who had not yet made their transition public or who had no local trans community.

Solace's interface and features reflect the values and experiences of its creator—a college-educated white trans woman with technical skills who views gender transition as an individual, rather than community-based, process. On the one hand, the fact that Solace's founder created and gathered funding for an app that allowed many others to mirror her own solitary transition experience can be seen as empowering. But at the same time, the design may not fully represent the needs and desires of the larger trans population, particularly trans people of color, those facing economic precarity, and others whose identities sit at the intersection of multiple forms of marginalization. I begin here with Solace not because it is a trans technology success story or a representative exemplar of trans technology. In fact, Solace is quite different from most trans technologies, in both its funding model and its individualist orientation. But it is representative of trans technologies in one way: Solace

---

4. When I refer to mutual aid, I use Dean Spade's (2020) definition: "collective coordination to meet each other's needs, usually from an awareness that the systems we have in place are not going to meet them."

highlights the complexities of technology designed specifically *for*—but not always *by* or *with*—trans people. Solace is the tip of the iceberg of trans technology—a visible part of the much larger world of technologies designed for, adapted to, or used by trans communities to improve their lives. In this book, I explore the world of trans technologies.

I come to the world of trans technology not as an outsider, but as someone who could have benefited greatly from technological support for my own gender transition. When I first decided to get top surgery in 2010, I had no idea how to find information and resources.[5] I specifically wanted to see photos of post-op patients from different surgeons to help me decide which surgeon to go to. I did Internet searches for surgeons and came across the name of a local surgeon who supposedly had experience conducting top surgery. However, I could not find any post-op photos of the chests of people he had operated on, and when I asked him for examples, he did not have any to share. I tried to register for Transbucket, an online trans surgery photo-sharing site, so I could look at post-op photos of trans people who had gone to various surgeons. But my Transbucket account was not approved. Perhaps this was because I was not sure I was trans at the time, I had not yet changed my name, and I had not yet started hormones. I knew that the resource—that trans technology—was there, but I could not access it.

Instead, I asked around to a few friends in the local trans and queer community. One friend brushed me off; he had little to say except "you should do research, and ask people in the community for advice." He did not seem to realize that that was exactly what I was trying to do with him—*he* was the person in the community I was asking for advice. I saw his post-op chest when, as the temporary drummer for our band, he took his shirt off at practice and at our first show. He had had a procedure that involved no scars, a procedure not available to me given my body type. Another friend had had double incision surgery and offered to show me their scars. After a gathering at my house, we went up to my bedroom and they awkwardly removed their shirt to show the visible pink scars on their pale chest, scars that I realized I would be happy to one day have.

Both of these friends had gone to the same surgeon—one of the well-known ones on the East Coast—and both recommended her, but she was

---

5. "Top surgery" refers to a double mastectomy, a chest-masculinization procedure that many trans men and transmasculine and nonbinary people undergo.

expensive and not local to me. I did not know then just how bad a mistake it would be to go to a lesser-known surgeon who shared no post-op photographs of his work.[6] My chest did not end up looking like either of my friends', nor any of the photos that I eventually saw online when I finally got access to Transbucket with my new name and email address. My surgeon, it turns out, did not have the expertise he claimed. He removed tissue haphazardly and stitched me up carelessly. Five years later, after doing exhaustive research online using sites like Transbucket and Facebook groups, I went to one of the big-name top surgeons near the ocean to get my revision. I was still paying off the loans I had taken out for the first surgery.

When I got my first trans surgery, I was already part of a trans and queer community, but it was not enough. I could not find the information I so desperately needed just by asking the two post-op people I happened to know. I needed a much larger pool of information and experiences—resources that are most developed and most accessible online, where many people use digital technology to join together and share resources. In other words, I needed both technology and community. I posit that trans technologies—like online trans support and information communities—are most powerful when they join technology and community together.

In 2010 and 2011, I was part of a "transition cohort." Here, I mean "transition" in two senses: we were a group of people transitioning gender, but also, the broader world was in a moment of social and technological transition. At this time, the Internet was mature and there was a (limited) set of online trans resources available, but the close-knit offline support groups that had existed years earlier were less available than they had been, and the wide range of digital trans technologies that exist today had not yet emerged. During the research I conducted for this book, after I had interviewed over fifty creators of trans technology, it struck me that the vast majority of the trans technologies I discuss in this book did not exist when I was transitioning. This absence made a material impact on me—I was affected physically, emotionally, and financially by this technological lack when I settled for a shoddy surgeon because I did not have the tools or resources to make an informed decision. Lack of access to trans

---

6. The number and geographic spread of surgeons who perform gender-affirming procedures have greatly improved over time, so trans patients are now more likely to find a competent surgeon in their area. Yet many other care barriers remain.

technologies must have also hindered many others who transitioned before me and along similar timelines.

How would things have been different if I had had access to these forms of technology-mediated support? A decade after my first top surgery, Mod Club was launched—a website that offers surgery photos for multiple different surgeons and an online community full of people like me. If I had transitioned nine years later, I could have joined Trans Peer Network, a trans online community on Discord, and discussed my surgery decisions with other people in similar situations. When I began my transition, Trans Lifeline, the peer support hotline, would not be founded for several more years. Transition apps like TRACE would not be created until over a decade later. There were no online maps of trans-inclusive health care providers. I could not track my hormone dosages via apps like ShotTraX, launched eight years later. Mutual aid networks did not yet exist in the way they do today, with technology (particularly social media) extending people's reach far beyond their local in-person networks. Instead, I took out personal loans and extra student loans to pay for my surgery (this was possible for me as a relatively privileged person, but the loans still took over ten years to pay back; many trans people have far less access to institutional credit). The only tool that I had was Google search—and that was how I found the surgeon who botched my first top surgery. The trans technologies I discuss in this book are actively helping many trans people, and I wish they had been available to me early in my transition and to others who needed them before they existed.

This examination of the world of trans technology shows what happens when technological innovation seeks to redress a social problem—society's failure to provide for, or its active mistreatment of, a marginalized group. Typically, new technologies are created to solve problems that their creators see in the world. A can opener responds to the need to get to food that is sealed in cans, and Google Maps was created to help people find their way in unfamiliar settings. Most technology responds to fairly mundane problems like these—problems that are rarely critically related to their creators' identities and life chances. With trans technology, though, technological innovations are frequently created in direct response to the oppressive conditions trans people face in the social, legal, and medical spheres: transphobia, violence, antitrans legislation, difficulty identifying supportive resources, and lack of access to medical care. Because these common trans experiences are not ones that many mainstream technology developers share, trans people often must create our own technologies to meet our needs. Trans-made and trans-centered technologies and the design processes that brought them to life can illuminate what is needed for truly meaningful technological inclusion. What we learn from studying the world of trans technologies can inform inclusive design for other marginalized individuals and communities in the broader world of technology design.

This book looks at trans technologies: apps, games, health resources, supplies, art, and other types of technology designed or adapted to help address some of the challenges transgender people face in the world and to create spaces for trans communities and individuals. My original interest was in digital technologies like those I mentioned above (Transbucket, TRACE, ShotTraX). However, when I asked creators of trans technologies (often, but not always, trans people themselves) what they would classify as trans technologies, they offered answers that went beyond apps and digital tools, and sometimes these answers fit uneasily into the category of technology as I had conceived of it. Other people I spoke to resisted or were ambivalent about the very idea of a trans technology and were reluctant to classify their creations under that heading. This book attempts to do justice to the wide range of ideas and experiences of technology that interviewees shared with me. *Trans Technologies* seeks to illuminate the broad landscape of trans technology, the design processes that produced the trans technologies in this book, and the ways trans people rely on technology and community to meet their most basic needs and challenges. The stories I report here about how and why trans technologies were created, in often-precarious conditions and in an increasingly antitrans political moment, show why trans technology matters.

What Is Technology? What Is Trans Technology?

While I was recruiting trans tech creators to interview for this research, I found myself confronted with a definitional question: What is (and is not) "technology"? In conceiving this project, I had originally thought mostly about apps and websites—digital technologies. But things like prostheses, supplies, and medical interventions are incredibly important technologies for trans people. Where should I draw the line? I struggled to find or formulate a clear definition of technology for quite a while. It was not until my interview with trans studies founder and digital performance artist Allucquére Rosanne "Sandy" Stone that I heard a definition that reflected the ways

I had been thinking of and bounding the category of technology. During our interview, Stone casually stated the simple, elegant definition of technology that I had been searching for: *"Technology is anything that extends your agency."* Stone's definition draws from media scholar Marshall McLuhan's (1964) definition of technology as "any extension of ourselves." To me, Stone's wording is a particularly useful way of thinking about technology in relation to transness, because trans people and communities need and seek out ways to extend their agency to address the challenges that they face in everyday life. For example, a transition app extends a trans person's agency by enabling them to track aspects of themselves (moods, physical changes, etc.) that help them better understand their changing body and self; a virtual reality (VR) system provides realistic access to trans experiences and stories, giving a questioning trans person the agency to explore new aspects of their identity.

Transness and technology are deeply interconnected (Shapiro 2015). The trans experience is, by definition, technologically mediated: whether one's trans experience involves medical technologies like hormones and surgeries (Gill-Peterson 2014), appearance-changing technologies like makeup and clothing, or digital technologies like transition apps that record gender changes, trans experiences always in some way involve using tools to extend one's agency. In our conversation, trans media scholar Cáel Keegan described technologies as "ways of extending the capacity of the human body" and stated that "transness is already constantly demonstrating that. What we think the human body is capable of, and what it's actually capable of, are two different things." As Keegan makes clear, gender transition necessarily involves extending one's agency beyond biological and social barriers using technology.

If we define technology as an extension of the self and the self's agency, what then, is *trans* technology? Is it any technology a trans person uses? Under Stone's definition, almost any tool could be considered a technology, including a can opener or Google Maps. Are these trans technologies because trans people use them to open cans or navigate new places? Not by either of my definitions of trans technology. I offer two interlinked definitions that, taken together, define trans technology.[7] First, and most pragmatically, *trans technologies are technologies built or adapted to address the specific concerns and*

---

7. These definitions are addressed in detail in chapter 1.

needs of trans people and communities. By this definition, a can opener and
Google Maps are not trans technologies, because while trans people do use
can openers and Google Maps, these tools are not specially adapted to the
unique needs and challenges of the trans community.[8] Second, and more
theoretically, *trans technologies are technologies that embody or support themes
or characteristics of transness*—such as mutability, change, crossing, and new
worlds and possibilities. The plasticity and volatility at the heart of transness as a category and concept inform and shape the categorical boundaries
of trans technology. This second definition is capacious; it is by this definition that the games and art discussed in this book fall under the umbrella of
trans technology. By this definition, too, can openers and Google Maps are
not trans technologies, for they do not push the boundaries of what technology is or can do, or focus on change, or enable people to explore their identities in new ways.

Why two definitions of trans technology? Stone's further discussion of
her definition of technology points toward this complexity and duality: "I'm
inclined to say that technology, at this point in our evolution as a culture,
as a species: technology is whatever you say it is. You can talk about any discourse as a technology, if you look at it right. So, in a way that makes things
simpler—and of course, in a way it makes them horribly complex, but I'll
take the simpler." Ultimately, I decided who to interview for this research
and what technologies to include in the book, and so in one way, in this
book, technology is what I say it is. But my view of technology evolved and
shifted as I talked with each trans tech creator, and my definitions of trans
technology were ultimately impacted by each of the people I interviewed. So
perhaps in the end, we might say that trans technology is whatever a trans
person using or creating it says it is—whatever technology addresses their
unique trans needs and challenges, aligns with their changing and complex
identity and body, and to some extent just *feels trans* to them.

---

8. When I write about the "trans community," I do not mean to imply that there is
only one trans community. In reality, there are many different trans communities both
online and in the physical world that coalesce based on identities, locations, interests,
and other factors and do not have strict boundaries. Further, community itself if a fuzzy
concept that is not easily delineated (Bruckman 2022; Plett 2023). While referring to the
trans "population" might be more precise, I keep the "community" language because
I learned in this research how community is vitally important to trans technology creation and use.

Trans Technology Design: Care, Ambivalence, and Marginalization

This work is grounded in in-depth interviews with creators of more than a hundred trans technologies (listed in Appendix A, along with the estimated time ranges each was active), conducted in 2021 and 2022, aimed at exploring the current and past landscape of trans technologies. I examined how these technologies were envisioned and designed, looked for areas for future innovation, and considered what it means for a technology to be a trans technology by asking interviewees what trans technology means to them. Because I interviewed *creators* rather than *users* of trans technologies, this work primarily provides a backstage rather than a frontstage view. I complement this view by drawing from years of my own and others' research on trans experiences using technologies, along with my own trans technology use.

I call this group of interviewees "trans tech creators," but I do not mean that all of them were necessarily trans themselves—I mean that they were creators of trans technology. While 80 percent of the creators in my study were trans and/or nonbinary, some were cisgender.[9] It is also important to note that not all the people who I would categorize as trans tech creators would necessarily use this label for themselves. Indeed, some were ambivalent about the idea of trans technology, and a few were resistant to it. Most participants in this research explicitly wanted to be identified rather than anonymous, so I use their full names in this book, with their permission. Other participants requested that I use first names only, or pseudonyms, or wanted to remain anonymous. I report names based on participants' wishes in every case, except for a few instances where I anonymize to avoid publicly critiquing an individual.

This book is written for anyone who feels that they cannot fit into a box or that they inhabit multiple contrasting truths at the same time, whether related to identity, gender, scholarly discipline, or something else entirely. My primary (though not only) disciplinary audiences are human-computer interaction (HCI)/social computing and trans studies (both traditional and applied), with some chapters (e.g., chapters 2 and 4) and arguments likely speaking more to the former and some (e.g., chapters 1 and 5) to the latter. The book is also written for nonacademics interested in trans identity,

---

9. "Cisgender" (or "cis" for short) means that a person's current gender is the same as that assigned at birth.

technology, social justice, and the intersections between them. I hope that *Trans Technologies* will speak to each of these audiences.

I study technology to learn more about transness, and trans identity to understand more about technology. Most importantly, I examine the spots where technology and transness meet because that is where vital tensions arise surrounding what is created and by whom. One of my primary arguments in this book is about the tensions between community-oriented and more individualist trans technology creation. Trans technology design processes are often deeply personal and focus on the technology creator's needs and desires; they are often solutions to a problem that the creator faces. Trans technology design can therefore be empowering, because technology creators have agency to create the tools they themselves need to navigate the world. But when larger trans communities are not involved in design processes (as with Solace, the app I opened this introduction with), it can lead to overly individualistic design that speaks primarily to the needs of privileged trans people—that is, those who have the skills and resources to create technology, who are more likely to be white and well educated—rather than to the needs of the larger community of multiply marginalized trans people.

I hope that *Trans Technologies* can help to address this problem—that it can itself serve as a kind of trans technology, one that attunes trans tech creators to the needs of the larger community of trans people. The book thus articulates which trans needs and challenges are currently being addressed by technology and which ones still need to be addressed. By highlighting the areas where innovation is still needed, I hope that the book can help to prompt positive social change. Identifying how trans technologies sometimes better serve the more privileged members of the trans population helps us understand how to address these limitations. By describing and drawing from past and current innovations in the trans technology space, I show how we can innovate in the future in ways that can improve trans people's lives.

I also develop an understanding of what trans technology means and what the future of trans technologies might look like—a future that is, I hope, grounded in community articulations and experiences. As digital trans studies scholars like Cassius Adair, Alex Ahmed, micha cárdenas, Tee Chuanromanee, Avery Dame-Griff, Michael Ann DeVito, Whit Pow, K.J. Rawson, Sandy Stone, and others have demonstrated, trans technology is all around us, and looking closely at trans technology can help us learn what happens when technology design processes have deeply personal implications.

I argue here that trans technologies make visible and unite two threads: *care* and *ambivalence*. First, trans technology is a way to care for one's self and one's community—a form of what Hil Malatino (2020) calls *trans care*, the innovative and inventive ways that trans people show up for each other when society and family fail them. There is a long history of work on care more broadly. According to Bernice Fisher and Joan Tronto (2003), care involves "everything that we do to maintain, continue, and repair our 'world' so that we can live in it as well as possible," a world that includes "our bodies, our selves, and our environment, all of which we seek to interweave in a complex, life-sustaining web." Care as a concept inherently contains within itself a duality or ambivalence: it is at the same time both a "warm pleasant affection" and a type of gendered and racialized labor that disproportionately falls on women (Puig de la Bellacasa 2017), gender minorities (Aizura and Malatino 2019), and people of color (Duffy 2011). Care work is undervalued by capitalism, as it has historically been considered women's work and thus unproductive (Care Collective et al. 2020), but capitalism relies on it: capitalist systems typically disregard people's well-being, which manifests in their refusal to provide social services, and care work must fill in the gaps (Nadasen 2023; Piepzna-Samarasinha 2018). For instance, in trans contexts, lack of access to health care and surgical after-care leaves many trans people reliant on community members for care (Malatino 2020). Rather than just traditional care work—care that fills the gaps left by society—we need radical care, care that seeks to change the system that both demands and undervalues it: "alternative and transformative care practices emerging from and connected to social movement organizing" (Nadasen 2023). Trans care, then, must not only aim to meet immediate needs but also seek to change the systems that continually produce those needs while refusing to meet them.

In technological contexts, care takes many forms. For instance, personal information management technologies can be used both for self-care and as a way of caring for others by sharing one's information with them (Cushing 2023). Technological care can also manifest as what Cynthia Bennett and colleagues (2020) call the care work of access (the ways that people collaboratively complete technological tasks by attending to each other's access needs) or in the ways that participants in technology-focused spaces mutually care for each other as a form of community maintenance (Toombs, Bardzell, and Bardzell 2015). I show here another facet of technological care: technology creators can practice care for others by creating technology that helps users meet their needs. Care work, while potentially transformative, often becomes invisible, which leads to overburdening; it also risks disrupting the autonomy of care recipients (Toombs et al. 2018). These are considerations that trans technologies demonstrating trans care must take seriously.

What happens when we combine technological care with trans care? If, as María Puig de la Bellacasa (2011) argues, care involves a "commitment to neglected things," we can consider trans people, often neglected by mainstream society and social services, as deserving recipients of commitment and care. Trans technologies are one way of providing this care. Trans care, as a utopian care ethic, has a long history of being expressed both in physical spaces and via technological means (e.g., newsletters, listservs, transition crowdfunding) (Malatino 2020). As this book shows, the creation of trans technology can be a form of what I call *technological trans care*: trans people (and sometimes cisgender allies) creating innovative technological mechanisms to address the needs that they and their communities face in the world. Trans care draws from the disability justice concept of care webs, in which disabled people reciprocally care for each other (Piepzna-Samarasinha 2018). But trans technology's one-to-many distributive nature, while it may hinder reciprocity, enables technological trans care to reach wide audiences and extend far beyond its creator's immediate networks.

Trans technologies can thus be seen as "care structures," which Andre Cavalcante (2018) describes as "invisible" structures, "hidden in the design and functionality of technology," that are "rooted in human creativity and careful concern." As Cavalcante's definition indicates, care goes *into* making trans technology and then later comes *out of* the technology in its profound impacts on its users. Note here the dual structure of care; this duality is another form of ambivalence. As Puig de la Bellacasa (2011) contends, "Transforming things into matters of care is a way of relating to them, of inevitably becoming affected by them, and of modifying their potential to affect others." This is borne out in the relation of trans tech creators to their creations: creators are personally affected by their own technological care practices (as many trans technologies are created to address a need the creator has themselves experienced), and at the same time, they affect other users of their technologies via those technological care practices. Digital technologies can enable people to care for people they do not know and may never meet (Care Collective et al. 2020). What, then, is the creator's responsibility toward those others affected by the trans technologies they create? This is a difficult question, for care takes different forms in each context (Puig de la Bellacasa 2011). In many trans contexts, creating technology to address trans needs and challenges is an important way to care for others, as I show in the examples throughout this book. Yet trans technological care work is also necessarily limited (and limiting), for care requires going beyond technology design, and even beyond technology deployment; it also involves long-term sustainable technology maintenance, which requires substantial time and effort—things that trans tech creators often cannot provide.

Trans technology thus encodes and makes apparent the ambivalences that permeate trans communities and trans technology creation. The word "ambivalence" for me has a peculiarly trans quality to it. I distinctly remember learning the word when I was thirteen and how it so meaningfully captured my own feelings at the time about my gender and sexuality. I was drawn to the word partly because of the disconnect between what it seems to mean at first glance and what it actually means. On the surface, "ambivalence" seems to mean basically "uncertainty" or "unsureness." While uncertainty and unsureness can be part of ambivalence, I think of ambivalence as involving two or more distant (maybe opposite) poles between which a person wavers and that they contemplate simultaneously. The word embodies a sense that multiple opposing things can be true at the same time. For example, as a thirteen-year-old, I was female, yet I had a different (secret, future) gender too—one that I would not understand for many more years. I felt pulled back and forth between the two without really understanding what was happening. I did not feel in-between; I felt multiple. I think ambivalence captures multiplicity well—and the complexity of having two or more competing orientations simultaneously.

Ambivalence, as feminist theorist Clare Hemmings (2018) describes, enables us to embrace complexities and contradictions in research about gender, sexuality, and race: "In imagining that we know how to ameliorate gendered, racial, and sexual inequalities, or indeed what gender, race, and sexuality are, it is easy to miss the profound ambivalence about these terms and the inequalities or pleasures that cluster around them." In research about gender and technology there is never only one truth, and imagining a simple orientation toward these phenomena flattens people's experiences. Hemmings (2018) argues that ambivalence is "fundamental to both the present and the past" and that researchers must embrace uncertainty and resist the urge to resolve paradoxes. Instead, as we move toward understanding inequalities, we must let go of certainty and singularity.

It is from this ambivalent stance that I contend with trans technology's many ambivalences. In chapter 1, I explore the ambivalence in thinking about trans technology as both practical and theoretical; in chapter 2, the ambivalence in designing to address individual trans needs when structural inequities remain; in chapter 3, that of designing with privilege and for inclusion; in chapter 4, the ambivalence of designing in isolation and designing for/in/with community; in chapter 5, that of designing for community good within a fundamentally capitalist landscape; and finally, in chapter 6, the ambivalence of technological inclusionism and separatism: Is the future dystopian or utopian, and should future trans technologies integrate into the mainstream or remain separate and alternative? None of these are binaries or true opposites, and in each case, trans tech creators gave ambivalent answers: they wavered between the two seeming poles, expressing multiple seemingly opposite orientations at once. This embrace of multiple viewpoints that seem to contradict one another does not signal inauthenticity but instead highlights the complexities inherent in designing trans technology.

Marginalization and Technology

Marginalization plays out both uniquely and familiarly in digital spaces and systems. Digital technologies have always been ambivalent spaces for marginalized groups, as technology can both amplify the inequalities faced by marginalized people[10] and foster connections with others like them, allowing them to explore and affirm their identities, find resources, and engage in activism.

In the days of the early Internet, because people's race and gender were not apparent online, many assumed that the inequities we see in the physical world would not exist in online spaces (Kendall 1998; Nakamura 2002). That techno-optimistic view did not come to be. Instead, as Lisa Nakamura (2002) argues, the view of the Internet as "raceless" created an online world in which whiteness was the default—that is, every person was assumed to be

---

10. Recently, online platforms have been shown to perpetuate heteronormativity and marginalize LGBTQ+ people and communities through overly restrictive policies that overblock trans and queer content (Haimson et al. 2021, Monea 2023).

white, and likely male, unless shown to be otherwise. When race or gender did become visible, people often used the same stereotypes they relied on in the physical world. In online settings, then, people with multiply marginalized or otherwise "messy" identities often became illegible (Nakamura 2002).

Yet at the same time, digital technologies can also be supportive and affirming for marginalized groups. Online spaces on the early Internet were important places for people to experiment with identity, especially gender—to be ambiguous and inhabit multiple identities rather than only one (Stone 1995). The Internet, social media, and online communities have helped LGBTQ+ people find names and labels for the gender and sexual identities they had already been experiencing in daily life in the physical world but had no name or label for (Cavalcante 2016; Delmonaco and Haimson 2023; Gray 2009a, 2009b). Digital media expand possibilities for LGBTQ+ people, allowing them to think more critically—more ambivalently—about seemingly binary categories like male and female, gay and straight, and so on (Gray 2009a). Trans people especially have used digital technologies and online spaces to connect with similar others, share information and resources, and exchange support (Cavalcante 2016; Chuanromanee and Metoyer 2021; Haimson et al. 2020a; Jackson, Bailey, and Foucault Welles 2020; Shapiro 2015). The Internet has great potential to "address gaps of power and privilege" because it enables "exploration, secrecy, connection, and community" (Lingel 2017).

Intersectional tech, a concept introduced by Kishonna Gray (2020), describes how marginalized people (Gray focuses on Black people in particular) use digital technologies in new ways, often ways unintended by developers, that complicate digital/physical boundaries and make racialized and gendered labor and oppression more visible. Gray draws from the concept of intersectionality, first introduced by the Combahee River Collective (1983) and popularized by Kimberlé Crenshaw (1991), which describes the ways that people with multiple marginalized identities, such as Black women, experience not additive but multiplicative marginalizations. In other words, they experience marginalization, oppression, and discrimination from each separate marginalized identity (e.g., as Black people and as women) and also from the combination of those identities (e.g., as Black women).

People with multiple marginalized identities experience particular precarity in online and other tech-focused spaces, which are often claimed and dominated by cisgender and heterosexual white and Asian men (Gray 2020).

For instance, as Gray describes, mainstream online gaming spaces reflect embedded racialized and gendered stereotypes and the perpetuation of whiteness as default, and Black gamers (especially Black women gamers) experience substantial overt racism. As a result, marginalized people often create their own separate online spaces. This allows them to support each other, survive online misogyny and racism (Gray 2020), and center their own identities—to, as Catherine Knight Steele (2021) puts it, "unsettle the centrality of whiteness in technology." As Steele (2021) shows, Black women's experiences with technology are illuminating because of their history of existing in multiple worlds, using multiple disparate types of technologies, maximizing resources by necessity, and experiencing unique oppression due to their multiple marginalizations. Something similar happens with trans people online. Trans people also face substantial harms in online spaces, including harassment, doxing, and trolling (Scheuerman, Branham, and Hamidi 2018), and have created alternative technological spaces in response to the marginalization and oppression they experience with mainstream digital technologies.[11]

Marginalized groups have two paths when it comes to using technology: the first is to create new technological systems specifically for that group (we might call this *technological separatism*), and the second is to attempt to fit into, and potentially improve, existing systems (we might term this *technological inclusionism*).[12] These paths are not mutually exclusive: as Gray (2020) describes in her book, Black women gamers often exist both in mainstream online gaming spaces and in their own smaller, separate spaces. Some researchers studying trans experiences on social media, such as Michael Ann DeVito, have aligned with a technological inclusionist approach; DeVito's work has made important recommendations for how platforms like TikTok and Facebook can improve their design to be more inclusive for trans and queer users, without requiring trans and queer people to change and become more palatable (DeVito 2022; DeVito, Walker, and Fernandez 2021). I myself, in my social media research, have been more aligned with and excited about

---

11. Trans people's technological experiences can differ substantially due to intersections with race, and many mainstream technologies and trans technologies can thus feel safer for some trans people than others. For example, trans people of color, who are multiply marginalized, are less likely to feel safe in mainstream online spaces.
12. Jessa Lingel (2017) makes a similar observation, describing how communities can either "work within mainstream platforms to make them more legible, flexible, and authentic" or use their own standalone technologies.

technological separatism, which motivated me to start studying the (now defunct) trans-specific social media site Trans Time (Haimson et al. 2020a) after years of researching more mainstream platforms like Facebook and Tumblr (Haimson et al. 2015; Haimson 2018).

Trans people are not unique in creating or repurposing technology to address our needs: Indigenous people (Nakamura 2014), Black people (Fouché 2006; McIlwain 2019), and disabled people (Buehler et al. 2015) have also done so, to name only a few examples. Yet trans identities are unique in being conceptually tied to crossing over gaps or boundaries and to change over time.[13] This often creates exceptional challenges in using mainstream technological systems (for example, many online systems continue to display one's deadname in unexpected places long after the user inputs their new name).[14] Trans technologies, often examples of technological separatism, are technologies built by a marginalized group to account for and foreground change and transition in response to mainstream systems that do not.

From Technology to Trans Technology

For almost half a century, trans people have been deeply involved with the world of digital technologies: for instance, trans technology pioneer Lynn Conway invented a revolutionary microchip in the 1970s that is still used in many electronics, and Mary Ann Horton, also trans, created the first tool for email attachments in the 1980s. In the 1990s, trans people started gathering in online communities on bulletin board systems (BBSs) (Dame-Griff 2023) and America Online (where they had to fight to even be allowed to use the word "transgender" in what was billed as a "family-friendly" online space (Leveque 2017)). Also during the 1990s and early 2000s, trans women were building trans resource websites: Lynn Conway's Website, Andrea James's Transgender Map (then called Transsexual Road Map), and Anna-Jayne Metcalfe's Anna's Place shared information about transitioning long before social media sites. As Avery Dame-Griff (2023) shows, an important shift occurred

---

13. We can see an important parallel to transness in Anzaldúa's (1981) conceptualization of borderland identities, which she applies to her own identity as a queer Chicana.
14. Deadname: a trans person's previous name that they no longer use (sometimes their birth name).

when social media emerged as the dominant form of online interaction: trans people shifted from creating their own online communities in the early days of the Internet to attempting to fit their identities into mainstream platforms.

Mainstream technological systems often cause substantial harm and exclusion for trans people. Credit reporting systems, for instance, perpetually connect trans people with their previous names and genders. This has several downstream effects: trans people often must disclose this information to creditors, which creates barriers to rental housing and employment; in addition, these systems frequently flag trans people as fraudulent due to name and gender mismatches over time, and sometimes trans people must effectively start over because their credit history exists under a different name (Mackenzie 2017). Trans people also face other technological barriers to employment. For example, ridesharing services like Uber require that one's current appearance match their drivers' license photo, and because trans people's faces often change as part of transition, they can be effectively blocked from working as drivers (Hussain 2021). These types of technological harms are likely amplified for trans people of color.

Trans people are also excluded when technological services use facial identification or gender binaries. These are both problems in air travel. Airport screening increasingly uses facial identification, and airport security scanning systems (which often rely on binary gender systems) flag trans bodies as suspect, leading to embarrassing and time-consuming body searches (Costanza-Chock 2020; Currah and Mulqueen 2011). Airline travel systems generally impose binary gender options; while one interviewee in my study told me about a hack in which they edited the airline company website's HTML code to change their title to "Mx." instead of "Mr." or "Mrs.," most trans passengers do not have the technical know-how to edit code to accurately represent their gender identity on their boarding pass.

The gender binary also structures mainstream social media and dating platforms, excluding trans people.[15] Many social media sites encode binary genders into their site design, making it difficult for gender minorities to use digital spaces (Bivens 2017; Bivens and Haimson 2016). For example,

---

15. In addition to the problems caused by these sites' structural reliance on gender binaries, trans people also face substantial harassment on social media sites (GLAAD 2023; Scheuerman, Branham, and Hamidi 2018), with little protection from site owners or moderators.

Facebook has a "real name" policy that harms trans people: it is against policy to have multiple accounts or names that do not align with one's ID (Haimson and Hoffmann 2016). Dating apps like Tinder often remove trans women from their platform when cisgender people complain about matching with them, and apps often fail to include nonbinary people in search results (Costanza-Chock 2020; Hoffmann and Jonas 2017; Rude 2019).

These technologies that exclude trans people show, as Viviane Namaste (2000) argues, how processes and policies make trans people impossible, gradually erasing them from the world. Safiya Umoja Noble (2018) contends that "racism and sexism are part of the architecture and language of technology"—a problem that urgently "needs attention and remediation." I extend Noble's argument to trans people, for transphobia and trans-exclusion are similarly baked into many mainstream technologies.

It is no wonder that the vast world of trans technologies emerged in response to the technological harms and exclusion trans people face. Trans technology is now a small but growing area of design and study. Designers have harnessed a wide range of types of technology to support trans people in creative ways: via virtual reality (VR) (cárdenas 2011; Paré 2022), prostheses and wearable technologies (Baeza Argüello et al. 2021; Bolesnikov, Cochrane, and Girouard 2023; Riggs 2024; Starks, Dillahunt, and Haimson 2019), medical technologies (Blasdel et al. 2020; Shakir and Zhao 2021), and apps and systems to support various aspects of trans experiences (Ahmed et al. 2021; Beirl et al. 2017; Chong et al. 2021; Chiang and Bachmann 2022; Liang et al. 2020; Lima et al. 2022; Pereira and Baranauskas 2018). Several researchers besides myself (Haimson et al. 2019a; Haimson et al. 2020b; Haimson et al. 2023; Starks, Dillahunt, and Haimson 2019), mostly researchers in HCI, have started to refer to and study trans technology explicitly (Baeza Argüello et al. 2021; Chuanromanee and Metoyer 2022, 2023; Feuston et al. 2022; Gentleman 2021; Lima et al. 2023; Liu 2023).[16]

Certainly, then, some technologies are trans technologies—designed to meet the unique needs and challenges of trans people. But there is another, perhaps more radical claim here: we can also think about technologies

---

16. There have been two systematic reviews of trans technologies, one examining "technology-mediated interventions for or inclusive of transgender and gender-expansive youth" (Skeen et al. 2021, Skeen and Cain 2022) and one studying "information and communication technology-based health interventions for transgender people" (Wong et al. 2022).

themselves as trans. This claim (which I expand in chapter 1) builds on a long history of thinking about queerness and transness in relation to technology. As Bo Ruberg (2019) shows, games (one type of trans technology) can be queer, or at least can be "interpreted through queer lenses," even when they do not feature explicitly queer content or characters. When we queer games, we look at elements of design, narrative, and game play mechanics that push boundaries and work outside of normative ideas of what games are and how they should look and function (Pow 2018; Ruberg 2019; Ruberg and Shaw 2017). More recently, Ruberg (2022) has begun to consider how we might trans games as well as queering them: "To trans game studies is to lay claim to games as always-already trans while also making the field of game studies something new—to transition, transgress, transform, and transmogrify in the continual process of transing media."

Ruberg (2020) discusses the work of what they call the "queer games avant garde," a group of game designers and developers who create queer and trans games; they decide what games they want to see and then create them. This is the ideal video game world envisioned by trans game creator and scholar Anna Anthropy (2012), who wants games created by and for community members rather than by publishers. As Anthropy argues, digital games are especially suited for telling stories, and there should be more game creators to produce more personal narratives. In her vision, each person should be able to easily create their own games and distribute them directly from creator to player. In many ways, we are approaching that vision. We can see it in the game designers interviewed in Ruberg's book and in mine, and in the rise of platforms like itch.io, which enable players to purchase games directly from creators.[17]

Like the game designers interviewed in Ruberg's book, the trans tech creators I interviewed are living out Anthropy's vision for game design, using their agency to create the technologies they want to see in the world and making very personal creations to tell their own stories. Some of the creators interviewed in Ruberg's (2020) book also appear in mine, but I document many other types of trans technologies beyond games, especially those that align with the needs of the larger trans community. Next, I detail what some of these needs are.

---

17. itch.io is an online marketplace for digital creators, including many independent video games.

Trans people face substantial challenges in the world, and technology can help to address or ameliorate some of them. Working in collaboration with trans community members, my research team (Dykee Gorrell, Denny Starks, and Zu Weinger) and I determined fourteen categories of these challenges (Haimson et al. 2020b):[18]

- Access to society (e.g., access to restrooms, being safe/welcome in physical spaces)
- Document-related challenges (e.g., difficulty changing name, gender, and identification; complexities around X gender marker)
- Financial/employment challenges (e.g., financial disparities, barriers to employment, binary job applications, lack of trans-inclusive workplaces)
- Gatekeeping (e.g., not feeling "trans enough," transphobia within LGB spaces, exclusionary behaviors, nonbinary erasure, pressure to disclose)
- Health care (e.g., lack of trans-competent providers, access to insurance, addiction, HIV)
- Housing (e.g., housing discrimination, affordable housing, homelessness)
- Lack of access to resources (e.g., health care, housing, food, education, clothing)
- Lack of respect for one's identity (e.g., people using incorrect names and pronouns, forms with only binary gender options, systems that do not allow name changes)
- Legal issues and police (e.g., harassment by police, challenges with legal systems, targeting by police, incarceration)
- Online identity (e.g., difficulty expressing trans identity online, privacy and anonymity challenges, "real name" policies, sites that do not allow name changes)
- Pressure to educate cisgender people about trans identities (e.g., lack of existing educational resources, lack of media representation)
- Racial injustice (e.g., white supremacy, anti-Blackness, transmisogynoir[19])

---

18. I revised this list based on topics that have come up in our more recent studies.
19. Transmisogynoir describes the oppression that trans women and transfeminine people of color face due to the combination of transphobia, racism, and sexism (Krell 2017).

- Violence (e.g., murder of trans women of color, sexual assault, harassment, coerced sex work, domestic violence)

- Miscellaneous challenges (e.g., lack of access to trans history, trans experiences being marginal to cisgender experiences)

Some of these challenges can be more readily addressed with technology than others. Technology cannot "fix" or "solve" systemic issues like racism and transphobia; it cannot create solutions to complex social problems (Lindtner 2020; Strohmayer, Clamen, and Laing 2019). I therefore see trans technologies not as solutions but as stopgaps—as tools to address these challenges in a limited fashion until systemic change can be achieved, and sometimes as mechanisms to push society toward social change.

Although technology cannot solve many of these challenges, it can materially improve trans people's lives on individual, community, and societal levels. As Jean Hardy and colleagues (2022) put it when discussing participatory design workshops with rural LGBTQ+ communities, "people grappling with the complexities of visibility, safety, and resources access . . . wanted to be able to use and create sociotechnical solutions that could help them navigate these complexities." Trans technologies are most impactful when trans tech creators begin by understanding the needs and challenges of the larger trans community rather than drawing only from their own individual experiences.

Searching for Trans Technologies: Research Methods

In 2019, several years before beginning the research project that would result in this book, I started a list titled "trans technologies" in my note-taking app. Every time I came across something that might be a trans technology (usually on social media, at conferences, or via word of mouth), I added it to the list. Some technologies on the list were already deployed and in use, some were in the prototype stage, and some had been sunsetted or were no longer compatible with modern operating systems. The first four items on the list were MyTransHealth (a health care resource site), Solace (the transition app I described at the beginning of this introduction), Transdr (a trans-focused dating app), and TransTech Social Enterprises (a community focused on helping trans people learn skills to work in the tech industry).

When I began the study interviewing trans tech creators in summer 2021, I hired research assistants Kai Nham and Ollie Downs, and they searched for more trans technologies in app stores, web searches, browser extension directories, and research articles. The list, now kept in a collaborative spreadsheet, grew to include more than one hundred trans technologies. Kai started reaching out to creators of the technologies on the list, and we began conducting interviews that summer.[20]

After that summer, Kai left to start his PhD at UCLA, and I became obsessed with the project. The data was just so exciting! I had expected to do an interview study with roughly twenty-five participants that might result in a few journal articles or conference papers, but the project started to expand in my mind. I wanted to include *every* trans tech creator who existed and would talk to me, and after preliminary data analysis, I began to realize that the results would be far too in-depth and complex to be compressed into a journal article. Throughout the end of 2021 and the first half of 2022, I contacted all of the trans tech creators on our ever-growing spreadsheet. At the end of each interview, we asked interviewees to recommend other trans technologies or trans tech creators. Through this snowball sampling method, our list finally maxed out at a total of 238 trans technologies. Of these, we ended up interviewing the creators of 104 trans technologies,[21] a response rate of 44 percent. I conducted eighty-four (80 percent) of the interviews, and research assistants Kai Nham, Hibby Thach, Aloe DeGuia, Ollie Downs, and Daniel Delmonaco conducted the rest.

---

20. We used criterion sampling (Maxwell 2012), an approach in which we selected participants who met a particular predetermined criterion—in this case, being creators, designers, or developers of some type of trans technology. Additional inclusion criteria included the ability to speak and understand English (all interviews were conducted in English) and being eighteen years old or older. We conducted semistructured interviews, primarily via Zoom, that lasted approximately sixty minutes. We asked participants about the story of their technology's ideation and creation, their design processes and who was involved, challenges they faced, their conceptions of trans technology, and more; interviews focused on topics most salient to participants. Participants were compensated with a $100 gift card or check. This study was reviewed and deemed exempt by the University of Michigan's institutional review board.

21. Some of the interviews included two or three creators who had worked on one technology (e.g., we interviewed both Laura Horak and Evie Ruddy from Transgender Media Portal in one interview), so the total number of trans tech creators we spoke with was 115.

The snowball sampling method meant that the list of potential interviewees never stopped growing. Several times I got close to completing the
list, but then an interviewee would suggest contacting someone new who
opened up a whole new world of trans tech creators. Trans technology was
blowing up, constantly expanding and attracting new people. People who
had not created any technology at all when my research team and I were
first building our list learned new skills within the time frame of our data
collection and created multiple trans technologies by the time our study
ended![22] It was impossible to keep up. I finally realized this when I was
nearing a hundred interviews. The ninety-third interview was with Sasha
Winter,[23] a game creator and organizer of the Trans Fucking Rage Jam. The
game jam received eighty-three entries. Each of these could be considered
a trans technology, each of them had been created in the past month, and
we had scheduled interviews with only three of those creators (including
Winter). It was at this point that I realized that it would never be possible
to cover the full landscape of trans technologies. I reached out to the final
few who remained on the existing list, aiming for a sample size of roughly
one hundred.

After I stopped collecting data, I came across many more trans technologies. I still add them to the bottom of the spreadsheet; I still have the urge
to be complete. I wish I could interview them all. But I know that the vast
dataset that we collected for this study—about 106 hours of audio recording
and over 1,800 pages of interview transcripts—is more than enough to gain a
substantial understanding of the world of trans technologies. I will continue
documenting trans technologies that emerge after this book's publication
through my Instagram account (@transtechnologies), where I highlight one
or two trans technologies each week; it serves as an archive and a visual companion to this book.

During the interview period and afterward, in 2021–2023, I also conducted
a digital ethnography of trans technologies. I personally tried out many of
the trans technologies in the dataset, followed as many trans technologies as
possible on Instagram and Twitter[24] and read/viewed their content regularly,

---

22. Simone Skeen and Demetria Cain (2022) attribute trans technology's recent
growth to the Covid-19 pandemic, which hit trans communities particularly hard.
23. Sasha Winter publishes her work as stargazersasha.
24. Though Twitter has since changed its name, I have left the references to Twitter
as is.

signed up for and read email updates for many trans technologies and followed links included in the emails, and attended the TransTech Summit online conference in 2022 and 2023. I also conducted extensive background research on each of the trans technologies before and after my interviews with creators. I was thus deeply immersed in the trans technology world for several years.

I am an academic researcher with expertise in technology, trans identity, and online communities, a white trans man living in the US, now highly educated and class-privileged but who spent much of my life under economic precarity. This is my first time fully disclosing my positionality in print, something I have shied away from in this dangerous political environment. Yet I did not think it would be possible to write a book about trans technologies without making clear my own stake in the game. My trans identity was something I had in common with many participants, as was my technical knowledge; these similarities helped me build rapport with interviewees, allowed us to leave unexplained much of the background information surrounding trans experiences and technology, and added depth to my data analysis beyond that of an outsider. However, I do not share the experiences of trans tech creators of color, or of trans women and nonbinary people, or of those facing substantial financial challenges; there may be things that I missed in conducting and analyzing those interviews due to my privileges. Most of the researchers on my team were people of color, some of whom were trans women and/or nonbinary, and their positionalities added depth and complexity to the data collection and analysis.[25] However, we were all affiliated with top-tier universities, all living in the US, and we conducted interviews in English, the latter two of which restricted our ability to find out about trans technologies in non-Western parts of the world, talk with their creators, and center non-Western perspectives—a limitation of this work.

In addition, the trans tech creators themselves were a relatively privileged group in many ways: people with the skills and resources to design

---

25. To analyze the interview transcripts and field notes, I followed an iterative inductive qualitative coding technique drawing from open coding and axial coding techniques (Corbin and Strauss 2008) and reflexive thematic analysis (Braun and Clarke 2021). Several members of my research team—Kai Nham, Aloe DeGuia, and Hibby Thach—collaborated with me on making sense of the data, creating and revising codes, and generating themes.

and develop technology tend to be more highly educated, of higher socio-economic status, and more likely to be white or Asian than the trans population overall.[26] As I show in this book, many trans tech creators designed technologies based on their own experiences, so the sample's whiteness and relative financial and educational privilege limits our understanding of trans technology experiences for people who are racially, economically, and/or educationally marginalized. Though I cannot know for sure, my guess is that more trans tech creators of color might have agreed to an interview if they had been invited by another person of color instead of me, a white man. People of color often (rightfully) mistrust white researchers (Rhodes 1994), and in this sense, my whiteness limited the study.

As I mentioned at the beginning of this introduction, there are a wide variety of types of trans technologies included in this book, ranging from apps and games to health resources, from supplies to art and beyond. When I first started considering trans technologies years ago, my thinking was much narrower; I began by exploring social media as a trans technology (Haimson et al. 2019a), but I found that trans technology extends far beyond social media. There are trans technology apps and websites, but there are also wearable technologies and extended reality and any number of different things that I myself would have never thought of creating. Many of the technologies I have come across while conducting this research are nothing short of brilliant, and the world of trans technology is so much bigger than I had initially imagined. The technologies included in this research can be broadly sorted into the categories listed in table I.1, which are ordered by prevalence (most prevalent to least).

---

26. Interviewees were 34 percent trans women and/or transfeminine people, 28 percent trans men and/or transmasculine people, 23 percent nonbinary, 15 percent cisgender women, 5 percent cisgender men, and 2 percent who self-identified only as "trans" when asked about their gender. Interviewees were 78 percent white, 15 percent Asian, 10 percent Latinx/e, 5 percent Black, 3 percent Indigenous, 2 percent Middle Eastern, 2 percent self-identified as "other," and 15 percent multiracial. Many participants described their gender and race as falling into multiple categories, so percentages add up to greater than 100 percent. Their average age was thirty-seven, and their ages ranged from twenty-one to eighty-five. Most trans tech creators in this study were living in the US (75 percent), with 9 percent in Canada, 7 percent in the United Kingdom, and the rest in Australia, Brazil, Ireland, Japan, Spain, and Switzerland.

Table I.1
Types of trans technologies

Technology type	Description	Number (%) (total sample size = 104)	Examples
Resource	Provide a particular type of resource for trans people and communities, such as information (e.g., about transition, trans language, or instances of violence) or tangible support	15 (14.4%)	Trans Language Primer, Transgender Map, Transgender Day of Remembrance website, Trans Family Network, TransTech Social Enterprises
Health resource	Provide resources that are related to trans people's health and well-being in some way, including resources related to gender-affirming care and trans-specific health care	15 (14.4%)	Erin's Informed Consent HRT (Hormone Replacement Therapy) Map, RAD Remedy, Plume, QueerDoc, Trans in the South, Gender Infinity Resource Locator, Trans Lifeline, Mod Club
Game	Video games, analog games, tabletop role-playing games, extended reality games	14 (13.5%)	Games by creators including D. Squinkifer, Tabitha Nikolai, Victoria Dominowski, Llaura McGee, Seanna Musgrave, Logan Timmins, micha cárdenas
Archive or database	Provide digital archives of trans content or classification systems for categorizing trans content	9 (8.7%)	Digital Transgender Archive, Transpedia, Transgender Media Portal, Transgender Usenet Archive, Trans Reads, Museum of Trans Hirstory & Art (MoTHA), NYC Trans Oral History Project, Homosaurus, Trans Metadata Collective
Body technology	Technologies that in some way involve adjusting or changing trans people's physical bodies (e.g., biohacking, prosthetics, surgeons)	9 (8.7%)	Open Source Gendercodes, Hacking Biopolitics, Dr. Nabeel Shakir

(continued)

Table I.1 (continued)

Technology type	Description	Number (%) (total sample size = 104)	Examples
Art	Artists who create digital art related in some way to trans identity	9 (8.7%)	Art by creators like Heather Dewey-Hagborg, Edgar Fabián Frías, Sandy Stone
Transition app	Enable people to track various aspects of their transition and sometimes to connect with others who have similar transition experiences	6 (5.8%)	TRACE, Solace, Transcapsule, ShotTraX, Patch Day
Extended reality	Virtual reality (VR) angd augmented reality (AR) systems, which combine the physical and digital worlds in creative ways	6 (5.8%)	*Through the Wardrobe, Machine To Be Another, Creative Futures, We Are All Made of Starstuff*
Browser extension	Extensions for web browsers that adjust HTML code to change sites in ways related to trans identity	5 (4.8%)	Deadname Remover, Gender Neutralize, Name-Block, Jailbreak the Binary
Safety technologies	Help to address trans safety concerns	4 (3.8%)	Arm the Girls, U-Signal, Trans Defense Fund LA, LGBTrust
Social media	Enable people to gather in trans-specific online platforms	4 (3.8%)	Flux, Trans Women Connected, TRACE
Supplies	Assist trans people in modifying their bodies in different ways	3 (2.9%)	Trans Tape, Transguy Supply
Voice technology	Help trans people adjust their voice to match their gender (usually mobile apps)	3 (2.9%)	Christella VoiceUp, Project Spectra, PRYDE Voice and Speech Therapy App
Podcast	Hosts curate stories and interviews about trans experiences	3 (2.9%)	*Gender Reveal, Genderful Talk Show*
Online community	Online spaces where trans people gather to form connections and find support	3 (2.9%)	Trans Peer Network, Transgender Community Forum

Streaming	Trans-related streaming channels or "stream teams" on platforms like Twitch	3 (2.9%)	Gender Federation, The Transverse
Dating app	Dating platforms focused specifically on trans people and those who want to connect with them	2 (1.9%)	Tser
Appearance-changing technology	Help people adjust their appearances to better align with their gender	2 (1.9%)	Makeup support system, Apple Face ID for new hybrid identities
Crowdfunding	Digital platforms enabling trans people to raise funding, often for transition-related expenses	1 (1.0%)	To Be Real
Hackathon	Event where people come together to create technology focused on trans issues	1 (1.0%)	Trans*Code Hackathon

Note: Many technologies fell into multiple categories, so percentages add up to greater than 100 percent.

Why Trans Technology Is Critical

As I write this book, trans rights are under attack. In the US in 2023, forty-eight states proposed or passed laws targeting trans people's rights to receive gender-affirming health care, access public restrooms, be referred to using the correct name and pronouns, access books that involve trans topics, choose when and how to disclose one's trans status to parents, participate in sports, be discussed in classrooms, present as visibly gender-non-normative in public, and more (Chapman, Caraballo, and Reed 2023). Twenty-three states, including Texas, Missouri, and Florida, have enacted laws banning or restricting gender-affirming care for trans young people or laws intended to legislate trans people out of existence (Dawson and Kates 2024; Reed 2023). One state, Florida, has been declared unsafe for travel for trans people: its laws strip parental rights from parents who are supportive of their children's gender-affirming health care, require trans people to use restrooms aligning with their sex assigned at birth rather than their current gender, and ban discussion of gender identity and sexual orientation in schools (the infamous "Don't Say Gay" bill) (Chapman, Caraballo, and Reed 2023; Reed 2023). Antitrans legislation has tangible impacts: the 2022 US Trans Survey found that almost half of respondents had considered moving to a different state, and 5 percent actually had, due to state laws (James et al. 2024). At a recent conservative conference, political commentator Michael Knowles called for "transgenderism" to be "eradicated from public life entirely" (Wade and Reis 2023)—a call that summarizes much current right-wing sentiment and confirms many trans people's fears that the recent wave of transphobic legislation aims at elimination. This antitrans climate is not limited to the US—trans rights remain precarious in the UK, and nine countries worldwide, including Malaysia, Saudi Arabia, and United Arab Emirates, criminalize some forms of gender expression (Human Rights Watch 2023)—but it is very pervasive here. Trans people in the US consistently experience precarity around housing, employment, and health care at rates far higher than the general population (James et al. 2016, 2024). Violence against trans people, especially trans women of color, continues to increase, with 420 reports of trans people murdered in 2023 (Remembering Our Dead 2024), and reports suggest that roughly 94 percent of them were trans women or femmes, 80 percent people of color, and 48 percent sex workers (TGEU 2023). Antitrans restroom legislation became a life-or-death issue in 2024 when nonbinary teenager Nex Benedict died by suicide after classmates brutally beat him in a high school restroom in Oklahoma, a state legally requiring people to use school restrooms aligned with their sex assigned at birth (Goodman and Sandoval 2024). One of the interviewees in this study, Dr. Izzy Lowell, was the victim of arson when her trans health clinic QueerMed's Georgia headquarters was intentionally burned down in late 2023 (Monteil 2024). And trans people are consistently targeted, both online and off (James et al. 2024), by TERFs (trans exclusionary radical feminists) who promote so-called "gender critical" antitrans disinformation (Billard 2023; Hines 2019) and many other harassers.

In this hostile political climate, trans people are drawn to creating and using technology that addresses needs and challenges related to basic rights and life chances. Many new trans technologies respond to the recent legislative crises (e.g., websites documenting antitrans legislation, apps that connect people in especially antitrans states with those able to provide support), and trans technologies related to tracking violence and helping maintain safety are as important as ever. Yet I also see trans people creating technologies like games, art, and online communities that can serve as an escape, a way to temporarily distract oneself from the weight of the antitrans landscape that surrounds them. Trans people are angry, scared, and exhausted, and every trans tech creator responds to these emotions differently. Some of them manage their fear and work toward resistance by meticulously tracking legislative changes and creating resources that map these laws and their outcomes, helping to spread information about the state of trans rights. Some of them organize game jams to channel their anger into creativity and community. It is inspiring to see what trans people can create when they must, when they cannot sit back and watch as antitrans rhetoric spreads and its tangible impacts ripple outward. I hope one day we will live in a world where trans tech creators can move beyond these immediate threats and instead channel more of their time and motivation toward the technologies that they *desire* to create, rather than those that they *must* create to avoid eradication.

Outline of Chapters

In chapter 1, I define and theorize what trans technology means to present two interlocking definitions for trans technology, one practical and one theoretical. In the practical definition, trans technology is technology that helps to address the unique needs and challenges that trans people face in the world. In the theoretical definition, trans technology embraces transition and change to create new trans worlds and new possibilities, expanding the limits of what technology can do.

Chapters 2, 3, and 4 are a three-chapter arc that demonstrates both the power and limits of trans technology. Chapter 2 describes both the trans marginalization that often determines trans people's and community's needs and the agency of trans tech creators, who share empowering experiences of identifying a need and then creating a technology to fill that need. I argue that when trans tech creators use their agency to create new technologies that go beyond what society provides, they can increase not only their own agency but also the agency for users of that technology—a form of technological trans care.

Yet in chapter 3 I argue that when trans tech creators (who are more likely to be white and highly educated) do not involve trans community members in design, especially those who are multiply marginalized, the isolationist technologies created can reproduce privilege and exclude those who most need support. Instead, as I show in chapter 4, trans technology creation can have the most impact and best address trans needs if diverse community members are meaningfully involved in design processes.

In chapter 5, I describe how trans technologies function financially. Some trans technology creators rely on community and mutual aid; others are more grounded in capitalist systems, even sometimes receiving venture capital funding. I show how different financial orientations amplify or limit trans technologies' impact and potential: underresourced trans technologies often have more freedom to pursue their goals but also suffer from limited scope, while well-funded technologies often face different limits related to funders' values. I discuss *trans capitalism*, which describes how trans identities are increasingly monetized, commodified, and marketed to.

In chapter 6, I move beyond the current landscape of trans technologies and toward trans technological futures. I examine trans tech creators' ambivalent visions for the future of trans technology. Some of these visions are utopian, enabling new trans worlds and trans liberation, and others describe dystopian futures in which trans technology is increasingly commercialized. Trans futures may involve trans-specific technologies that more effectively meet trans needs; yet perhaps trans people will be included in mainstream society to an extent that explicitly trans technologies will no longer be necessary. Here, I argue for a temporality of transness: transness is inherently future-focused, both personally and politically, and trans technologies enable trans people to augment present experiences—adjusting bodies or working toward social change—such that we move toward the future that we want.

In the conclusion, I show how as individual creators design trans technologies to meet their own needs, the technologies they produce end up working together to make up a collaborative trans technological landscape. But there remain areas for future innovation. Some trans needs that could be addressed by technology are still unmet, and I identify some of these areas. In addition, I call for trans tech creators to use human-centered and community-based design processes. This is because not everyone has the privilege and skills to create technology, as many trans people struggle to meet their most basic needs. By including less privileged trans people in design processes, trans technologies can come closer to meeting the needs of those who cannot create their own technologies.

This book offers a journey through the world of trans technology. By telling trans tech creators' stories about how trans technologies were envisioned and designed, I highlight the care that creators feel for their fellow trans people, expressed by creating technology that makes trans lives more livable. Trans tech creators' stories also make visible the structural ambivalence that permeates trans technologies: around isolation and community, privilege and inclusion, capitalist and anticapitalist approaches, inclusionism and separatism, dystopian and utopian futures, and more. But the root "trans" means "across," and I show that trans technologies do indeed cross the gaps that separate these seeming opposites, erasing or expanding binaries in favor of multiplicity and richness—in other words, transing the world a little at a time with each piece of trans technology dreamed up and then made real. In a world where trans people are continually stripped of basic needs, rights, and life chances, and where trans people cannot rely on mainstream society for help, technology creation is one way to fight back and address some of these challenges—to make the world a somewhat more hospitable place for trans people. In doing so, trans technology both changes what technology means and expands the technological possibilities for trans liberation. Trans technology can be, I hope, a way forward through a hostile world into the future that we dream of.

My optimistic stance is tempered by the fact that the trans technologies I discuss in this book are often precarious, short-lived, or never actually deployed. Further, they often do not meet or consider the needs of multiply marginalized trans people. Thus, the exciting trans technological world I hope for, and the one that some interviewees speak of—in which trans technologies truly do meet people's needs and create new possibilities and new trans worlds—is in some ways a trans technological imagination, an idealistic and utopian vision, not a reality. As you continue reading, stand in the ambivalence that trans technology's potentiality is both real and imagined.

1 What Is Trans Technology?

"You use 'trans technology' as if it were a thing. But that's not a well-defined phrase now," said trans technology pioneer Lynn Conway during our interview. Conway was correct—trans technology is a new concept, one that I proposed around 2018 (Haimson et al. 2019a) and that I have been on a journey to better define and understand ever since.[1] One of this book's goals is to create a definition of trans technology that is grounded in the perspectives of trans tech creators. I therefore asked each interviewee directly how they would define "trans technology" and then analyzed and characterized the meanings articulated by trans tech creators into several different categories (shown in figure 1.1 and table 1.1) and two primary definitions. First, the more pragmatic or applied definition of trans technology is technology that addresses trans people's needs and is made by, for, and/or centering trans people. A second, more theoretical definition is that trans technology changes what technology means and opens up new possibilities for what it can do by foregrounding change and transition. Trans technology's meaning also depends, in part, on design processes (the extent to which a technology is designed by, for, and centering trans people) and the role of community in its creation.

Some technologies are explicitly aimed at meeting trans needs (e.g., Safe Transgender Bathroom App and the transition-tracking app Transcapsule), while others are more inherently trans (e.g., games like Llaura McGee's *If Found . . .* , which *feel* trans and include themes of change and transition but are not as explicit about their transness). It is important to define this second category. What does it mean for a technology (or a type of technology) to be trans? This is a question that is worthy of academic study, and the answers can

---

1. I was not the first person to discuss trans technology; see Appendix B for a lineage of the term.

What is trans technology?

practical meanings

addresses trans people's needs and challenges	facilitates trans community and connection
facilitates trans healthcare, body changes, and medical transition	facilitates trans identity formation and exploration
facilitates access to trans resources	for trans liberation and resistance

theoretical meanings

adapts or reconfigures existing technology for trans purposes	combines multiple technologies to meet trans needs
imagines new possibilities and creates new trans worlds	breaks down barriers and boundaries
is flexible and fluid	

design-process-related meanings

centers trans people	created by and for trans people

community-centric

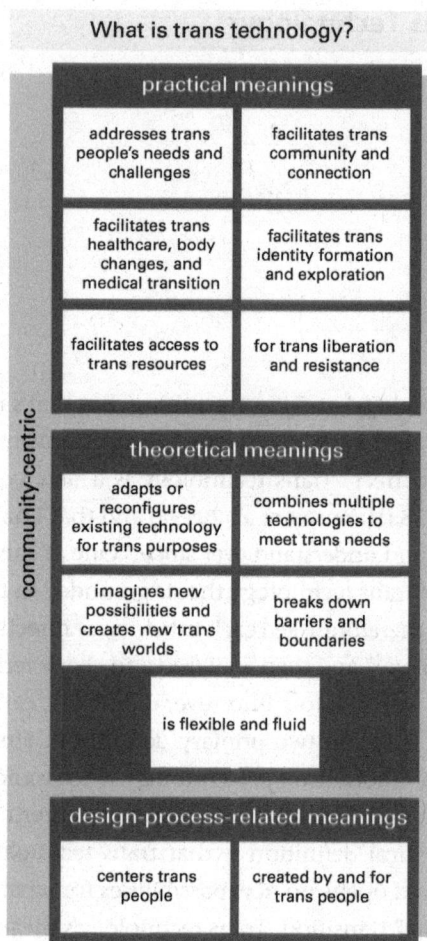

Figure 1.1
What is trans technology?

drive design and innovation. Paradoxically, despite the value in these definitions, "trans technology" cannot be nailed down to a singular comprehensive
meaning: not only does trans technology mean different things to different
people, but trans *as a concept* itself defies precise definition. For this reason,
the practical and theoretical definitions I offer in this chapter must be considered together. These definitions describe different types of trans technologies
that interlock to show us how to address a wide spectrum of trans needs and
how to think about and design in trans ways. The two definitions of trans

Table 1.1

Trans technology meanings and examples

Trans technology meaning	Example
Practical meanings	
Addresses trans people's needs and challenges	Sophie Debs, creator of the Gender Neutralize browser extension that replaces unnecessarily gendered words, defined trans technologies as "technologies that trans people create to help them survive in a largely cisgendered, cisnormative world."
Facilitates trans community and connection	Streamer and podcaster GenderMeowster (they/them)[2] stated, "We have our online spaces to console each other and keep each other company and tell each other to keep the faith and don't give up on being alive because it's fucking hard right now. I hope that these trans technologies continue to save lives and also make those lives worth living because you have community and you have connection and you have your stories as a community."
Facilitates trans health care, body changes, and medical transition	Dr. Nabeel Shakir discussed medical technologies for trans health care:[3] "I would define [trans technology] as any implementer tool that is used to help further care of trans and nonbinary folks. That doesn't necessarily have to be a piece of software or novel piece of equipment or invention. It could be anything that's appropriated or redirected for the space of trans medicine and trans care."
Facilitates trans identity formation and exploration	Malaya Mañacop described a Discord server she moderates for transfemmes and trans women in San Diego: "This Discord server, to me, has shown just how technology can be used as a tool for people to connect and explore their identities in a virtual space, whether or not they're able to express their gender identity openly in the real world. It allows for . . . I don't want to say an escape, just an alternative."
Facilitates access to trans resources	Taylor Chiang, creator of the gender-affirming health care resource app TranZap, said, "I think trans technology would involve anything that is aimed at trans folks being the user in order to gain information to anything that they wanted to . . . and giving trans folks either equal or better access to something. So in this case health care, but maybe it's housing, maybe it's grocery stores or other services or areas and neighborhoods that are safe or unsafe, or something like that."

(continued)

---

2. GenderMeowster (they/them) explicitly requested that their pronouns be included along with their name.
3. While many interviewees held doctoral degrees, in this book I use "Dr." only for medical doctors.

Table 1.1 (continued)

Trans technology meaning	Example
Theoretical meanings	
Adapts or reconfigures existing technology for trans purposes	Gaines Blasdel cocreated a user interface that helps trans men and transmasculine people determine nipple and scar placement for top surgery (Blasdel et al. 2020). The tool used existing technologies—things like drag and drop interactions, 3D modeling, and Javascript—to create a tool that would give people more control over their surgical options and a new visual way to communicate with their surgeon. This is a form of what Sara Ahmed (2019) calls queer use: "how things can be used in ways other than for which they were intended or by those other than for whom they were intended."
Combines multiple technologies to meet trans needs	Charlotte Danielle from The Transverse used a LEGO analogy to discuss how combining multiple existing technologies can form a trans technology: "We may be using LEGO, taking this piece and putting it to this piece and putting it to this piece. . . . When you put something together in the right way, it looks pretty darn good and works nicely. . . . It's using their stuff, and it's putting it together. But it's something new. I think saying *carte blanche* that doing that is a trans technology, no, but I think in the situation of how . . . trans people take things and block it together making use of these other pieces to get there, is demonstrating trans technology."
Imagines new possibilities and creates new trans worlds	Rob Eagle, creator of the *Through the Wardrobe* interactive augmented reality (AR) exhibition, described how AR technologies change the way people can view themselves, which creates new possibilities, especially for young people: "What I've seen with AR in the last few years since we did *Through the Wardrobe* is . . . the pervasiveness of AR, that it's in Zoom, it's in Teams, it's in so many platforms. It's built into these platforms. It's increasingly part of TikTok. So we're going to have a whole generation of young people who have all sorts of ways of layering their environments and layering the way that they see themselves in their environment, on the screen. If that's not trans, I don't know what is. That's being able to see yourself transforming and playing." AR, then, becomes a tool for trans worldmaking (Rawson 2014a), allowing trans people to reconfigure their surroundings to create and inhabit new worlds in which they can better explore their identities.
Breaks down barriers and boundaries	Game creator Ryan Rose Aceae discussed how trans games help players think about their own identities and bodies in new ways that extend beyond binaries. "I think [trans

Table 1.1 (continued)

Trans technology meaning	Example
	games] are games that explore . . . it might be gender and it might be identity and bodiliness in general. [Games that] dismantle that and step outside that and challenge us to think about our own bodies, and others' bodies and lives, in ways that step outside of (I'm trying to not say this in super cliché terms) binaries and boxes. . . . I think trans games also can . . . push boundaries of what games can be."
Is flexible and fluid	Manali Desai, cocreator of Flux (a prototype transition and social media app) said, "It's about catering to fluidity in people's growth and evolution." Because transness is, at its core, about *change* (in identity, body, etc.), technology for trans experiences must also be flexible so it can account for identities in flux.
Design-process related meanings	
Centers trans people	"I think that it's not being an asterisk, but the main show," said the product manager for a queer-focused social media platform and dating site (who wished to remain anonymous). "I think that, in general, dating apps have always been like, 'and it's for queer people too.' But it's really just for straight people and it's not designed at all for queer people. I see [trans technology] as trans people being the number one thought. All of the design is being considered for trans people."
Created by and for trans people	Yana Calou, formerly of Trans Lifeline, a trans community support helpline, said, "I think that everything at Trans Lifeline, from the actual operators and the care that's given, to the tech built, has very much a *for us, by us* feel. I think that that is maybe one of the defining characteristics of trans tech, is that it's built by trans folks who have shared lived experience of the ways that technology intersects with our lives, in ways that can often be harmful to trans people."

technology are not mutually exclusive but fluid and overlapping meaning categories. We can see many trans technologies as having several different meanings—some practical, some more theoretical. For instance, *Through the Wardrobe*, an augmented reality (AR) exhibition in which visitors try out new identities via clothing and other artifacts, is a trans technology that both facilitates identity exploration (more practical) and enables users to imagine new possibilities and create new trans worlds (more theoretical).

Today, there are two primary orientations within the academic discipline of transgender studies: traditional trans studies, which draws from queer theory and often takes humanistic approaches, and the newer applied trans studies, which comes from a wide range of social science and related disciplines and tends to take empirical approaches (Billard, Everhart, and Zhang 2022; Keegan 2018). My work in this book aligns with and contributes to both—it embraces multiplicity and entanglement, crossing the gaps between the two trans studies orientations and participating in both, sometimes simultaneously and sometimes separately. My practical definition of trans technology aligns with TJ Billard and colleagues' (2022) call for more emphasis on applied transgender studies, which moves "toward addressing the material conditions of transgender existence and the issues transgender people face in the world," and with Vivian Namaste's (2000) call for research that considers the actual experiences of trans people and that may lead to meaningful positive change. My theoretical trans technology definition, as I describe in more detail later in this chapter, draws from trans theory and the traditional trans studies canon (Stryker, Currah, and Moore 2008; Prosser 1998) by examining what it means to *trans* technology. I am committed to combining these two orientations—to applying the theory that lies at the core of traditional transgender studies to help address real trans problems and improve trans lives via technology and research. Studying trans technology might be considered a subfield of trans studies—*trans technology studies*—which addresses both the material and theoretical implications of trans people's relationships with technology.

Yet as many of the examples in this book show, trans technology is often created by and for trans people far outside of the constraints of academia. The definitions of trans technology that I offer here are thus grounded primarily in what I learned from trans tech creators and their groundbreaking work, which pushes the boundaries of what technology can be.

This chapter's definitions of trans technology also align with the two recurring central concepts in this book: *care* and *ambivalence*. First, I argue that trans technology, in both its practical and theoretical meanings, is fundamentally about trans care (Malatino 2020)—the care that trans people provide for each other in the absence of care from mainstream society and technologies. In practical ways, trans people and allies practice trans care by creating trans technologies to address their own and each other's needs.

In addition, by *transing* technology, trans tech creators push the boundaries of technology, making it flex and change so as to embody and account for trans experiences—another vital form of care.

As these two definitions of trans technology make visible, there is an *ambivalence* between practical and theoretical ways of thinking about trans technologies. Thinking about trans technology in practical ways allows us to understand how it can be directly applied to make a real-world impact on improving trans people's lives. At the same time, each trans technology, even those that are highly practical, enables us to think about technology and transness in new ways and consider how it contributes to theory. Trans tech creators need not choose between practicality and theoretical depth, for they are not contradictory and can exist simultaneously. An example of this concurrent ambivalence can be seen in Trans Boxing's description on its website: it is "an ongoing co-authored art project in the form of a boxing club." A boxing club is practical and helps trans people in tangible ways. An art project is theoretical and expands our knowledge about transness and technology. Trans Boxing does both, and its two orientations exist in harmony.

A Practical Definition

When Erin Reed, now a prominent trans activist and journalist, first made up her mind that she was ready to begin her medical transition and start gender-affirming hormone therapy (GAHT), she was unsure where and how to access the care she needed. Some providers of transition care require a letter from a therapist or psychiatrist attesting that the prospective client is eligible, but there is an alternative—what is known as informed consent, which allows a trans person to weigh the risks and benefits and decide for themselves that they are ready to access trans medicine like GAHT or surgery. For someone like Reed, who had put substantial thought and research into her decision to medically transition, it can be frustrating to be required to jump through hoops to access care. It was very important to her to find an informed consent provider. But finding such a provider was difficult:

> I knew that informed consent existed, that it was a way of handling hormone therapy that would avoid the need for me to go to a therapist for a year and a half and get a bunch of letters, and then try to work with my insurance company. I was thirty years old at the time, and while that might have made sense if I were

thirteen or something, trying to go through at the age of thirty, I knew that I was trans and that I knew that I wanted to start hormone therapy. And so the thing is, it was very hard to find an informed consent place, not because they were rare, but because the resources didn't exist as far as learning where one place was informed consent, whereas another wasn't.

With no simple way of finding nearby informed consent GAHT providers, Reed traveled three hours to access care throughout the first several months of her medical transition.

Reed had identified a need, and she "spent basically a solid three days, nonstop, every waking hour in front of my computer" using the Google Maps MyMaps interface to address that need. She created Erin's Informed Consent HRT (Hormone Replacement Therapy) Map (see figure 1.2). Erin's resource now chronicles almost a thousand informed consent trans health care providers around the world. Using Erin's Map, trans people can now easily find the informed consent provider closest to them.

When I asked Reed what the phrase "trans technology" meant to her, she said, "A trans technology would be anything that trans people can use to aid them in their transition or make life easier and address concerns that trans people have . . . technologies that I think help navigate the trans experience and help make it a safer, more enjoyable, and affirming experience for trans people." Many other trans tech creators articulated similar definitions, and these inform my first, more practical definition of trans technology: *trans technology is technology that addresses the unique needs and challenges faced by trans people and communities*. Trans technology is usually created *for* trans people and in many cases is created *by* trans people, and it often centers trans community both in the design process and in how the technology is used.[4] Trans technologies address trans needs and challenges such as facilitating trans community and connection; trans health care, body changes, and medical transition; trans identity formation and exploration; access to trans resources; and trans liberation and resistance (see figure 1.1 and table 1.1).

---

4. A definition is helpful in part because of what it excludes. An antitrans group called the Gender Mapping Project allegedly used the Copy Map feature on Google MyMaps to create a duplicate of Erin's Map, but for a very different purpose: to surveil, threaten, and harass gender-affirming care providers (Everhart, Gamarel, and Haimson 2024). Despite using the same technology as Erin's Map, the Gender Mapping Project could not be considered a trans technology, because its aims run counter to addressing trans needs.

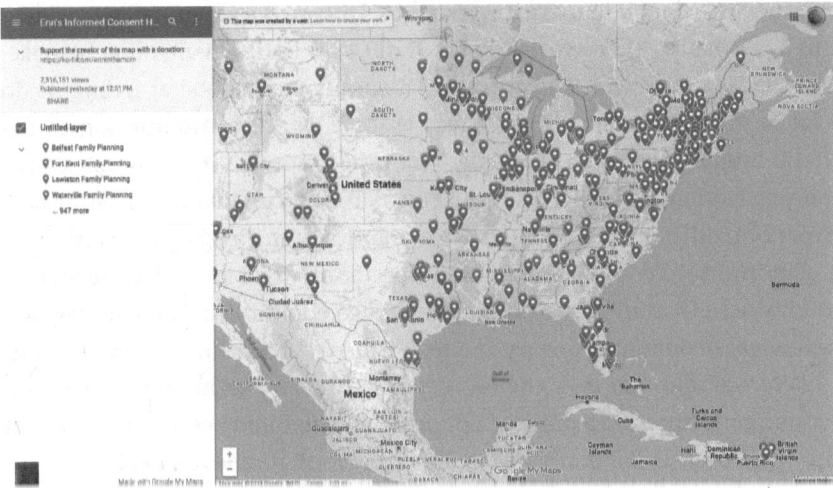

Figure 1.2
Erin Reed's Informed Consent HRT (Hormone Replacement Therapy) Map. Screenshot by the author, 2023.

A Theoretical Definition

Technologies can also be trans in a more theoretical sense. For instance, several trans tech creators discussed how they used existing technologies to create their trans technologies; they said that the original technologies were not trans in and of themselves, but they became trans through use toward trans purposes. Laur Bereznai, founder of the online community Trans Peer Network, described this through the example of Trans Peer Network's Notion (an online workspace platform) page and Discord server: "I don't think necessarily that there's tools that are very specifically only trans, but it's who uses it and for whom is it being used, that makes them trans. My Notion page is very trans, . . . but Notion isn't trans in itself. It's just mine [my Notion page]. That is, [it's trans] because that's what I turn it into." In this quote, I note the ease inherent in Bereznai's description of transforming Notion into a trans technology and the agency they take in "turn[ing] it into" something trans. Simply by being trans and using the site to coordinate trans organizations and activism work, Bereznai transed Notion—and so could other would-be trans technologists.

Bereznai also described how they adapted Discord, another nontrans tool, for trans purposes: "We take something that is not meant specifically for us and then we adapt it to make it work for us. Discord is a very good example for this. . . . What we do is we have a lot of different bots that are more bespoke, and that interface with Discord, and Discord is pretty good at letting us do a lot of things with that. That's a way that we work Discord into something that is useful for us as trans people." Transing Discord is more complex than transing Notion, and for Trans Peer Network the process involved creating bots to perform different tasks—much more technically challenging than just using a platform. Yet Bereznai noted several specifically trans ways that their community used Discord bots, including enabling people to enter and display pronouns and maintaining privacy and security to resist potential antitrans actors.

Bereznai said that they themselves were not very technologically savvy, "coming mostly from a place of not being able to build bespoke things," yet they and their collaborators were able to reconfigure several existing platforms to be used for trans benefit. Doing so, in Bereznai's view, is "a form of piracy maybe; it's adapting things to our own purposes even though they are systematically and fundamentally not made for us or with us in mind. So it's always a form of resistance for me, it's always a form of fighting back, it's always a form of taking away something that was meant to be not ours and making it ours." Because technologies are so rarely built with trans people in mind, creating trans technologies by transing existing platforms is political, a form of resistance that can help work toward trans liberation, even for trans tech creators with minimal technical skills.

For Bereznai, trans technology is both about meeting trans people's needs and about changing, adapting, and reconfiguring technology in ways similar to how trans people change their bodies and identities by crossing gender boundaries. These ideas are at the heart of my more theoretical definition of trans technology: *Trans technology is technology that embraces change and/or transition, fosters the creation of new trans worlds, and opens up new possibilities for what technology means and what it can do.* This definition describes technologies that adapt or combine existing technologies to meet trans needs, that imagine new possibilities and create new trans worlds, that break down barriers and boundaries, and that embrace flexibility, fluidity, and plasticity in their designs (see figure 1.1 and table 1.1).[5] Trans technologies that

---

5. Plasticity describes the "capacity to both receive and give form"—that is, to be both changeable and to change one's environment, while flexibility only includes malleability (Malabou 2011; Sanabira 2016). When identities are plastic, they can enable body transformation (Sanabria 2016).

meet this definition are often futuristic, strange, and infeasible, but they can be life-changing and can help people see their identities and bodies in new and exciting ways. These technologies have potential to change the world by extending the limits of what technology can achieve.

Transing Technology

When I asked tech creators what "trans technology" means, a number of them brought up the concept of *transing* technology. I am particularly grateful to K.J. Rawson, creator of Digital Transgender Archive (an online archive of historical trans materials), who was the first interviewee who really helped me to think through the two primary facets of trans technology—the practical and the theoretical—as I have been articulating them in this chapter. When I asked Rawson how he would define trans technologies, he replied:

> I'd say that there's kind of a simple answer, which would be technologies that facilitate trans community building, trans identity formation, access to trans related care, etc. . . .
>
> As an academic, I want to take the next move to be like, okay, in what ways are trans people, but also trans as a theoretical concept, able to move our understandings of technology, or radically reformulate technology.[6] And that is so fascinating to me. I hope you're going to go there at some point.

So, yes, I am going to go there and discuss how trans as a theoretical concept can expand our understandings of what technology can be.

First, why do we need to think about transing technology? Others have already worked on *queering* technology—what do we stand to gain from *transing* it? Quite a bit. Queering involves viewing through a queer lens and questioning dominant conceptions and narratives—and not only those of gender and sexuality. For instance, queer lives often take place in fundamentally different temporalities than heterosexual and cisgender lives, embracing different timelines for life milestones like marriage and parenthood or rejecting such goals entirely (Halberstam 2005; Warner 2000). But it is reductive to attribute all differences to strict distinctions made between queer and heterosexual, for identities are intersectional, and many heterosexual people are marginalized along some of the same dimensions (race, class, etc.) that queer people are (Cohen 1997). Queering is thus theoretically expansive, relating

---

6. These two dimensions—material and theoretical—also align with Rawson's (2014b) conceptualization of trans archives.

to much more than just gender and sexuality: it emphasizes ambiguity, fluidity, and multiplicity, seeking to challenge and break down dominant categories and assumed binaries of all types (Butler 1999; Sedgwick 1990).

A number of previous researchers have considered what it means to *queer* technologies (Blas 2012; Keeling 2014; Landström 2007; Light 2011; Ruberg 2019; Sender and Shaw 2017). According to Ann Light (2011), queering human-computer interaction requires that we problematize and critique its structures and foundations, challenging forms of essentialism that are embedded in technologies. Bo Ruberg (2019) discusses queering games in a similar way, saying that to queer games is to "imagine alternative ways of being and to make space within structures of power for resistance through play." For Kara Keeling (2014), "Queer OS" involves both "embracing *queer* and *gender* as technologies" while recognizing how facets including gender, race, sexuality, and class cannot be separated from digital technologies or from each other. Other scholars contend that a social media site like Tumblr can be considered queer because the site's affordances enable queer identity presentations (Cavalcante 2019; Cho 2015).

How is this different from transing? First, queer theory tends to view trans people in more theoretical and abstract ways, while trans studies focuses on materiality, accounting for trans people's material circumstances and changing physical bodies (Gentleman 2021; Halley 2006; Keegan 2018; Namaste 2000; Prosser 1998; Stryker 1994;). The concept of transing was first introduced by Susan Stryker, Paisley Currah, and Lisa Jean Moore (2008) as a way to move beyond traditional notions of gender, identity, and categories, considering them not fixed but "porous and permeable." According to these theorists, transing can "function as an escape vector, line of flight, or pathway toward liberation": as a vector, transing requires not just change but also direction. This is thus a useful formulation for thinking about how *trans* as a concept can have material effects, positioning trans technology as both an escape route away from mainstream technologies and a pathway toward trans liberation. In my view, transing is characterized by both an emphasis on materiality and a sense of movement—of change, crossing, and separation. Here, I draw from Dunbar-Hester and Renninger's (2013) distinction between queering and transing: queering technologies means *questioning* technical, social, and bodily borders, while transing technologies means *crossing* these borders. I also draw here from my previous research (in collaboration with Avery Dame-Griff, Elias

Capello, and Zara Richter) describing differences between queer and trans theory in relation to technology (Haimson et al. 2019a):

> Trans is different from queer because, in addition to the multiplicity, fluidity, and ambiguity that accompany queerness, transness involves movement or *change* from one gender to another, and often a temporary *separation* from one's existing, everyday network (Haimson 2018). Further, as Prosser (1998), Halley (2006), and Keegan (2018) have argued, many trans people require a material and embodied realness of the gender they transition into, while queer theory instead emphasizes gender's social construction and performative nature (e.g., (Butler 1999)). That is, for some (though certainly not all) trans people, gender transition involves moving from one gender category to another rather than breaking categories down.

Finally, I draw from the work of Cáel Keegan and Laura Horak (2022), who call for transing cinema and media studies by centering trans people, trans methods, and trans knowledges; transing technology requires the same alignment around the concerns and wisdom of trans people, particularly in relation to design processes.

When transing technology, then, we must take seriously the elements of change (including material and bodily changes) and transition, along with queer elements like fluidity, ambiguity, and resistance to binaries and dominant categories. By examining, learning from, and embracing trans technologies, we can understand how to trans technology—how to change technology into something new that can improve trans lives in material ways and open up new possibilities for what technology is, means, and does. For example, Seanna Musgrave's game *Dysforgiveness*, which involves swapping gendered body parts, allows us to envision a future in which health care technologies and policies make trans surgeries more accessible; prototype trans safety apps like U-Signal and LGBTrust help us imagine a future in which technology, combined with community, may help keep trans people safe. Although the material changes that some trans technologies allow us to play with are currently speculative and not yet feasible (e.g., the ability to exchange body parts or to remain safe), their focus on change and materiality, and thus their transness, remains salient. Trans needs and desires can feel impossible, and trans technologies are often future-oriented when the present lets us down.

Change and transformation, then, are what make trans technology different from other technologies that may on the surface seem similar. For instance, an app that tracks a diabetic's insulin injections may appear similar to an app that tracks a trans person's hormone injections—but the former is oriented toward managing a chronic health condition, while the latter works toward fundamentally changing and transforming a body. One may also see similarities between trans technologies and body modification technologies, for both of these change and transform bodies in material ways (Shapiro 2015). While body modifications (such as tattoos or ear pointing) may technically be trans technologies in the theoretical sense, they do not meet the practical definition of addressing trans needs and challenges—which is to say that their function might not directly address marginality and need.

Many interviewees viewed change and transformation as vital aspects of trans technology. These were the values by which Avery Dame-Griff manages Transgender Usenet Archive, an online archive of trans-themed Usenet groups. For Dame-Griff, it is important to consider how the archive attends specifically to "how identities change over time, and respecting that change as a part of the archives. Instead of just being like 'the archive is what it is, it does not change, it cannot change, and it will just be there.' . . . This is an archive that is meant to change. It's meant to be fluid, that is expected that it might change, and that's fine, and that doesn't make it any less valuable." For instance, sometimes people whose messages are included in the archive want those messages removed or deleted. Dame-Griff views deletion as a responsibility, as an expected part of archival work, because change and fluidity are values built into this specifically trans archive (trans in both content and structure): "If I take messages out—maybe somebody wants them out, or they want something changed—that does not make it less valuable, because I have made that commitment." A trans view of digital archiving requires the flexibility to make changes in accordance with the changing identities and visibility preferences of the people represented in the archive. This commitment values change, transformation, and agency in self-presentation above traditional archive values like completeness and accuracy.

In other words, there is a difference between technology that is *for trans people* and technology that is *trans*—the difference in the practical and theoretical definitions of trans technology. Nolan Hanson, founder of Trans Boxing, intentionally incorporated both into their boxing club: "Trans Boxing, I always thought about it as not just transgender, but *trans* as the prefix, and how can the project really speak to that? Yes, transgender people are part of it, but it's not the whole thing. I think about *trans* as an approach, and the way that I personally orient myself in the world. Yeah, I think it comes from my experience as a transgender person, but not all transgender people approach the world or are oriented in a trans way. Transness I think is a quality that not all transgender people have." In a practical sense, trans technology speaks to the needs of trans people—even those trans people who do not embody transness in the more theoretical sense. But as Hanson's quote indicates, there is another dimension to transing technology—something related to centering trans values of crossing and multiplicity. For Hanson, a trans approach to Trans Boxing meant incorporating tension and complexity into the boxing club and not attempting to reduce or simplify things: "I don't want to be totally vague. But I also don't want people to be able to totally pin it down. I like it to remain in this interdisciplinary space in which it's multiple things. And I think that that in itself, for me, feels like a trans approach to a project like this." Rather than being just a boxing club, Trans Boxing is explicitly "an ongoing coauthored art project in the form of a boxing club." Art and boxing do not naturally fit together and may even seem discordant— yet Trans Boxing is both at once, changing from one into the other, back and forth, crossing over and transforming the boundaries of sports and art.

Some trans tech creators described trans technology as specifically transing or queering categories like gender, sexuality, and race. Homosaurus cocreator Bri Watson described how trans technologies "are disrupting the established hierarchies and norms of gender," and Gender Neutralize creator Sophie Debs considered trans technology to be anything that is "queering normative structures of sexuality, gender, and race as well, I think addressing those and addressing the inequalities and conceiving of something better." She continued, "I think I would also consider things that just inherently deconstruct or queer gender in some way, would also be pretty valid there. . . . I think things that attempt to denormalize cisgenderedness and a binary would be valuable trans tech. Less practical tools and more ideological tools would be the other part of trans tech." Similar to Rawson, Debs's quote also pointed at the two definitions of trans technology—one more practical, one more theoretical. It is worth noting that Watson's and Debs's descriptions point more toward queering and queer theory (Cifor and Rawson 2022), rather than incorporating the aspect of change that I posited as important for transing technology. However, both of their technologies (Homosaurus and Gender Neutralize) serve important functions toward change and creating new worlds—Homosaurus by creating and updating a vocabulary of LGBTQ+ terms and Gender Neutralize by adjusting HTML code to remove gender from one's Internet browser.

In our interview, trans studies pioneer and performance artist Allucquére Rosanne "Sandy" Stone described transing as involving rearticulation, inversion, and calling attention to previously invisible elements. "When it came out the other side," Stone explained, "it was inverted, it had all its guts on the outside, and they were clearly visible to you. We're making structure the primary thing here. So that's my idea . . . of what trans theory means for this. A trans art is one in which you call attention to the invisible, that relates to the particular cultural situation in which trans people find themselves at this point in . . . history, time." For Stone, transing involves the change of articulating something differently and thereby making the invisible visible. Stone's conception of transing thus aligns with mine: by emphasizing change and creating new ideas for what technology can be, trans technology makes visible aspects of both trans experiences and technology that were once invisible. That is, a technology that is built to embrace change and transition would necessarily uncover parts of a trans person's experience that might be muted or suppressed by a mainstream technology (e.g., their complex life narratives) and would also uncover parts of technologies that are often unnoticed (e.g., mainstream technologies' often rigid structure).

Designers can trans technology by employing new creative approaches that lie outside of normative design. In Rawson's words, "You take something and you say, 'Okay, we've tried it your way, we've tried it within this normative framework.' But maybe we need to push against and find fissures and make fissures in order to open up this work or adapt this work or create new technological approaches, because the way the system is built was not for us in mind." Because most technologies are not designed in consideration of trans people, transing technology requires adjusting technology by trying unique new design approaches—by experimenting to find out how technology can be designed in a trans way. The trans technologies in this book are examples of such experimentation with transing technology—experimentation with what processes and outcomes work and with how trans technologies can be designed and built to change the world.

Conclusion

In this chapter I have distilled trans tech creators' thoughts about what trans technology means into two primary definitions, one practical and one theoretical: trans technology addresses trans needs and challenges in some way, and/or it enables us to envision new possibilities and build new trans worlds, sometimes by reconfiguring or combining existing technologies—in other words, by transing technology. As my research assistant Aloe DeGuia noted in one of her memos during our research process, "Technology occupies an interesting space of having potential for practical, tangible future implications, while also making people rethink or examine larger social structures." When technology is trans, it exhibits what philosopher Catherine Malabou (2011) calls plasticity—it must be malleable and flexible to effectively address trans needs and center the complexity of trans identities, and it must have the capacity to change the world around it in some way. My definitions of trans technology show how creators can make a technology trans: by building it in trans ways, by orienting it toward helping improve trans lives in material ways, or by shifting and challenging what technology (or a particular type of technology) was meant to do.

Though I have sought to separate and distinguish them here for clarity's sake, these definitions and transing mechanisms overlap and blur together in existing trans technologies, as will become clear in the remainder of the book. The next three chapters discuss how trans technologies were designed. In chapter 2, I show how trans technology design can be empowering, giving trans tech creators the agency to meet their own and their community's needs. Yet in chapter 3, I discuss how trans technology design sometimes relies on individualistic processes and thus excludes multiply marginalized trans people, who are less likely to have the technical skills needed to create technology. Then, in chapter 4, I describe how trans technology design can avoid this individualistic approach and make more impact by involving trans people and communities in meaningful ways.

2   Agency and Empowerment in Trans Technology Design

In 2022, trans people were angry. Trans people had long been angry about the many injustices they faced, but in 2021 and 2022, their anger became more urgent as many antitrans laws were proposed or passed in the US that limited trans people's access to basic rights like health care and public restrooms.[1] While most Americans ignored or overlooked the legislation, trans people felt under constant, increasing attack; many interviewees in my study described feeling not only frustrated but enraged. Some of them channeled this rage into technology design to support community-building, advocacy, and activism against the proposed legislation. Others channeled their rage into creative outlets.

Sasha Winter, a game designer, game jam organizer, and creator of a trans Discord community, did both (see figure 2.1):

> I was at work on a Tuesday night. It was the night Idaho was trending because of that legislature that made it a crime to leave the state with a transgender child for whom you helped get gender affirming care. It was just the latest in a series of really terrifying [legislation]. I probably don't need to tell you this, but really, really, really terrifying news about trans legislature.
>
> I went on Twitter, because I was gonna say something about it. I was really angry. I got really frustrated because it felt like no matter what I said about it, I didn't have a good call to action to put at the end. That made me want to just disengage and not say anything at all. I was just really frustrated and angry. . . .
>
> I decided, 'If I can't do anything else, I might as well put it into my art.' So, I made a couple of simple graphics. I tweeted, 'Trans Fucking Rage Jam, make whatever you want as long as it's angry.' I woke up the next day, and it had a

---

1. For a full list of antitrans legislation and proposed legislation in US states, see https://www.transformationsproject.org/state-anti-trans-legislation or https://www.erininthemorning.com/.

sasha winter ☀ 🌙 ⭐
@stargazersasha   ...

right then:

🗡 🔥 📢 TRANS FUCKING RAGE JAM 📢 🔥 🗡
MARCH FUCKING 10TH – APRIL FUCKING 10TH

📢 MAKE IT LOUD 📢
🔥 MAKE IT ANGRY 🔥
🗡 MAKE IT UGLY 🗡

LINK IN REPLY

10:12 PM · Mar 8, 2022

234 Retweets   **22** Quotes   **370** Likes   **22** Bookmarks

Figure 2.1
"MAKE IT ANGRY." Sasha Winter's tweet announcing Trans Fucking Rage Jam, 2022.
Screenshot by the author.

hundred retweets. I made a Discord server for it that night. I didn't expect it to become big; I thought that it was going to max out at thirty or forty people. There are now 150 people on that server, and it's still going.

Winter felt helpless sitting around and doing nothing, so she exercised her agency to make something creative happen in community with other trans people. By "agency," I mean capacity to take action and *do something*. Agency involves responding to problems in deliberative ways depending on context and requires the "capacity to imagine alternative possibilities" for the future (Emirbayer and Mische 1998).

Trans Fucking Rage Jam received eighty-three entries, mostly from trans people who were relatively new to designing games. Scrolling through the jam's page on itch.io is an adventure in trans anger channeled into trans agency;[2] it includes games with titles like *& With My Anger I Will Grow, rage and hope*, and *TERF Defence*. Winter was surprised that the effort was so successful, but clearly many other trans people felt similarly angry, pessimistic, and frustrated and needed a creative outlet to channel their feelings. Technology design became an outlet for exercising agency when it felt impossible to fight back but intolerable to do nothing.

Trans rage can be a powerful motivator, catalyzing marginalized people to fight back against dominant systems (Benavente and Gill-Peterson 2019; Malatino 2022; Stryker 1994). For marginalized groups, "bad sentiments" like anger and rage about an unacceptable present situation "can signal the capacity to transcend hopelessness" (Duggan and Muñoz 2009; Butler 2018). For instance, trans activist Sylvia Rivera used anger and rage as a form of trans activism in her 1973 "Y'all Better Quiet Down" speech at New York City's Christopher Street Parade (Benavente and Gill-Peterson 2019; Gossett 2013). Similarly, trans studies scholar and historian Susan Stryker, along with other trans activists, disrupted the 1993 American Psychiatric Association conference as a way to "harness the intense emotions emanating from transsexual experience—especially rage—and mobilize them into effective political actions" (Stryker 1994). In *Side Affects: On Being Trans and Feeling Bad*, Hil Malatino (2022) describes trans rage as "a legitimate response to significant existential impediments, to roadblocks that minimize, circumscribe, and reduce one's possibilities, and it is a response that seeks to transform, and destroy, such impediments." Malatino's description accurately describes

---

2. https://itch.io/jam/transrage

what I saw in my research with trans tech creators: they often channeled their rage into projects that sought to "destroy" impediments to trans well-being by addressing trans needs and taking care of other trans people. In trans contexts, says Malatino (2022), anger and rage, which are typically thought of as negative emotions, can be "transformative and worldbuilding," particularly when collectivized, as in the example of the Trans Fucking Rage Jam. Similarly, Bo Ruberg (2015) argues that games that focus on difficult emotions such as rage, sadness, and annoyance can be a form of queer worldmaking. This chapter draws from these ideas of trans rage as generative,[3] showing how trans tech creators channeled difficult emotions like rage into transformative and liberatory trans technologies.

Some trans tech creators created technology that would directly fight back against transphobic forces or support people who were most impacted by the proposed legislation. One of the most remarkable stories I heard was about the creation of Trans Family Network, an app that connects people in need of support with people who can provide that support. For instance, families with trans kids in Texas may need lodging, transportation, financial support, or legal services if they leave the state to access trans health care. The project started off as a spreadsheet where people stated their needs or their capacities to help. Laur Bereznai, one of Trans Family Network's founders, described it this way: "It was like, 'Hey, here's a spreadsheet, if you want to help somebody, if you need help, just put yourself in here.' That thing blew up to a point where it was not tenable. It was a spreadsheet, and nobody knew how to handle it anymore." The organizers soon realized that the spreadsheet was not only disorganized but also had no vetting mechanism to protect families from bad actors, for the spreadsheet was editable by anyone who accessed it.

In response, a group of software engineers (who met on Twitter) organized to build the Trans Family Network system, a web app that matched people in need with people who could support them in tangible ways. The team conducted rigorous manual vetting of potential supporters before the system would connect a family to them. Jaylin Bowers, another Trans Family Network founder, discussed the design and development process: "So, I started building an app and churned up an app in about an hour. . . . That was the

---

3. Yet trans rage does not always have to be generative; transness is fundamentally intertwined with negative emotions (Awkward-Rich 2022), whether or not they lead to motivation and worldmaking.

beginning of it. From there a couple other people were like, 'Hey, this looks interesting, I want to help.' All on the same day, later that evening." Bowers herself took two weeks off work from her software engineering job to create the Trans Family Network app. "It feels very much like everybody's really excited and anxious to use their skill sets that they've been holding for the last ten, twenty, thirty years to move the needle and make a difference in something they care about. It's all trans engineers. The whole thing. It's built for and by trans people." While many trans people work in the tech industry, they are not often given the chance to use their coding skills to make a difference in trans lives. With Trans Family Network, Bowers, Bereznai, and their collaborators Lyra Foster and Michaela Gallucci saw an opportunity and jumped on it. They had the skills and the means necessary to create a technology that would help address challenges that trans people and their families were facing. According to Bowers, using her skills to help people made her feel powerful in the face of injustice. Bowers and her collaborators used and extended their agency, and their privilege as people with technical skills and time, to make a difference for people who needed help.

On the ground in Texas, a state hit particularly hard with antitrans legislation, activists like Juniper Porter (in collaboration with Laur Bereznai and others) recognized a need for technology to help people find protests related to the proposed laws. In collaboration with the Trans Resistance of Texas organization, they exercised their agency by creating Tear It Up, a location-filterable website listing upcoming protests. Porter described the need for such a resource: "I've personally felt like we needed an organization like this in Texas and the [US] South all my life. We're finally doing it. It may have been in response to some really messed up political climate, but at least we're doing something." Like the Trans Fucking Rage Jam and Trans Family Network, Tear It Up was a way for trans people to exercise agency to create something to help fight back against the antitrans political climate. A similar desire was at work for Alexander Petrovnia and his collaborators, who created the Trans Formations Project, a site to track antitrans legislation, and an accompanying Discord server where supporters and those in need of support could connect. Petrovnia said,

> In the face of all of this horrible, hateful legislation, being able to do something that I materially know is going to make a difference, even if it's a small difference, that is going to actively fight back against these [bills]. Just not feeling helpless, having

something concrete and constructive to do with this nervous energy, anger, and fear, is just so powerful. I've talked to a lot of my volunteers who have expressed very similar things. . . . I've heard over and over again, people saying, "I'm so glad I found this group, because now I can do something constructive to protect my loved ones." Or, "Now I can do something constructive to keep myself safer."

By creating the Trans Formations Project legislation-tracking site, Petrovnia and other volunteers were able to channel anger into tangible efforts to address trans needs.

The examples above—Trans Fucking Rage Jam, Trans Family Network, Tear It Up, and the Trans Formations Project—are just a few instances of trans people creating trans technology to exercise their agency and address trans needs and challenges in response to oppressive social and political forces. In the rest of this chapter, I explore how trans technology design empowers creators, allowing them to exercise their agency to make a difference for their community. I argue that in creating trans technology, creators use their agency and skills to offer something that society does not readily provide to trans people—a form of technological trans care that empowers both its creators and its users. This chapter also examines how trans technological innovation reveals the marginalization that drives the needs of trans people and communities. I highlight an ambivalence faced by trans tech creators: they have agency to create technology that addresses some trans needs, but only as a stopgap; they are unable to address the large structural issues at the root of these problems. This ambivalence means that trans tech creators must simultaneously hold their desire and hope to create change with their frustration and helplessness in the face of widespread trans oppression and discrimination—what Duggan and Muñoz (2009) call an "educated hope."

Ambivalence creates a balancing act, giving rise to feelings of anger—the trans rage discussed above—and also joy. Several months after I interviewed Sasha Winter, I noticed that she had changed her Twitter screenname to include a reference to something called the Trans Joy Jam. Looking into this more, I discovered that Trans Fucking Rage Jam's sequel was the Trans Joy Jam, "a celebration of radical trans art" on itch.io. Participants were encouraged to submit "any art inspired by trans joy." While the Joy Jam received fewer than half as many entries as the Rage Jam, submissions included celebratory and joyful submissions about topics like change and transformation, cats, faeries, and tea, with titles like *An Actually Nice Time at the Beach, Manifest—A Game About Becoming,* and *Self-Care or Dare!* The pairing of Trans Joy Jam and

Trans Fucking Rage Jam embodies the ambivalence inherent in trans technologies. It is not that trans people were filled with rage in March and April but then in July and August were magically filled with joy; rather, in the face of oppression, trans people experience both rage and joy—multiple opposing but simultaneously true emotions and coping mechanisms.

The Need Is Dire: Trans Technology That Addresses Trans Needs

Trans technologies like those described above clearly address trans needs, providing mechanisms for trans advocacy, activism, resistance, connection, and support and drawing awareness to antitrans legislation. Each of these technologies helps trans people and communities in tangible ways. Many of the trans technologies I studied were like these: technologies created to address trans needs, such as those related to trans safety, survival, and mutual aid, access to health care and health resources, and safe and informative online spaces and media. But the needs addressed were often those that impacted the designer's life or the lives of their communities. These technologies rarely followed best practices recommended in human-computer interaction (HCI), which advocate objectively gathering information about users' needs and challenges before beginning to design and build technology (Nielsen 1993; Sharp, Preece, and Rogers 2019). I found that in the world of trans technology, designers usually create based on their own and their immediate community's urgently experienced needs. Thus, trans technology design involves personal stakes and agency typically absent from HCI research and design.

An example of these personal stakes is the story of We Are the Ones We've Been Waiting For, a trans collective focused on art, music, community, mutual aid, and social justice in Oakland, California. The collective was formed in response to local trans needs and problems: economic precarity (with many community members unable to cover their living expenses), violence, and a lack of positive trans representation. Cofounder Guerrilla Davis and their collaborators noticed that "the common narrative for queer and trans people is centered around violence and centered around death; the only time there's any kind of movement or any kind of solidarity building is when someone dies." We Are the Ones sought instead to take proactive action. They did not shy away from addressing violence and harm, but they worked to address the need for more positive trans representation, particularly for Black trans women: they created "a marketing campaign that would change the narrative into the hands of trans women and just start this conversation around trans people fighting back and trans people taking ownership of the narrative of their lives and saying 'we've had enough.'" This was not the positive trans representation of mainstream organizations, which often paint trans people as "normal" and "just like everyone else" and ignore or gloss over the violence the community faces. We Are the Ones' approach was far more radical, as it considered fighting back against violence and actively working to resist victimization to be vital aspects of positive trans representation.

As one way to fight back against violence, We Are the Ones runs a program called Arm the Girls, which assembles and distributes hundreds of self-defense kits for trans women and trans femmes of color in the Bay Area. The kits are both beautiful and expertly designed (see figure 2.2), including items such as pepper spray, a mini stun gun, and an evil eye pendant to protect against harm. Davis described having mixed feelings about the large reach of the Arm the Girls campaign; on one hand, it was great that the program helped so many people, but "also it's just kind of devastating, because it only got so big because of the need. . . . I have to remind myself, and remind people: it's only so popular because people need it. The need is dire." Arm the Girls is an example of a trans technology created in direct response to a substantial trans need as a form of trans care. We Are the Ones cares deeply for its community and demonstrates care by compiling and distributing self-defense kits that can increase people's safety in potentially violent situations. With their pastel colors and cute aesthetics (e.g., a sound alarm shaped like a cat face and a faux fur pom pom), the kits may invoke care more strongly than violence, serving as a thoughtful gift from the collective to its community, an item community members will treasure.

We Are the Ones also focuses on mutual aid and leads many fundraising efforts, each focused on collecting and distributing resources to meet a specific community need. Just as the self-defense kits are both useful and cute, the fundraising events provide both resources for vital mutual aid and fun gatherings for the community that feature DJs, music, and art. In Davis's words,

> What we focus on directly reflects the needs of the community at the time. . . . All of our parties are fundraisers, and there's always a beneficiary for why we're having a gathering. One of our first parties that we had (outside of supporting asylum seekers, which we were doing that every month for a very long time), there was

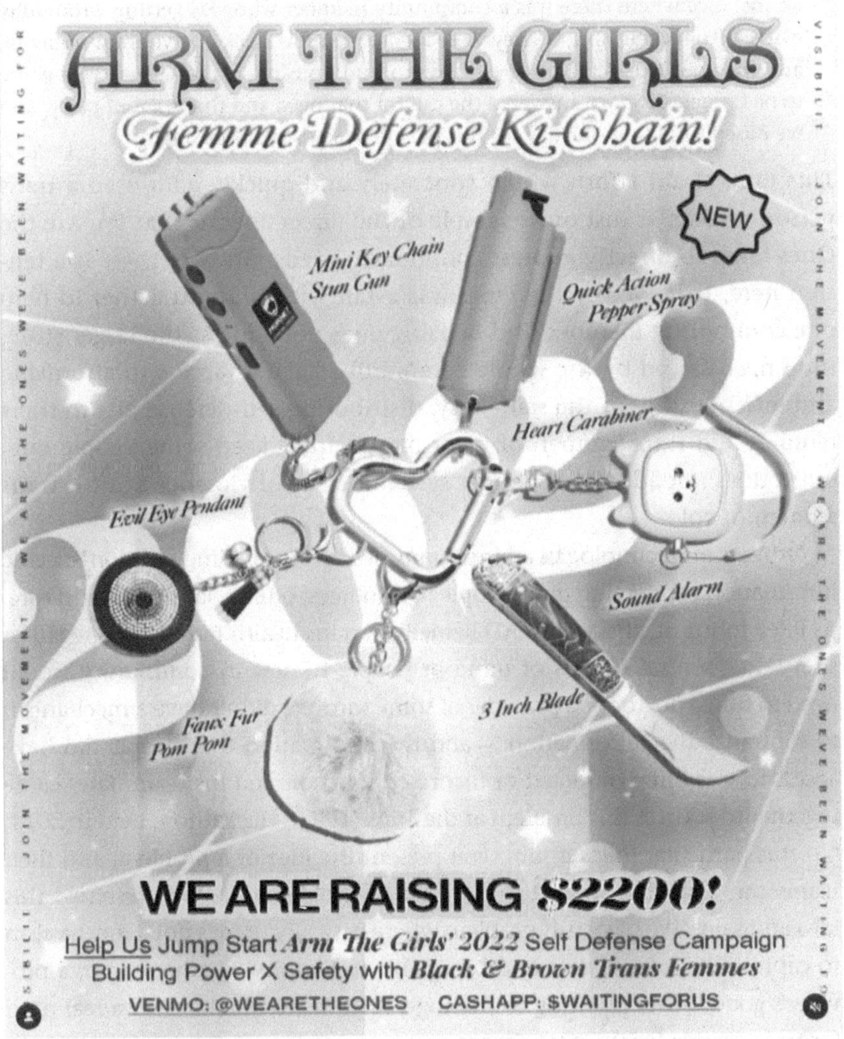

Figure 2.2
"Building Power X Safety." Instagram post showing the Arm the Girls self-defense kit for Black and brown trans femmes, 2021. Screenshot by the author.

an instance where there was a community member who was getting wrongfully evicted from their house. They were a queer femme Black Native from Oakland, and they needed $1,000 in seven days to find housing, because they were going to be homeless. So we answered the call for that need and threw a rent party, and we raised $1,000 in one day for this person to save their housing.

This mutual aid effort, which concretely and quickly addressed a trans person's needs, is just one example of the direct actions that We Are the Ones takes to directly address community needs. And yet there is a tension here, that We Are the Ones was aware of: coming together to help one community member find housing does not address the larger structural needs faced by the whole community, such as access to affordable and safe housing. In the same way, distributing self-defense kits to trans femmes and trans women of color may help to keep some people safe, but it does not address the larger systemic issue of violence against trans women of color.

Other trans technologies address trans needs by providing location-specific information connecting trans people to resources, often related to health care. As Riley Johnson, creator of RAD Remedy (a trans health resource aggregation site) said, "several friends of mine or people I knew in community would need to find a doctor or a provider of some sort. We didn't have a mechanism to centralize that information"—and the information that people did have access to was often outdated or incorrect. Johnson and his teammates came together to address this problem at the Trans*H4CK Hackathon, held in 2014: "In this particular [hackathon], you present the idea or a problem, and then teams can assemble around those ideas or problems. . . . We presented this idea and said, 'We have this problem where basically there's not a mechanism to capture the referral data and being able to identify whether or not a provider's good.'" The resulting technology, RAD Remedy, addressed a real need for trans people for the next six years.

Another trans technology, TranZap, was designed to meet the same need in 2020 by Rutgers University medical student Taylor Chiang, who said,

So that's really what it came down to, is that folks really wanted a way to find physicians . . . who at the very least understood what the term transgender means, what it means to be nonbinary, what it means to ask someone for their pronouns or potentially a different name than what's on their documents. Just someone who understands maybe the nuance of what the trans experience is. And so I thought, hey, it seems like a lot of people . . . seem to get these referrals by word of mouth. What if I took the word of mouth out of it? What if I created some sort of system, some sort of app, that would be able to house this information and people could share their experience in that way?

In response, Chiang created TranZap, an app (not yet launched as of 2024) that will enable trans people and allies to review providers and share information about how trans-competent health care providers are. Several other technologies fill similar health needs, each with a unique take on the problem and a different audience: examples include Erin Reed's Informed Consent HRT (Hormone Replacement Therapy) Map, Avery Everhart's spatial database of trans health care facilities, and regional health resource databases like Trans in the South and Transgender Resource Center of New Mexico's Provider Directory.

These trans technologies provide technological trans care by organizing information to help trans people connect with the health care resources they need. This is crucial, because not everyone has an in-person trans community to get word-of-mouth recommendations from, and even those who do receive only limited information, as my own experience looking for a surgeon shows. However, trans health resource technologies each serve different geographical regions, and they are at various stages of design, deployment, and (in some cases) sunsetting. Several people I talked to expressed the need for a new nationwide or global health care provider database; I heard rumors from participants that a tool like this is currently being created and may be launched in the not-too-distant future.

Telehealth services can be trans technologies when they increase access to gender-affirming care by enabling trans people to meet with health care providers via video chat at a distance (Dowshen and Lett 2022). Several telehealth trans health care providers described the trans needs that their services addressed, often in terms of their own personal identities and experiences. "I'm a trans person myself," said Dr. Jerrica Kirkley, founder of the trans telehealth platform Plume. "I have the privilege of being a physician, actually knowing how the system works for the most part, and still had struggles of my own in navigating some of this and getting the services that I needed. So that is really where it was all born out of." Dr. Kirkley wanted to "create a platform that truly could be accessed from anywhere, that could be safely accessed, conveniently accessed, and . . . could deliver high-quality and, most importantly, affirming care. And just essentially doing all those things that I didn't see the legacy health care system doing very well." I heard a similar story from QueerDoc telehealth provider Dr. Crystal Beal, who said,

I'm queer and gender diverse myself, and most of my personal friends and family and community are as well. And so I think I was just really tired of hearing all of our stories of bad health care, both health care I've gotten myself and that my friends were getting. I would always hear stories and be like, 'Oh gosh, this is just horrible.' It's sad that really the only criteria a lot of my trans friends had for going to the doctor was that the doctor could get their name and pronouns right. It wasn't even [expected that] the doctor would know how to actually take care of them.

Both Plume and QueerDoc—trans-affirming telehealth services with trans-inclusive intake procedures and systems—were created in response to the felt need for access to high-quality trans health care experiences.[4]

In addition to structural access, trans health care requires frequent personal tasks, such as taking gender-affirming hormone therapy (GAHT) shots. Several trans tech creators identified and sought to meet needs around these tasks. Braxton Fleming, creator of Stealth Bros & Co., described realizing the need for "dopp kits"—small bags to hold GAHT vials, needles, syringes, and alcohol pads. "As I was going through my own personal transition, I was watching YouTube videos of other trans men. . . . I realized there was nowhere for us to put our hormone replacement therapy. So I went to Marshalls, and I'm looking around for toiletry bags and things of that nature. I just couldn't find anything that really suited me that would hold the medication the way that I wanted it to be held. So that's when I had this idea spark in my mind." Fleming's personal needs, combined with watching other trans men on YouTube, helped him identify a community need.

Trans technology creators frequently mentioned drawing from their own personal experiences to identify trans needs. For instance, James Husband, cocreator of the ShotTraX transition-tracking app, described identifying the need for a technology to track his testosterone shots:

---

4. As antitrans legislation has increasingly targeted trans health care in the US, some trans telehealth services have been temporarily or permanently prohibited from providing care in some states or to people of particular ages. However, telehealth providers have more flexibility to adjust to new antitrans laws than in-person providers do. For instance, Plume has increased coverage in Florida ("We've hired more FL-licensed doctors . . . who can prescribe hormones such as testosterone or estrogen in compliance with new state laws," says their website; https://getplume.co/florida/) and has also started holding peer support groups for trans people impacted by the state's changing legislation.

The way that it started is, I personally struggle with remembering to do my shot, and I used to just put it in my phone calendar. That still didn't work. Then I also couldn't remember that I'd actually done it. Even if I had put it in my phone calendar, I noticed that I would have anxiety around doing it. . . . Then I would message . . . one of my friends and be like, "Hey, man, I did my shot." And he would do the same whenever his shot day would come around also. I really wished there was some way I could get people to know that they were not the only people [struggling with this]. I also help organize and run a transmasculine support group. So, I had heard these common feelings of anxiety around doing their shot. People forget, or they'll push it off because they're anxious. They're like, "Oh, wow, it's pretty cool to know that other people are also feeling these same things."

Husband's own experiences, and his interactions with friends and trans community members, helped him realize the need for an app like ShotTraX, a trans-specific way of tracking and remembering to take GAHT. The app is not simply a reminder app: it also incorporates a community element, displaying a list of people (friends, but also anonymized strangers) who have taken their shots recently, similar to Husband's experience of texting with his friend. Designing an app to address these needs, including social needs, can potentially help to reduce people's anxiety around GAHT injections.

Another trans-specific need is access to safe restrooms, a location-based problem. Karen, the cisgender creator of Safe Transgender Bathroom App, described how she discovered this trans need: "I have a friend who has a trans son. And while he was transitioning, he and his mom would be out in public and didn't feel safe using bathrooms. Well, I'd written one app. And my friend asked me if I would make a bathroom app for finding gender-neutral bathrooms or safe bathrooms. It seemed like a fun, interesting project, so I decided to take it on." While most trans tech creators are trans themselves, sometimes cisgender people like Karen come into contact with trans needs through their personal networks. Those with the skills and motivation sometimes address these trans needs via technology.

Other trans technologies address digital trans needs that are often not met in mainstream online spaces, such as dating apps. This was the case with Tser, a trans-focused dating app, which was created because its founder, Derek Fung, was harassed and told that she did not belong on Grindr (a mainstream gay dating app). She spoke to other trans people (some who would become her collaborators in creating the app) and found that her experience was not unique. She and her collaborators decided to create Tser, a new space for the trans community, as a "safe and comfortable place for trans people to meet."

"We ourselves face many challenges in life," Fung said. "It's exciting to create something to resolve the problems of the community." Fung's own individual experiences of harassment and marginalization in mainstream dating apps alerted her to the larger trans need, which she and her collaborators sought to address by designing the app.

Similarly, Tuck Woodstock described creating his podcast *Gender Reveal* after realizing that rich, nuanced conversations about gender were not taking place in mainstream media and were thus inaccessible to trans people in isolated settings who were not already involved in trans community. Woodstock said, "[*Gender Reveal*] was created to reach trans people who didn't have access to this conversation. So that could be trans people who live in rural areas, trans people who aren't out yet, trans youth who are living with parents who don't approve, disabled trans folks who couldn't leave the house. . . . And just thinking about trans folks of color who were not seeing themselves represented in this largely white trans representation that exists. We were seeking to show up for those people." *Gender Reveal* sought to address a trans need for media, which marginalized trans audiences generally had little access to; Woodstock's involvement in the trans community helped him understand both the need for this type of media and the asymmetry of access to such conversations. He created a technology to distribute the benefits of trans community more equitably to people who otherwise did not have access.

Each of the trans technologies in this section is an example of technological trans care: a creator identified a trans need, then created a technology to address that need. These creators may never have any contact with the end users of their technology, but their apps demonstrate care for them by helping them find health care, or safety, or public restrooms, or the voices and stories of other people like themselves.

But Why Do We Have to Train Our Voices: Trans Needs or Societal Failures?

Are trans needs indicators of societal failures—of trans marginalization? To explore this thorny question, I describe an example from the world of trans voice apps. Several trans tech creators I talked to had created voice apps to help address trans people's need to adjust their vocal patterns to match their gender. While some voice therapists are trained and willing to work with trans people, many are not, and there are huge infrastructural barriers to accessing this type of care. For instance, in the UK health care system,[5] voice therapy services are rare, and trans-competent speech therapists are even rarer. This is how Sam Brady, cocreator (with Christella Antoni) of Christella VoiceUp, described the difficulties: "I think it's a five-year waiting list now for . . . their first appointment . . . and then after five years, then they get referred to speech therapy. It's absolutely, it's beyond despair. It's really frustrating. So hearing those stories, and hearing those real-life situations and knowing that that's going on in the UK, that will have driven [our creation of Christella VoiceUp]. . . . It's not necessary to wait that long for voice therapy. That is personal. It's very personal." And there is even less access to voice therapists who have experience working with trans people: "Very often a client will see a therapist," Antoni said, "and the therapist would say 'I've not really done this before,' which isn't really ideal. . . . I thought, well, there's got to be something that could be done [so that] at least people can access it." Although Christella VoiceUp's creators are cisgender, they are speech therapists who work with trans clients, and so they still described feeling personally impacted by the frustrating trans health care situation in the UK. This frustration, along with their inability to accommodate the high demand for their services and their goal to increase access to trans-specific voice therapy, motivated them to create the app, in which Antoni models vocal training exercises for users. The trans population Antoni found was most in need of services—those who she most wanted to help—were trans women, who, in Antoni's words, "didn't get any voice change from hormones," unlike trans men, whose voices often deepen naturally with GAHT. Christella VoiceUp has a substantial user base: 40,000 people worldwide who had downloaded the app as of 2022.

As cisgender people, Antoni and Brady's awareness of the trans need that their app fills does not necessarily account for some of the complexities of actual trans experiences around voice apps. Trans creator Alex Ahmed described a much more complicated relationship with trans voice

---

5. While in the US, people are responsible for finding their own health insurance coverage (often through an employer) and can then go to any provider that their insurance covers, in the UK a central organization called the National Health System covers all health care costs for most of the population. People are placed on waiting lists for the particular types of provider(s) they need. For most types of trans health care, the waiting lists are many years long, causing substantial barriers to care (Pearce 2018).

app technology. Ahmed created a voice app, Project Spectra, in a human-centered design process with other trans people (Ahmed et al. 2021).[6] At the beginning of the multiyear design and development process, Ahmed was optimistic about the technology's potential to help trans people, though she was already critical of the stereotypically binary-gendered nature of voice-training apps. "I think then I was like, 'This could be cool. This might be helpful for some people.' That's all true. That could be true of any of these apps, even the shitty ones . . . the ones that are pink and blue, extremely uncritical, with a super stereotypic view of what voice is and what gendered voice is. Those may certainly be helpful for some people." But after several years working in the trans voice app development space, Ahmed described a shift in her attitude toward voice training: "I think my outlook changed so much over time. I now feel that the technology, despite it being possibly helpful or possibly harm reduction for some people, doesn't mean that it was successful. I don't even really know what that would mean anymore."

Ahmed acknowledged that many trans people use voice apps to address what they feel is a need; but she questioned, Does that need come from the trans person themselves, or is it imposed by cisgender society? Ahmed worried about whether creating technology in this space might actually reinforce people's "need" to change their voice: "There's personal reasons why one might want to, but among the people I talked to . . . they feel like they have to, or they feel it's a safety thing." Ahmed continued, "I feel like the central question is, does the technology actually address the social conditions that are that are causing the problem in the first place? Because a voice app can help a trans person train their voice, but why do we have to train our voices?" Ahmed wished for a more liberatory technological tool, one that might encourage critical thinking and "help people think a little more about the various ways that they stereotype voice." As Ahmed's comments here show, trans technology often meets trans needs that are intertwined with pervasive systemic transphobia, discrimination, and violence.

Ahmed's critical stance helps us to think through technology's limitations and its undue power in both personal transition and in society, and the ambivalence inherent in the position of the technology creator: technologies

---

6. A human-centered design process is one where a technology's users are involved throughout the design process (IDEO 2015; Sharp, Preece, and Rogers 2019). I discuss this in more detail in chapter 4.

can address specific trans needs, but they are always only stopgaps that cannot address larger structural inequities. No matter what technology a person or community uses, societal and structural issues remain. A self-defense kit may help a Black trans woman to scare off an attacker, yet it cannot address the larger issues of transphobia, racism, and misogyny[7] that place her at great risk of assault. A curated and vetted database can help a young trans man find a doctor who will use the correct pronouns for him and prescribe his first dose of testosterone, but this does not fix the problem of many other doctors mistreating or refusing to treat trans people. A voice app can help a trans woman be recognized as a woman, but as Ahmed points out, this brings up bigger, more foundational questions about why society requires that a woman have a certain kind of voice. These are the complexities of technologies that address trans needs. Trans technologies are, all at once, liberatory and yet defeating, helpful and yet distressing, radical and yet assimilationist. With trans technology, the world is so much better for trans people; and yet there is still so much to fight for.

I'm Going to Fix It: Agency to Create Trans Technology

As a young trans person, Mia (a pseudonym for a participant who wishes to remain anonymous) identified problems that trans people were facing in the world, and she was not satisfied to wait for solutions to appear:

> I came out when I was eight, and very few trans resources whatsoever were around . . . I mean there weren't any organizations led by trans youth at the time, and almost none that were even focused on trans youth. So there was this huge need. I didn't feel supported. So I saw a very big need for supporting trans youth, and I also realized that as a trans person in the rural community, I wasn't going to have the sort of queer gender and sexuality centers or alliances that I would need to get support. So I would need an online resource. There were also thousands of other young trans people who would need that online resource too. So I worked with some friends that I knew from the Internet and we started [anonymized educational resource for trans young people]. . . . I'm one of the two cofounders. We were both sixteen-year-old trans girls at the time. We didn't know how big it was going to grow or how long it was going to last, and it's still running strong.

In the rural US in the early 2010s, Mia faced many barriers to creating her trans technologies—both the online educational resource for trans young

---

7. A combination known as transmisogynoir (Krell 2017).

people and also several personal websites related to her trans identity. "At my home, we had dial-up speed Internet until about 2015," she recounted, "but I still . . . I was writing code on TextEdit, and then I had to upload it through an FTP because the regular uploading things were too slow. Thankfully, my school finally got satellite Internet, which is less than high speed, but good enough to code on when I was a little younger. I made my first website when I was eight, as many trans girls do." Despite Mia's modest assertion that "many trans girls" are making websites at eight, I did not hear from any other participants who had created technology at such an early age. However, I did hear from many who did so as teenagers. Mia's experiences here—an eight-year-old creating her own website, a sixteen-year-old creating an online trans educational resource—highlight the agency felt by many trans people when they create technology to address trans needs. Those who had the skills and the resources—even very limited resources, as in Mia's case—did not have to simply accept existing problems but could start to address them.

It can feel incredibly powerful to see a problem that needs to be solved in the world, to conceive of an idea, and then create technology to address the problem—to take concrete steps toward solving it. Many of the trans tech creators in this study described feeling that they had *agency to create technology*—the combined motivation and ability to take action to address a need or solve a problem by creating technology. This notion of agency to create technology appeared again and again in interviews with participants when I asked them to describe their technology and tell the story of how it came to be. Clair Kronk, creator of Transpedia (an online encyclopedia of trans topics), expressed a sentiment I heard from many creators: "We're like, 'Oh, well, this should be available. No one else is gonna make it. So I'll take it into my own hands.'" Kronk's annoyance at society's failure to properly use, define, and categorize language was (like the trans anger I described at the beginning of this chapter) a motivation for creating trans tech. Agency feels empowering, but it is frustrating to be forced to create the things one needs rather than to simply use existing tools, as so many cisgender people can.

Often, trans tech creators' agency extended to other trans people in the form of technological trans care. Creators used their relative privilege to help those without the skills, resources, and time to create technology. For instance, Jaylin Bowers of the Trans Family Network app exercised her agency to create technology not for herself but to help trans children and their parents living in hostile environments. "It's not so much I imagine myself there," she said. "I imagine that happening to someone I care about, and I have the power to fix it. So, I'm going to go fix it." As a software engineer, Bowers was accustomed to "fixing" things with software and computer code. She saw an opportunity to fix consequences of the antitrans legislative crisis, and trans access to resources more broadly, by creating Trans Family Network.

Similarly, Delilah D'Lune, creator of a trans social media site and a new site for sharing porn content, said,

> There are a lot of things about this world that are really just so awful. And I live a very comfortable life at this point. I'm an engineer, I have a full-time job, I have an apartment to myself, I have a lot of things. A lot of people don't have that experience. And it's very easy for me to just sink into that comfort . . . while all around me people are struggling. I . . . feel . . . this awareness of it, and not doing anything about the very real problems that some people face today [is not an option]. And so committing myself to doing something helps me feel alive again, because I don't have to just actively be turning myself off in order to exist in such a hostile world. So that's, I think, the main thing that keeps me going.

Applying technological trans care by "doing something" helped D'Lune to find purpose and meaning in a world that is so often hostile for trans people and "keeps [her] going" in a way that her full-time software engineering job (or creating technology that meets only her own needs) does not. Relatively privileged members of the trans community like Bowers and D'Lune use their software engineering salaries and programming skills to help others, who may not have the skills and resources to create technological solutions themselves.

Other trans tech creators talked about using off-the-shelf software to exercise their agency to create technology. For instance, most people would not be capable of constructing augmented reality (AR) experiences from scratch, but a platform like Adobe Aero puts the ability to "build, view, and share immersive AR experiences" into the hands of anyone using the software.[8] As Chitra Gopalakrishnan, creator of the trans-focused AR exhibition *We Are All Made of Starstuff*, discussed, "The fact that a platform like Aero, or there are several that are making it so easy. . . . The ability to be producers of the content, not just consumers of it, that's a part of AR that I'm so excited for to see how it grows, and to see how content creators that have diverse perspectives can easily access this info. You don't need an immense amount of background,

---

8. https://www.adobe.com/products/aero.html

or technology, or resources to build something like this." Similarly, Wayne Temple, creator of the True Self browser extension that replaces a person's previous name with their chosen name, discussed the relatively low barriers of entry for him to create this trans technology: as someone with coding experience, he was able to borrow open-source code from existing extensions and pull it together to create a trans-focused extension. Temple was pleasantly surprised by "just how easy it was to make an extension that helped." Several other creators of browser extensions echoed similar sentiments, often saying that they created their extensions in just a few hours with minimal coding. These are only a few examples of how some easily accessible tools can increase people's agency by allowing them to create technology to address trans community needs, indicating promising futures in which a broader set of people can create trans technology with fewer skills and less time.

Slide the Nipple Slider: Technology That Increases Agency in One's Own Health Care and Body

Trans people, who are often at the mercy of cisgender health care providers, often lack agency in receiving health care and in making decisions about changes to their own bodies (Pearce 2018; shuster 2021; Stone 1991). In response, many trans tech creators designed technology that would allow them to exercise agency in their own health care and to help other people do the same—a form of technological trans care. These trans health technologies took several forms: the previously mentioned health care resource websites and transition-tracking tools, as well as hormone biohacking, DNA phenotyping, apps for communicating with surgeons to collaboratively craft medical procedures to meet one's needs, and supplies and training. Trans people can exercise agency in creating technology to address trans needs or by using other people's creations to access necessary health care and align their bodies with their identities.

Avey, who created an experimental project examining trans data tracking, autonomy, and surveillance, was interested in helping trans people track their transition metrics in a personally empowering way. They considered how technology could securely enable trans people to collect large amounts of personal health data while actively resisting the surveillance capitalism (Zuboff 2019) that permeates the health-tracking space: generally, tracked personal health data are collected by large corporations like Google, Apple, and Epic or medical systems like the UK's National Health Service, and users have no idea how the data are stored or used. Avey said, "It's a lot of actually surveilling not only trans bodies, but all bodies." Avey sought to disrupt these potential invasions of data privacy, designing "experimental ways of building activity trackers or other biometrics trackers that could allow trans and queer people to collect data about themselves and claim ownership over their data." Their trans-built, privacy-conscious tracking mechanism for biometric data is a form of technological trans care that enables trans people to exercise agency over their own health care and data.

Another more futuristic mechanism for exercising one's agency over health care and body is trans biohacking. Hil Malatino (2017) defines biohacking as "the practice of manipulating biology through engaging biomolecular, medical, and technological innovations" to, in trans cases, change some aspects of biological gender. There are many forms of biohacking, each currently at different levels of feasibility and prototyping. Some trans biohacking directions are not yet fully possible—for instance, it is not yet technologically possible for a person to create their own gender-affirming hormones. But it seems that the process of trying feels empowering, offering trans people a sense of agency over their own health care and medical transition journeys.

I spoke with Rian Ciela Hammond (creator of the hormone-development project Open Source Gendercodes), who told me that they "really wanted to try and create a hormone-producing plant that could facilitate something like a community co-op producing their own hormones at cost." Through experimentation, Hammond determined that it was not yet technologically feasible to create hormones with plants, and yet they found that the experimenting itself enabled them to better understand their own identity and gender outside of the limits of medical practice. "I was going through the early stages of understanding my own transness at the time, going through transition and thinking about hormones, how I wanted to engage with that. Thinking about what it would mean for me as a person to engage with the medical system and try to access hormones, especially specifically as somebody who is nonbinary. I felt there was this pressure to present as a binary M to F person." When medical systems engage trans identities at all, they often privilege binary trans identities, and nonbinary trans people sometimes must misrepresent themselves to receive trans health care—another barrier to medical transition (shuster 2021). Thus, the attempt to create one's own medical transition supplies such as hormones can increase one's sense of agency and can be a form of trans care for oneself and others. Other experimental projects like Mary Maggic DIY Estrogen and Umico Niwa's plant-based hormone art experiments similarly challenge the existing medical establishment while opening up new ways of thinking about what trans medicine is and how it can work.

DNA phenotyping is an example of how technology can help trans people exercise agency over their gender at a chromosomal level. In 2015, *Paper Magazine* wanted an image of famous whistleblower and trans woman Chelsea Manning to accompany an interview with her that they were publishing. But Manning was in prison and had not been allowed visitors or photography since before her gender transition. There were no photos of her. As a creative solution, the magazine hired Heather Dewey-Hagborg, an artist who works with DNA phenotypes, to create a portrait of Manning using Manning's DNA. "Immediately I was excited about the idea of working with her," said Dewey-Hagborg. "I . . . thought that this could be an interesting opportunity to start to show some of the reductionism in DNA phenotyping technologies." After Manning mailed Dewey-Hagborg her cheek swabs and hair clippings, Dewey-Hagborg used software and code to generate what would eventually become a piece called *Probably Chelsea*, a series of different possibilities of what Manning's face might look like given the variety of different instantiations of her DNA (see figure 2.3).

As Dewey-Hagborg described, current police surveillance tools (as well as her own past projects) used a binary understanding of gender. The *Probably Chelsea* project enabled her to challenge and move beyond that binary: in the software and code that Dewey-Hagborg used to create Manning's portraits, gender could be specified on a sliding scale between –1 and 1. Manning and Dewey-Hagborg decided to create both female and gender-neutral versions of Manning's portrait, with the technological affordances allowing them to exclude male versions of Manning entirely. Manning was thus able to exercise agency over her public appearance even from a prison cell, denied any type of physical representation to the public. By enabling Manning to exercise this agency, Dewey-Hagborg was practicing technological trans care.

Other trans technologies foster trans agency by giving users tools that let them imagine and experiment with how they want their bodies to look. In consults with gender-affirming surgeons, it can be difficult for a trans patient to communicate and advocate for their preferences for their body's appearance. Trans people are often assumed to want standard cisgender versions of

Figure 2.3
"Probably Chelsea." Chelsea Manning observing artist Heather Dewey-Hagborg's DNA phenotyping of Manning's face at an exhibition, 2020. Screenshot from https://www .exploratorium.edu/exhibits/probably-chelsea by the author.

bodies or are given only limited options. While the three surgeons I inter-viewed in this study (Drs. Mang Chen, Geolani Dy, and Nabeel Shakir) all sought to involve patients in their surgery decision-making and innovated to include patient input, not all surgeons are as forward-thinking and patient-centered as these three. Accessible tools are needed to help trans people decide and communicate how they want their bodies to look. I have exam-ined this in my past research; in participatory design workshops, trans people described wanting a "body changing laboratory" where they could view and adjust on a screen what they wanted their bodies to look like after medical transition (Haimson et al. 2020b). Gaines Blasdel, a former researcher at NYU Langone Health's Transgender Surgery Services who is now training to be a gender-affirming surgeon, described his vision for a tool that would help patients communicate their preferences for nipple placement after gender-affirming mastectomy ("top surgery") (Blasdel et al. 2020) (see figure 2.4): "I think it should be a Sims-style applet with sliders. And you can slide the nipple slider, the scar to be curvier, straight, or higher, lower." This is quite different from current practice: currently, each surgeon who performs top surgery has their own standard nipple placement and scar shape. Blasdel's team's tool would allow patients to decide and communicate what they want their post-op body to look like.

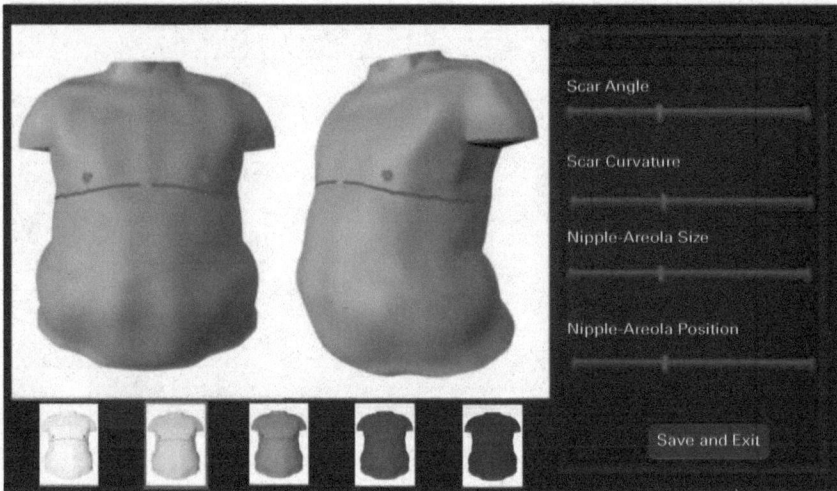

Figure 2.4
Gaines Blasdel and colleagues' (2020) tool to communicate patient preferences for gender-affirming mastectomy surgery. Reprinted with permission from Blasdel.

Trans people also exercise agency over their bodies by augmenting them with supplies and training. For instance, Trans Boxing, a trans boxing class and community, offers training that enables people to learn and practice new ways to move and inhabit their bodies within a supportive community of other trans people, and Transguy Supply provides supplies for trans men and transmasculine and nonbinary people—"any sort of product that might help make [them] feel more comfortable and safer in their bodies," said cofounder Scout Rose, ranging from "binders and packers to stand-to-pee devices." I talked with people from a number of companies offering different types of devices, supplies, and training to help trans people align their bodies with their identities, and each of them described a goal of helping trans people achieve more agency over their own bodies. For example, Leo from TransFormaGear[9] described his experience creating prosthetic penises:

> It was just a case of me tinkering and making the things that I needed for myself. So making the Rod, which really is just an attachment that you can use in situations where you are going to be naked, things like shower rooms, etc. And then the

9. Pseudonyms for this person and company.

Joystick was, I guess, the most important one for me personally, because I do just consider myself to be actually a fairly boring heterosexual man who wants to have sex the way most men do. So it was important that I could create something that also stimulated the wearer and felt as natural as possible, both to the wearer and the receiver.

Leo, like many of the other trans tech creators described in this chapter, drew from his own experiences, creating technology to increase bodily agency for himself and his customers. These tools and trainings from companies like Trans Boxing, Transguy Supply, and TransFormaGear are forms of technological trans care.

I Don't Want to Wait: Fast Design, Fast Deployment

Many trans tech creators found agency in creating trans technology rapidly. The creators of browser extensions went from idea to deployment in one to twelve hours, because many used "boiler plate code and code snippets found online," said Willow Hayward, creator of the Deadname Remover browser extension. Sophie Debs, creator of the Gender Neutralize browser extension, said, "Yeah, actually it was really quick. It took me probably six hours to get the core of it built, set up, and deployed on the web." Similarly, when creating the NameBlock extension, LemmaEOF "decided, 'Hey, that might be nice to make.' I just threw it together." ShotTraX was the most quickly deployed app in my dataset: in James Husband's words, his cocreator (who wished to remain anonymous) "cranked it out in an hour or so." This rapid creation aligns with game studies scholar and game creator Anna Anthropy's (2012) call to prototype quickly, rather than attempting to create perfect game designs.

Hayward discussed the benefits of quick deployment for trans technology projects: "In particular, when you're making something that could help vulnerable people, prototype quickly. The first version of Deadname Remover was an absolute hack job. It had bugs left, right, and center, but it worked. . . . I think that that's a really important thing for anyone who's creating to keep in mind, is get something out there and improve on that. Rather than waiting until your product is the perfect little darling that you want." When a technology can vastly improve the lives of the people who are using it, in Hayward's view, the best approach is to deploy that imperfect software so that people can use it. Other creators described similar sentiments: Avery Everhart's spatial database of trans health care facilities was created quickly, rather than perfectly: "At pretty much at every turn, I was just like, 'This should exist.' Then when it didn't, I was like, 'I don't want to wait for somebody else to do it. I'm gonna make an imperfect version, and then let that be that. If other things come of it, fantastic.'" Everhart focused not on perfection or completeness but on deploying a version that others could access and use. However, quick deployment requires creators to be responsive to user complaints and to rapidly release bug-fix updates; otherwise, users may feel more frustrated than cared for.

These same quick, imperfect deployments often characterized technologies designed and developed as part of hackathons and game jams. Zoe Nolan said of To Be Real, a prototype crowdfunding site she and her collaborators created at Trans*Code Hackathon, "It was very chaotic, and very much thrown together. If you look at the code, it's not the best-designed code in the world, but I think [it] hopefully got the point across." As long as it runs and does not put users at risk, chaotic and messy code can be good enough, especially for preliminary versions of technologies that will improve in future iterations. To do the most good and to most effectively practice technological trans care, sometimes it is more important for technology to exist quickly than be designed perfectly.

Rapid creation and deployment are especially important in technology responding to antitrans efforts. For example, Trans Family Network started up just a few weeks after the Texas antitrans legislation was proposed. Jaylin Bowers described the process: "So we basically took two weeks off work. We pushed to get something coherent, cohesive out the door. . . . That took about a week. It took about two weeks to get that to a stable point where we could basically be like, 'You should go to this, this is a thing that works.'" It was crucial that Trans Family Network (and many other trans technologies) mobilize rapidly to respond to a crisis. Having a working version of the app three weeks after the proposed legislation was announced meant that people could access the resources they needed; families in Texas could pull together the support to quickly travel out of state and access health care.

Even when technology took a bit longer to create, trans tech creators were often highly motivated and powered through the design and deployment processes quickly, with few breaks and little breathing room. For example, when Erin Reed was creating her map of informed consent GAHT providers, "the way that I did it was I kept it secret at first from everybody, I was just building it myself, and it took three days of literally twelve hours a day. I was only getting up to use the bathroom when I created it." When someone has an idea for a way to really help people, and has the skills and resources to bring that idea to life, they often work extremely hard over a short period of time. Quick design and development enables people to get their ideas out into the world and allows other trans people to access the outputs of those ideas with minimal delay.

However, not all trans technologies in my study were designed quickly. Many were designed slowly, often because they included communities in meaningful ways. For instance, the NYC Trans Oral History Project was intentionally designed slowly, said cocreator AJ Lewis: "One of the things that we did was . . . we got going really slowly. For our first couple of years, we really only produced a handful of interviews, because we were really emphatic about working with activists to see how they would want a project like that to work." Rapid solo design and deployment run counter to human-centered, participatory, and community-based design processes, which require building connections over time and sustained engagement. Trans technology design processes depend on many factors, and urgency to address a trans need is only one. Sometimes trans needs can be addressed most effectively with slow and deliberate, rather than rapid, forms of technological trans care. Here, we see another ambivalence: to make a rapid impact, creators must sometimes create and deploy technologies quickly and urgently, but to create the most impactful community-based technologies, creators need time and space to work intentionally. To some extent this ambivalence can be addressed with iteration—that is, by deploying a quick imperfect version and then taking the time to improve that technology in future iterations—but urgency and timeliness versus slowness and deliberation remains an important tension in trans technology design.

Conclusion

As the stories I shared in this chapter demonstrate, trans technology is a way to care for one's self and one's community, a form of what I call *technological trans care*—the ways that trans people use technology to fill care gaps left by mainstream society. Each trans tech creator creates their technology with a substantial focus on care for themselves and their users, seeking to meet trans needs they identify typically based on their own experiences. Trans tech creators exercise and build agency by designing technology that highlights and helps to address trans marginalization. Trans technology can also empower its users, the recipients of technological trans care, by helping them meet their needs in new ways. Engaging in trans advocacy via technology is a form of what Cait McKinney (2020) labels information activism: commitment to the "ongoing, everyday work of managing information," which is itself a form of care that marginalized people practice toward each other.

Trans people are not the only ones who use technology to address needs they see in the world; technological innovation often comes from technology designers who create products and systems that address a need that they personally experienced. Sometimes these creators are also marginalized people designing for themselves and their communities. More often, though, technology creators tend to be privileged people, and their innovations seek to create profit. Innovations are often incremental, and the needs they address can be minor—for example, a new razor that shaves a little bit better than existing razors. Other technological innovations may improve people's lives by providing excitement or fun, such as a drone that enables people to take aerial photographs in exciting new ways, rather than by addressing an actual problem related to day-to-day life. This is not the case for trans technology, where creators often design things that are critical to their lives or the lives of trans communities—a self-defense kit, a map to find trans health care. Trans creators often *need* to innovate to meet their needs—both day-to-day needs and the need to experience agency in a world that seems built to shut them out.

We can blame societal factors for the disparities between trans and cisgender needs being met. As discussed above, some trans "needs," such as voice apps, may be needs only because society expects women's and men's voices to sound a certain way, and trans health databases are needs only because not all doctors are trans-competent or even trans-inclusive. This creates an ambivalence for trans tech creators: they are often angry about the societal issues they are designing technology to address, but they still find joy and empowerment in creating technology. Rage and joy exist simultaneously, and both are motivators. Many trans tech creators in my study spent countless volunteer hours of their "spare time" creating their technologies, often on nights and weekends after working full-time day jobs doing something else. They were highly motivated to create technology, both for themselves and for others. Many interviewees' eyes lit up when describing other trans people using and finding value in their technology.

Ambivalence is at the heart of trans technology: trans technology fills needs that exist because our society does not take care of or even acknowledge the needs of trans people (a source of anger), but it is also empowering and fulfilling for trans tech creators (a source of joy). Anger, need, and urgency, though, are more likely than joy to motivate trans technology creation. But as we can see from the trans technology design processes I have described in this chapter, it is empowering to identify a need and then design a technology to address that need. As LemmaEOF described after creating the NameBlock extension, "It made me happy. I have been interested in programming for just about my whole life at this point. Being able to use it in a way that will help people or make people feel happy with themselves is what I have wanted. It's basically what I've always wanted to do ultimately." Using one's skills in technology design to create a trans technology can be motivating, inspiring, and empowering.

Many trans tech creators' processes resemble a method in HCI called autobiographical design, defined as "design research drawing on extensive, genuine usage by those creating or building the system" (Neustaedter and Sengers 2012). Trans tech creators often used autobiographical design processes, creating technology to meet their own needs. This self-focused process can be a useful way to use a technology in depth and quickly iterate (Neustaedter and Sengers 2012). But without involvement and feedback from other people, creators can miss important things. Personal agency and empowerment are important, but they can also be isolationist and lead to exclusion of people with multiply marginalized identities. I examine these topics of privilege and exclusion in the next chapter.

3 Privilege and Exclusion in Trans Technology Design

TransFormaGear[1] is a prosthetics company that creates genital prosthetic devices for trans men. Leo, the company's founder, described his initial approach to designing and creating these technologies:

> It was basically me just really trying to solve a problem for myself, which was that when I transitioned, there really weren't a lot of options available on the market. And I guess I was just frustrated with that. So I thought I could experiment and see if I could do better. And yeah, basically just started off by trying to make myself a stand-to-pee device. And it literally was just a case of me spending a few months trying to figure out how to do this and experimenting and finally after a few months, having something that I was relatively happy with and literally just posting in a Facebook group, "Look, what I made."

Leo, a white trans man, described feeling strongly that people should design based on their own experiences and not try to generalize further—an approach he called "people scratching their own itch." He continued, "I feel like the person that would come up with the best solutions would be a person for whom it actually solves their own personal problem." Individualist design processes begin with an idea for technology developed out of the creator's own experience.

However, individualist design processes can create trans technologies that exclude multiply marginalized trans people, such as trans people of color. For instance, while TransFormaGear offers three different skin tone colors for its products (light, medium, and dark), Leo opted not to customize his products more than that. "As a small business, I just can't. There's just not the bandwidth for that. . . . When you start to customize, costs become so,

---

1. I have pseudonymized this company and its founder to lessen potential negative personal impact of my critique.

so cost prohibitive that I can't make that sustainable. So I really don't do any customization." Customized skin tone colors may be less important for white trans people using prostheses, who are closer to the prototypical user that Leo envisioned when creating the products (and to Leo himself), but it can be more difficult for trans people of color to find a match. Leo's choice to limit his product's skin tones highlights both the privilege he and other white creators bring to trans technology design and the racist implications of a capitalist system in which meeting minoritized people's needs is financial unsustainable.[2]

TransFormaGear is just one example of many cases in which trans technologies were designed primarily for users with identities similar to the creator. The majority of trans tech creators (78 percent of my sample) were white, and creators tended to be more highly educated than the overall trans population; the trans technologies they created thus potentially exclude multiply marginalized trans community members, such as trans people of color and those with less education. In this chapter, I argue that individualist design processes create technologies that meet individual needs, which sometimes do not align with the common needs and challenges of the trans population more broadly and especially seem to overlook the needs of multiply marginalized trans people such as trans people of color. Trans technology design can thus further marginalize some trans people. Here, I want to acknowledge research assistant Kai Nham, whose initial data analysis and insights inform many of the ideas in this chapter.

Ultimately, this is an argument about intersectionality—the ways that multiple forms of oppression work together to impact the experiences of those who hold multiple marginalized identities (Crenshaw 1991). Being trans is challenging enough on its own, and by definition trans technologies are designed to help address some of these challenges. Yet multiply marginalized trans people—such as people who are also racial minorities, economically disadvantaged, disabled, or a combination of these—face additional challenges that require an intersectional approach to trans technology design. In many ways transness is inextricably linked with race (Snorton 2017) and disability (Awkward-Rich 2022), and these ties must be taken seriously in trans technology design.

---

2. As we also see with Band-Aids skin tones (Oyesiku 2021).

In this chapter, I discuss instances of trans technologies that were limited in demonstrating trans care. As I show here, when creators use individualist and isolationist design processes and produce technology that excludes or further marginalizes trans people with multiple marginalized identities, the creators are practicing care only toward people who are similar to them. A liberatory technological trans care ethic would require a technology to demonstrate trans care for those who need it the most—those who face oppression on multiple dimensions.

This chapter makes clear an ambivalence that many trans tech designers experienced: how to design technologies that addressed their own needs while accounting for their relative privilege and the ways their technology may not be inclusive for trans people with multiply marginalized identities. Some people leaned into their own experiences, simply relying on individualist design approaches rather than making conscious efforts to design for the needs of trans people with less privilege. However, these same creators often acknowledged the importance of inclusion and had ideas about how to make their technology useful to a larger group of trans people. This ambivalence is apparent in Leo's discussion above: he is aware that offering more skin tones would include more people, but he ended up designing for people like himself, primarily because of financial constraints. For Leo and other creators, these two seemingly conflicting orientations were both true at the same time: individualism, exclusion, and privilege existed in tension with attempts toward inclusion and (in some cases) acknowledgement of privilege.

A Space for Trans People That They Never Asked For: Trans Technology That Addresses Designers' Needs, Not Community Needs

People who are drawn to programming also tend to be drawn to problem-solving (Dunbar-Hester 2019) and creating technology to solve problems that they encounter. As I described in chapter 2, many trans tech creators design and develop technologies based on their own personal experiences navigating being trans. Often, these experiences extrapolate to trans community needs more broadly. However, when designers' needs were more individualistic, they tended to prioritize their own trans experiences, which did not always reflect the most pressing needs of the larger trans community.

Anna-Jayne Metcalfe observed this issue playing out year after year at the Trans*Code Hackathon. She described wanting to see future trans technologies that were less focused on individual daily needs (even needs shared by many trans people, like the need to find trans-affirming local businesses) and focused on more pressing trans needs: "More activism, because we need more and more activism. More community engagement." Hackathon projects tended to focus on small workaround-type apps (especially those that are feasible to code in a day or two) rather than more unique projects that could help multiply marginalized trans people. For example, trans people of color are at very high risk of police violence, and Metcalfe saw the need for technology that enabled "ways of reporting violence that don't involve the police. There'll always be a place for those sorts of applications. . . . There's a need to produce, to apply and think of, solutions that involve the wider community, raise awareness, and do advocacy on our behalf. With a much wider community. Individual solutions are not going to be able to push back against legislative attacks." Especially in the current hostile antitrans political environment, we need technologies that can keep the most vulnerable trans people safe and help the trans community fight back in collective ways. But each year, hackathon participants overlooked politically responsive advocacy- and activism-focused technologies and focused on creating stopgap technologies such as trans-affirming-business finders. In Metcalfe's view, this is because of a narrow view of what the trans community needs: "That's the problem, people immediately think about their own experience" rather than starting first with determining community needs and then designing to address them. Of course, hackathons are inherently time-limited, which lessens the likelihood of creating a groundbreaking new technology with broad impact. But there could be ways to scaffold hackathons, perhaps by prearticulating community needs and providing support for technology deployment and maintenance after the hackathon ends.

Some trans tech creators were self-aware, realizing that their technologies did not necessarily address a broader trans need. Delilah D'Lune was a cocreator of Royal Jelly, a porn content site being developed with a community-based approach that involves many trans content creators. D'Lune described how Royal Jelly was different from her previous project, a now-defunct trans social media site: "There's . . . a need for [Royal Jelly], unlike [social media site], which was trying to create new space for trans people that they didn't really ask for." D'Lune acknowledged that her previous project had taken more of an individualistic rather than a community-based design approach and that the final product had not really addressed a pressing community need; as a result, the site had only a small user base and never fully gained momentum. In contrast, Royal Jelly is being built with community buy-in, using a collective governance approach and an advisory committee. D'Lune hopes these structures will be "helpful in ensuring that people of all different marginalized categories are heard and accounted for."

Ash (the pseudonym for a creator who wished to remain anonymous) used automatic gender recognition technology to create a makeup support system aimed at helping trans people determine whether they could be recognized as their desired gender. Ash was aware that their project did not necessarily address a trans community need: "In terms of need, I don't think there's such a need for this . . . but it would be to many of them, something that they will really want to have. . . . So is it necessary? . . . I don't necessarily think so. But I think some of the participants really appreciate it, the existence of the system." In user testing with trans participants, Ash noted, some participants directly stated that they would not need such a system. In our conversation, Ash implied that the tool did not even fully meet their own aspirations for it. But as Ash noted, the system could still be helpful for some people.

Other trans tech creators were less self-aware than Ash and D'Lune. Many did not speak directly to the fact that they designed primarily based on individual rather than community needs. Some seemed to assume that their technology must address a broader trans need, because it addressed one of their own needs. In chapter 2, I discussed the positive aspects of self-driven approaches and celebrated the agency that these approaches allowed trans tech creators to exercise. Here, I delve into some of the more negative aspects of such individualistic approaches. When design is based on people's individual needs, technology addresses the needs of those who have the skills and privilege to design and build technology. The subset of the trans population with these skills and privileges tends to be more white, more educated, and more affluent than the trans population overall. The individually motivated trans technologies that exist in the world are necessarily designed with more privileged trans people's needs at the forefront, often overlooking the needs of multiply marginalized trans people and communities.

A different approach to trans technology design and development would first determine the trans population's most imperative needs and challenges and then seek to design and develop technology to address those needs. This is the approach my research team (including researchers Dykee Gorrell, Denny Starks, and Zu Weinger) took in our 2020 participatory design study with a diverse group of trans people (Haimson et al. 2020b). Through a collaborative brainstorming and affinity diagramming session, participants determined fourteen primary challenges faced by the trans community (listed in the introduction): some were systemic issues that could not be addressed with technology (e.g., racial injustice and violence), and others lent themselves well to technological solutions (e.g., access to health care and resources). Then, we led participants in design activities, asking them to choose challenges from that list and envision potential technologies that might address those challenges. We categorized participants' designs into four main categories: technologies for changing bodies, technologies for changing appearances/gender expressions, technologies for safety, and technologies for finding resources (Haimson et al. 2020b).

When conducting the research for this book, I was struck by how little overlap there was between the trans technologies people were creating and the types of technology design that emerged from our community needs–based approach, which included many multiply marginalized trans people. This signals to me that trans technology, and trans people, would greatly benefit if trans tech designers took a more holistic and analytical approach to determining trans community needs, rather than jumping into design based on individual needs.

Playing from the Gut: Individualist and Isolationist Trans Technology Design Processes

Many of the trans tech creators I spoke with were creating small-scale technology that was very personal to them and reflected their own experiences. They were not particularly concerned about whether their technology would have larger appeal or be helpful for others with different identities and experiences. But it is important for trans technology design to include the most marginalized trans people.

Solace—part of the Euphoria suite of transition apps—exemplifies individualist technology design. Although Euphoria's apps are created by a small team, they draw extensively from their own experiences in designing technologies for people transitioning in isolation. Cofounder Robbi Katherine Anthony (who goes by RKA), a white trans woman, described the company's design process: "A lot of it's internal. We play from the gut, we take from our collective lived experiences as a team. . . . Really, the biggest litmus test when we design something new is, does it evoke a very strong emotion? And if so, what we refer to internally as our 'instincts' are right. Thus far, we found that when we conceive an idea, it's generally a much bigger problem that warrants a solution." Drawing from their "instincts" or "gut," the Euphoria team creates technology that they assume will also speak to the larger trans community. What is most important to the design team is their *own* feelings and emotions about the app, not the feelings of other trans people or even existing Solace users.

Indeed, the Solace app is designed to enable people to transition in isolation, without need for a trans community. In RKA's words, "The app is always designed around centering the individual, and just having a one-on-one conversation with the trans soul, versus . . . a collective experience. . . . We think it creates a better experience because it allows the user to revel in the specialness of their own transition, without creating opportunities for misinformation or the comparison game that we see on platforms like Instagram, Reddit, or other Internet congregation places for the community." Solace's resources are indeed a vetted and accurate source of gender transition–related information, and their individual-based approach may work very well for some trans people. Yet individualist approaches to transition can feel isolating (Chuanromanee and Metoyer 2023) and may not align with user needs and desires.

In fact, Euphoria's isolationist approach to transition and technology design ran counter to some of its own insights from initial user research. Euphoria conducted initial user research (as I describe further in chapter 4) and heard from trans community members that they were looking for technology to address four needs: access to reliable information about transition, financial support, safety, and community. Solace addresses the first, and Bliss, Euphoria's banking app, aims to address the second. Euphoria has thus far left the last two, safety and community, completely unaddressed; its other apps Clarity, Devotion, and Windfall do not seem aligned with any of these four themes.[3] Of course, each technology creator can choose what to focus on, and no one is obligated to follow recommendations from user research. But safety and community are extremely important trans needs that have come up again and again in my research with trans communities, and I worry that by looking past these and relying instead on their individualist priorities, Euphoria does a disservice to the community.

---

3. These apps seem to be either short-lived or abandoned as of 2024.

Many other technologies in this study had similar individualist orientations, and they almost always were designed based on needs that the creator had identified in their own life, whether as a trans person or, in some cases, a cisgender ally. For example, ShotTraX, the gender-affirming hormone therapy (GAHT)–tracking app, was created by two white trans people, James Husband and a collaborator who preferred to remain anonymous. They received minimal input or feedback from users or potential users, as Husband described: "I would believe that our user feedback is minimal to zero. . . . A lot of the changes, I think, come from me and [collaborator] seeing what the general community is worried about." Husband gave the example of the app's "Tea Time" feature, which switched the app's icon and interface to an image of a tea timer. This ensured that the ShotTraX app's icon would not out anyone to people in their life who were unaware of their trans identity. Husband's collaborator was stealth in her own life, and she designed features aimed at others who were trying not to reveal their trans status—valid concerns in the current antitrans political climate. Husband noted, "I think when . . . [collaborator] created this stealth feature, I feel like it was at a time of more heightened [anxiety]. People were definitely worried about being more out about [being trans]. Worried about getting caught or something." Husband and his collaborator did not seek out trans people to design with or to test the app with. Their only user feedback mechanism was reviews in the app store, but the app was seldom reviewed. The creators had little ability to identify and incorporate into the design the needs of users unlike themselves. I am not suggesting that the "Tea Time" feature is unnecessary for trans people more broadly; I suspect that it is an important feature for many, and indeed, a community-based collaborative design process focused particularly on the design needs of stealth or low-disclosure trans people could be generative. Without community or user input, though, the ShotTraX creators cannot know if they are prioritizing features that align with community needs.

Another GAHT tracking app, Patch Day, took a similar individualistic approach. Creator Juliya Smith stated, "Initial prototyping was zero care about anyone but myself. I'm a new coder, I need to just have something working. This was a fun project for me. I didn't do the whole 'investigating other people's problems.'" The app worked well for Smith and gave her joy as a user: "The most exciting part for me is that I have an app that works that I can use. I use this app every day. I love opening it up and seeing it. I made this and it's doing what I need it to do. I love that." While this speaks to the agency that trans tech creators experience when they create technology that meets their needs, Smith's individualist approach, and the app's lack of user or community input, means that Patch Day is not designed for those who do not share Smith's particular identity as a young white trans woman.

Mentions of individualist and isolationist design approaches showed up time and time again in my interviews with trans tech creators. For example, D. Squinkifer described their game design process as "a pretty isolating process actually, especially with the pandemic." Leo from TransFormaGear said, "I, in my 'willotorium,' as I like to call it, just experiment with making the initial prototype and testing it on myself, first and foremost." Braxton Fleming from Stealth Bros referenced himself as being "a one-man band" who "literally do[es] everything" himself. Sam Martin from QueerViBE designed their technology as part of a PhD dissertation process, a solo endeavor. Avey described their trans biohacking project as "slightly narcissistic." I could go on; individualist, solo design processes are pervasive in trans technology design.

Other types of trans technology, such as art, were relatively individualist by nature; according to many trans art creators, art creation was a rather solitary process, and inspiration came from inside rather than outside the artist. Artist Myra Day stated, "I like trying to do things that would normally take a large team and doing all of that work by yourself." Kaylee Koss, an art and music creator, described her creation process: "Almost always alone . . . Also, being extremely introverted, no matter how enjoyable it is, it can be exhausting to be around or talk to other people, especially new people." While Koss had collaborated with other musicians in some instances, her process felt much more comfortable in isolation. Art, as an expression of oneself, seemed to benefit from individual techniques. Perhaps this is because, in contrast to apps that solve practical problems like transition-tracking and voice training, art is less intended to materially address trans needs. Of course, trans people are drawn to each other's art and see elements of themselves in others' creative output. If trans representation and content inspire more trans people to explore identity and create art, then trans art could have a material impact, perhaps increasing trans cultural production and informing community and identity construction. But it seems less important to involve trans community members in art creation than in trans software or hardware design processes.

In some of the interviews, I started to think back to my own transition and the ways that I was pushed into a rather isolated transition, as I described in the introduction. I mentioned this to Kai McBride and Jackal, hosts of *Stealth: Transmasculine Podcast*, and they discussed the differences in transitioning since the ascent of the Internet. Before trans content was readily available online, they said, in-person community was more prevalent; with transition resources easily available online now, it is less of a practical necessity to find a solid community of support. As McBride and Jackal explained it, "We didn't have the Internet. We had magazines, and we had friends tell us, 'Hey, we're having this support group at this center, or this person's house next weekend, you should come!' We had to physically meet each other in order to talk about these things."

Perhaps individualist trans technology creation goes hand in hand with individualist transition—something that likely increased during the Covid-19 pandemic. This individualist orientation to both design and transition may in part stem from trans people's own lived experiences and learned comfort with isolation. "There's a lot of trans women involved in technology [but] we don't do collaborative stuff, if that makes sense," said Andrea James, a white trans woman and creator of the Transgender Map resource site. "I'll collaborate when it's helpful, but I'd almost rather not in most cases." When I asked her to expand on this, she continued, "I think it's because when we were little we learned to live with loneliness and we just ended up creating our own world and our own space. And so that has just kind of continued. So, I'm hoping it's a generational thing, but that's just how it was back then. I think that a lot of people who I really admire and respect were just kind of doing their own thing." As James hints here, trans people experience marginalization, particularly earlier in life, and isolation and self-reliance start to feel normal—even preferred. If isolation and oppression are pervasive in one's early life, then it is only natural that people turn to individualist approaches focused on solving their own problems in all areas of their lives, including their technology design approaches. James's experiences did tend to echo those of other white trans women I talked with, particularly those who grew up pre-Internet. But orientations toward isolation versus community may be far different for trans women of color and for other multiply marginalized trans people.

If You Are Not Safe for Black Trans People, You Are Not Safe for Trans People: Trans Technology's Potential to Exclude Multiply Marginalized Trans People

Shinigami Eyes is a browser extension that "highlights transphobic and trans-friendly social network pages and users with different colors."[4] In the example shown on Shinigami Eyes' website, trans-friendly Facebook pages like Everyday Feminism are displayed with green text, while Facebook pages deemed transphobic are displayed in red (see figure 3.1). The system uses a combination of manual labeling by its creator, machine learning, and crowdsourcing to determine how to label content. Shinigami Eyes is clearly a useful tool for many trans people. But it does not take race into account; thus, the extension may overlook content created by trans people of color and may recommend content that is racially insensitive or even blatantly racist. As a tweet by @NotThatHeidi points out, after installing Shinigami Eyes, "I immediately noticed how many Black trans folks and Black trans allies are not marked safe, [and] how many blatantly racist folks are."[5] In a follow-up tweet, she stated "If you are not safe for Black trans people, you are not safe for trans people."[6] Shinigami Eyes' creator did not respond to my request for an interview, so I was unable to discuss their design processes with them, and I have no information about their gender, pronouns, and racial identity. According to the Shinigami Eyes website, the creator, a trans person themselves, created the tool in response to their own experience online of not knowing which sites they could trust. But based on @NotThatHeidi's observation and other similar feedback on Twitter, it seems likely that in the process of manual data labeling and creating a training set for the tool's machine learning algorithm, Shinigami Eyes' creator relied on their own experiences and biases and ended up creating a tool that is more likely to consider white trans people "safe" and Black trans people dangerous. The crowdsourcing process could have also introduced or perpetuated biases, depending on who was involved in labeling content. A more human-centered approach that involved trans people of color in design, content labeling, and testing could help to decrease the inadvertent biases that crept into Shinigami Eyes.

---

4. https://shinigami-eyes.github.io/
5. https://twitter.com/NotThatHeidi/status/1600267542635118592
6. https://twitter.com/NotThatHeidi/status/1600267659089960960

Shinigami Eyes

A browser addon that highlights transphobic and trans-friendly social network pages and users with different colors.

- **Shinigami Eyes for Chrome**
- **Shinigami Eyes for Firefox**
- **Shinigami Eyes for Firefox for Android** *(experimental)*

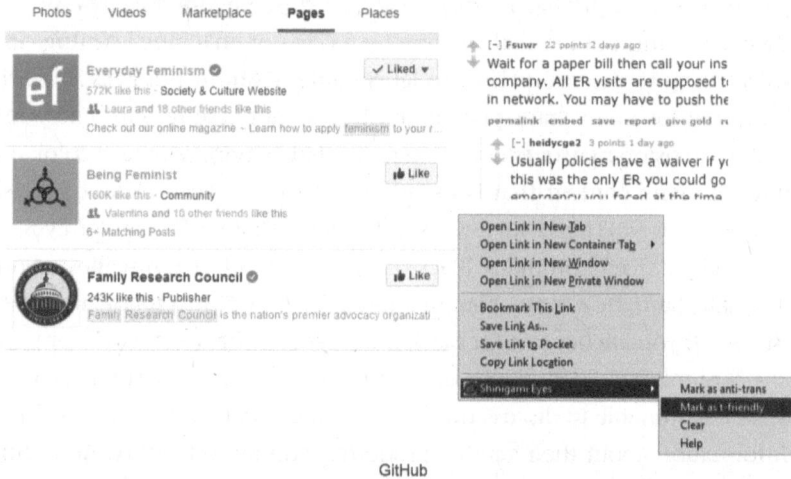

Photos   Videos   Marketplace   **Pages**   Places

ef   Everyday Feminism ✓   ✓ Liked ▾
572K like this · Society & Culture Website
Laura and 18 other friends like this
Check out our online magazine - Learn how to apply feminism to your r

Being Feminist   👍 Like
160K like this · Community
Valentina and 15 other friends like this
6+ Matching Posts

Family Research Council ✓   👍 Like
243K like this · Publisher
Family Research Council is the nation's premier advocacy organizati

[-] **Fsuwr** 22 points 2 days ago
Wait for a paper bill then call your ins
company. All ER visits are supposed t
in network. You may have to push the
permalink embed save report give gold r

[-] **heidycge2** 3 points 1 day ago
Usually policies have a waiver if yt
this was the only ER you could go
emergency you faced at the time

Open Link in New Tab
Open Link in New Container Tab ▸
Open Link in New Window
Open Link in New Private Window

Bookmark This Link
Save Link As...
Save Link to Pocket
Copy Link Location

Shinigami Eyes ▸   Mark as anti-trans
                     Mark as t-friendly
                     Clear
                     Help

GitHub

FAQ

How does it work?

Whenever you visit a social network or a comments section, this extension will color known trans-friendly (green) and anti-trans (red) users/pages differently.

Which sites are supported?

This extension supports Facebook, Twitter, Reddit, Tumblr, Medium, YouTube, Wikipedia articles, search engine results and all the sites with Disqus comments.

How does it know how to color each page?

The initial version has been created through a mix of manual labeling and machine learning, but you can contribute with your own labels.

Figure 3.1

Shinigami Eyes' website, describing how the browser extension works and how it determines which content is trans-friendly versus antitrans: "through a mix of manual labeling and machine learning, but you can contribute your own labels." Screenshot by the author, 2023.

Shinigami Eyes is just one example of trans technologies' potential to exclude and harm multiply marginalized trans people. As the previous sections have shown, trans tech creators often design technology for people similar to themselves—which, for trans tech designers as a group, tends to skew white and highly educated. This is exemplified by the whiteness-as-default orientation of the TransFormaGear prosthetics, described at the beginning of this chapter. Next, I offer several more examples of how designing for one's own needs can limit technological trans care.

The creator of a formative online trans resource, a white trans woman,[7] was forthright about her audience for the site: "I wanted to help the people who were kind of like me, who were college educated, competitive in white collar fields, because I knew if enough of them were able to keep their jobs and thrive, that we would be able to support things like artists and political activists and lobbying groups like NCTE [National Center for Transgender Equality] and things like that. So, that was my grand scheme. So, I was trying to make it for everybody, but I was really focused on people who I was most easily able to help." She was clear in her conviction that "I think really it was written from the point of view of a college-educated white person who was really trying to help the people who were best able to help themselves." I am not sure whether she still holds these views today, but this creator's comments imply an assumption that trans people who are not college-educated and white are less capable of helping themselves. While the site is a valuable resource for less-educated trans people and trans people of color, its creator's harmful assumptions likely inform the resource site and shape what resources it includes; for example, it may overlook resources that would be particularly useful to trans people who are not white, well educated, and affluent.

Trans technologies that are designed to work for certain skin colors and physical characteristics can exclude trans people of other races, as we saw with the US-based TransFormaGear example. Another example of racial exclusion is a makeup support system that uses automatic gender recognition to help trans people be viewed as their chosen gender. This tool was created in a Japanese context, by a team consisting of Japanese and Chinese people. To train the algorithm, the creators used primarily Japanese faces, and they focused on makeup colors that worked best for the skin tones represented

_____

7. I have removed this person's name to lessen potential negative personal impact of my critique.

in their dataset. As a result, creator Ash (a pseudonym) acknowledged that "whether it will work well for other populations is questionable at best." Ash noted that the system could be modified to work better for other races and skin tones by using different training data and "chang[ing] the makeup patterns to actually better suit other cultures." Ash thought that with those changes, the system would work well for non-Japanese people. For a tool deployed in Japan, for which the vast majority of users are likely to be Japanese, it seems reasonable to customize for Japanese skin tones and facial features, but it does limit the tool's usability outside of Japan and might feel exclusionary for those in Japan who do not fit normative beauty standards.

Alex Ahmed struggled with inclusion in creating Project Spectra, a trans voice-training tool. Most trans voice research was conducted primarily with white and Western populations, and Western notions of femininity are closely tied to whiteness as a product of colonization (Spillers 1987), so existing trans voice visualizations necessarily reproduce exclusionary practices (Ahmed, Kim, and Hoffmann 2022). In addition, Ahmed noted that trans voice training is accessed more by trans women "who are white and probably reasonably well-off to afford such a thing, and who are probably a little older." This created an inherently biased dataset: "Whatever categories that we've found that we could plot on an axis came from somewhere: probably white trans speakers," Ahmed said. "We just don't know whether the categories we're applying to people are even relevant. . . . Because we're so connected to the speech science and speech therapy world, we're reliant on what they have to offer us, which is normative crap, typically. So, that's a big limitation as well. Along race lines, class lines, there's no information on how trans people learn or understand their voices differently." It is likely that speech patterns, voice pitches, and resonances are different for nonwhite and non-Western populations, yet trans people of color and those in the Global South must still rely on voice-training apps that teach and measure based on white and Western standards. Because of the historic and systemic issues surrounding voice training, whiteness-as-default made its way into Project Spectra despite the creator's best efforts; Ahmed is herself a trans woman of color, and the app was designed using a community-based approach (described in more detail in chapter 4). As Ahmed lamented, the app ultimately could not conceptualize voice training outside of the constraints of whiteness.

Some white trans tech creators were self-aware about how their privilege could shape their tools, potentially baking in bias and exclusion. Clair

Kronk, creator of the online trans-focused encyclopedia Transpedia, considered including a disclaimer on her site that said, "I'm the only person making this as a white transfemme from the United States. I obviously have my own biases in creating this. . . . In an international context, absolutely use this with a grain of salt, because it was never intended for that context." Kronk acknowledged that her own positionality limited Transpedia's representation of indigenous topics: "Unfortunately, it's pretty lacking. I'm not gonna cover that up in any way. I think, for instance, for a lot of language translations, for a lot of indigenous terminology, the only sources that are really available are written by colonizers." I heard something similar from Digital Transgender Archive (DTA) creator K.J. Rawson, a white trans man, who said, "We're recognizing the ways that the Digital Transgender Archive is slanted toward otherwise privileged factions of trans communities, in ways that you can probably readily anticipate. . . . I'm sure that the DTA doesn't always feel like everyone's resource." Eryn Gitelis, creator of PRYDE Voice and Speech Therapy App, discussed how her own positionality impacted her app's potential lack of inclusivity: "It's a very unfortunately . . . I'm a [cisgender] white woman here, you know, here it is, I created it on my own. I would love to get trans voices on there. Even the design of it [is] very just kind of my personality. I tried to be inclusive; it's hard to do on your own." These interviewees' disclaimers resonate with me, as this book itself is also limited by my whiteness and my gender and class privileges. Like Gitelis I tried to be inclusive, but like Kronk my biases may creep in, and thus like Rawson I recognize that it may not feel like a book for everyone.[8]

Ryan Rose Aceae was similarly self-reflective about their experience as a white game designer and about the lack of explicit race-related content in their video games: "It also feels strange to leave [race] out of the conversation entirely. Because it's not like you can separate race from gender in any meaningful way. . . . It's something that I've continuously been grappling with that I haven't found a solution for yet. I'm not sure it is something that there's a solution for. I think it's something you have to think about continuously. . . . It's something that I'm trying to learn and think about and improve on." I appreciated Aceae's willingness to consider their own privileges, think deeply about race, and consciously reflect on the ways that their

---

8. Creating this book has also been somewhat of an isolationist process, I realize.

games may exclude some trans people and how they might work toward improving on those limitations.

Sam Martin, creator of QueerViBE, an online resource for trans youth, sought to recruit diverse participants when conducting research to inform the site but found it difficult. The online recruitment channels they used tended to include mainly white young trans people, and as Martin noted, "There's a huge amount of mistrust with trans people of color accessing . . . interventions from white people generally. And so I think I, myself, as a white trans person, potentially acted as a barrier [to accessing] more diverse communities that could potentially give me richer feedback about QueerViBE and how it didn't appeal to trans people of color, because it wasn't made with trans people of color." Martin makes an important observation here: involving trans people of color in trans technology design processes is crucial to increase inclusivity, but projects led by white creators are likely to meet resistance and mistrust from nonwhite potential collaborators.

Kronk, Rawson, Gitelis, Aceae, and Martin articulated awareness of their own limitations and of how they may perpetuate exclusion of people unlike themselves—such as trans people of color and trans people in non-Western contexts. The creators who explicitly acknowledged their limitations, and those who described ways to address their technologies' inclusivity blind spots, were a refreshing change from the many creators whose technologies involved similar limitations but who left them unstated and unaddressed. Including disclaimers on these technologies may not make them more inclusive, but it would help users look out for bias and for contexts in which they are unusable, lessening the technologies' potential for harm. Even better, seeking feedback from diverse people can make technologies more inclusive, though as Martin found, it is sometimes difficult to get buy-in from potential collaborators and testers. In the next section, I describe the methods that other trans tech creators used to design in inclusive ways.

Not Just a Vision for White Skinny People: Design for Multiply Marginalized Trans People

Many trans tech creators made conscious efforts to design specifically for multiply marginalized trans people—a form of technological trans care. For instance, while TransFormaGear quickly dismissed custom skin tone options as being not viable, trans supply companies Trans Tape and Transguy Supply both explicitly worked to diversify their offerings for nonwhite skin tones, even when doing so was financially costly. Scout Rose from Transguy Supply described their approach:

> I mean, our darker colors sell about 5 percent of what our lighter colors do, but we still know that we want to be able to offer them, and that we have no intention of taking them off of the platform, regardless if they don't ever take off. Yeah, and it's the same for every product we offer, for the binding tape, for prosthetics. The dark colors that are made for folks with darker skin colors, they sell much slower than the others, and same with the larger sizing in our Cake Bandit underwear line, like the 3XLs. We have a minimum, so we purchase large quantities of them, and they sell very slowly, but it's important to us that those people don't feel alienated. The idea of Transguy Supply being a space that was specifically for transmasculine folks to find things that made them feel better in their body wasn't just a vision for white skinny people.

Trans Tape also offered an extensive line of skin tones, influencing their manufacturer to create additional color options. Similarly, Gaines Blasdel and colleagues ensured that their top surgery nipple placement tool offered a wide selection of skin tones and body types—roughly 1,800 different combinations (Blasdel et al. 2020). These creators, all of whom are white, value inclusion and made sure that their technologies reflected this value by prioritizing options for trans people of color and plus-size trans people.

In creating U-Signal, a prototype safety app for people of color (see figure 3.2), creator Denny Starks based the design directly on the experiences of trans women of color, who experience substantially more violence and threats to safety than other trans people. Starks discussed being inspired to create the app by their own experiences as a nonbinary Black person and by observing a friend's experiences as a Black trans woman who faced frequent violence and threats of violence: "Just seeing and experiencing my own violence, with my own queerness, that inspired me. But it was really being out and about with my friend, and just I worry about her so much. And I'm not trying to come from a savior's complex. I'm always trying to check myself throughout the research, to make sure I'm not doing that. But that's what inspired it, was just going through my own experiences, but also looking at my friends' experiences, and what they're going through, and the lack of support that we have." U-Signal's design was based on insights gathered from initial research interviews with trans people of color, and so Starks was

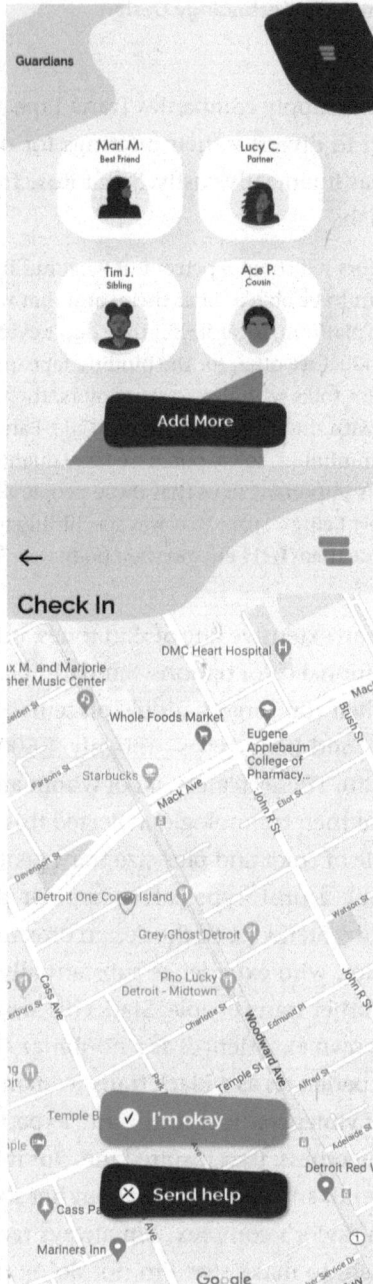

Figure 3.2
(top) "Guardians" and (bottom) "Check In." U-Signal prototype smartwatch and smartphone application to promote safety for trans people of color (designed by Denny Starks, 2021). Reprinted with permission from Denny Starks.

able to incorporate the lived experiences of many multiply marginalized trans people to create an app that spoke directly to their safety needs.

Malaya Mañacop, a Filipina trans woman/femme and bakla, described her approach to creating a gender-affirming surgery app prototype;[9] for her, it was crucial to involve multiply marginalized trans people in the planning and design process. "I think just really having an informed approach as far as including members of those marginalized identities at the planning table. Even before launching a project, making sure that it's accessible and inclusive for all communities." Mañacop also stressed the importance of hiring multiply marginalized people to work on trans technology projects and using community-based and participatory processes throughout. These practices enabled Mañacop to design an app that addressed the needs of multiply marginalized community members surrounding gender-affirming surgery—a perspective that is often overlooked.

In some cases, more privileged trans tech creators worked in collaboration with less privileged trans people, using their tech skills to support others. For instance, Anna-Jayne Metcalfe, a white trans woman in the UK, maintains a website to honor trans people who have been killed, which serves as a resource for the yearly Transgender Day of Remembrance (TDoR). She built and maintains the site in collaboration with a group of trans people of color from the Global South who choose to remain anonymous:

> I'm coming here from this position of privilege. I'm in the UK, which is a relatively safe place. . . . I don't face violence in the street, I'm not having to use GoFundMe to survive, I've got a decent job, I've got resources, and I'm white. So, I am never going to be able to, and wouldn't want to, put my voice over others. It's the voices of the marginalized, the people who are out in the streets who are facing all this shit every day, those are the ones we need to amplify. . . . I'd rather defer to somebody from Mexico, Brazil, Africa, who's got lived experiences of what's going on. Only by standing together, can we change all of this.

Metcalfe described how she centers trans people of color on the TDoR website:

> Mostly by telling their stories, learning from and listening to people who are in those communities. My coeditor, she doesn't want to be identified, is not from the white community. . . . Obviously, I'm not going to identify her and she's not going to come on camera. It's the same with the other activists outside of the Eurocentric world, outside of the Western world. Quite frankly, being able to write all this stuff

---

9. "Bakla" is a Tagalog term that is used to describe transfeminine identity/presentation and is also used colloquially as similar to "queer."

is currently a largely Western privilege. You can't devote time to spreading awareness, in the way that that I'm able to, if you're out on the street firefighting. So in
one way, I know that other communities need people like me to stand up and do
something. . . . They're too busy looking after people who are really facing some of
the horror.

Her collaborators prioritized everyday advocacy and groundwork and did
not have the time and resources available that Metcalfe does; they therefore
could not have created the website on their own. Metcalfe uses her privilege
to support these women, creating technology to meet their common goals of
sharing information about trans violence worldwide. Importantly, Metcalfe
let her collaborators take the drivers' seat in determining the site's direction
and goals, while she took over most of the "grunt work," working on the
technical site aspects and the tedious, emotionally challenging day-to-day
work of researching and chronicling trans murders.

I have described the powerful nature of inclusive technology design and
the importance of including multiply marginalized trans people in design
processes. Yet when design is more personal, as with game design and art
creation, it may be more impactful for creators to draw from their own experiences as multiply marginalized people rather than try to design to be explicitly inclusive of people with wide ranges of identity facets. Game designer
and Filipino-Iranian genderqueer and transmasculine person D. Squinkifer
described their approach:

I am a particular person with my own particular intersections, privileges, marginalization, everything, and it is impossible for me to create something that speaks to
everyone. I think the best thing I can do is create something that feels true to me.
Some people will necessarily relate to that more than others, some people may not
be able to relate to that at all. My solution to that is to position myself as more of
an example, rather than the solution to everything. I care about more marginalized people, more people with specific experiences, creating games of their own,
creating games to represent those experiences. It is not my sole responsibility to
be everything to everyone. . . . Because obviously, being one person who is responsible for all of the diversity and for getting everything right, that is exhausting. That
is, quite frankly, impossible, and that is not my goal.

As Squinkifer pointed out, it is not always possible for each technology to
speak to every facet of the trans community. For games and art, in which
audiences generally expect to be immersed in another person's vision, I agree
with Squinkifer that in an ideal world, many different types of marginalized
people would have the resources and time to create their own technologies

and communicate their own identities and experiences. But when it comes to technologies that are meant to help address trans challenges in the world, it is crucial to design in ways that are inclusive of multiply marginalized trans people.

In each interview, I asked trans tech creators how their technology might work differently, or be more or less effective, for people of different races, genders, abilities, socioeconomic statuses, and other identity facets. Many interviewees focused mostly on the "ability" part of the question, discussing web and app accessibility standards, how their technologies were built and tested to ensure they were accessible for disabled people, and accessibility limitations and ways they planned to improve accessibility in the future. Very few, especially among the white participants, chose to talk about race and how their technology design may not meet the needs of trans people of color. I suspect that race, and designing for racial inclusivity, feels like a more challenging topic for white creators to consider and address. When designing for accessibility, designers have standardized guides that they can reference (e.g., W3C Web Accessibility Initiative 2022). Designing for racial inclusion is not as easily distilled into checklists and guidelines. With recent advances in thinking about race and technology (Benjamin 2019; Gray 2020; Noble 2018), and with an increased focus on including trans people of color in design processes, I hope that trans technologies can improve to better account for nonwhite trans experiences.

Conclusion

In this chapter, I have argued that individualistic and isolationist trans technology design processes sometimes lead to technologies that respond more to the needs of their designers than to the needs of the larger trans population. Because trans tech creators are disproportionately white and well educated, the technologies they create are likely to mirror this privilege, excluding trans people of color and trans people who are less educated and affluent. To be more inclusive of and practice trans care toward multiply marginalized trans people, trans technologies should use community-based design approaches. Creators should involve multiply marginalized trans people in design processes, foregrounding broader trans needs and challenges rather than the creator's individual needs, and explicitly take an intersectional approach to design. These arguments build on prior work by micha cárdenas (2022) and

Sasha Costanza-Chock (2020) arguing that community-based approaches require that designers listen to trans people of color about their experiences rather than imposing designers' own ideas on communities. It also draws from the work of researchers calling for more intersectional and explicitly antiracist approaches to technology design (Erete, Israni, and Dillahunt 2018; Erete, Rankin, and Thomas 2023; Gray 2020; Ogbonnaya-Ogburu et al. 2020) and from those working on designing antiracist technology (Erete, Rankin, and Thomas 2023; To et al. 2021).

If technology is something that extends a person's agency, then we must think about *whose* agency is extended and, more importantly, *whose is not* (Lawson 2010). A new technology may extend agency for some people, meeting their needs and empowering them, but leave other people's needs unmet, disadvantaging them in comparison. If certain types of trans people consistently reap the benefits of trans technologies, then gaps in life chances and access to resources needed to survive will continue to widen between those with more and less privilege.

Moving forward, how can we work to ensure that trans technologies are designed not only for the more privileged facets of the trans community? Trans tech creators do not choose or intend to be discriminatory or to bypass the needs of multiply marginalized trans people. They fall into creating technology alone or in small groups because it is convenient and it feels comfortable and empowering. Many of them never learned about human-centered design; some that have learned about it lack the time and resources to apply it. Human-centered, truly inclusive design is *difficult*. It is actually quite rare, not only in trans technology, but in technology broadly. But even though it is difficult to design inclusively, trans tech creators should still try. There are steps forward. For instance, when deciding what to create, trans tech creators can increase their technologies' impact and inclusion by intentionally working to understand the broader trans population's needs and challenges, rather than drawing primarily from their own experiences. Doing so requires forming community connections and building partnerships with people unlike oneself.

Above, I described how trans hackathons often lead to the same "solutions" over and over again, such as apps to find safe and affirming local businesses. Indeed, many have observed that hackathons in general are less about creating usable solutions that will actually be deployed and more about networking and building community among programmers and designers (Broussard 2015). What if trans hackathons sought to take a more community-based and needs-centric approach? I can imagine hackathons that bring together people with technical and design skills with multiply marginalized trans community members—people who have good ideas but lack the skills, resources, and time to create technology to put their ideas into practice. Such efforts would require hard work to make sure multiply marginalized people feel comfortable and explicitly welcome in these spaces. By brainstorming needs first, or by drawing from the community-generated list of trans challenges that I presented in this book's introduction, designers can create technologies that actually fill needs gaps and can make larger impacts on the trans people who could benefit most from technological solutions to their challenges. Previous community-centered design research in an antiracist context has taken this approach, seeking to understand needs before designing, and this has led to promising design contributions (To et al. 2021). Such approaches may not be feasible within a day-long hackathon, but requirements gathering and community-building work could be done in advance, and there could be follow-up for the most promising hackathon projects, offering support for further human-centered design processes, development, deployment, and maintenance after the fact.

Another approach to making trans technology more inclusive would be to increase the number of multiply marginalized trans people with technical skills, who would then be able to exercise agency to create technology that meets their own, and their communities', needs. Programs such as TransTech Social Enterprises are working to help trans people, especially trans people of color, gain technical skills and succeed in tech careers. Yet we still have a long way to go until the most marginalized trans people are on par with the most privileged in terms of access to the training, education, resources, and networks necessary to succeed in tech design and development. Further, as Ruha Benjamin (2019) shows, efforts to diversify the tech industry often only result in surface-level changes that leave structural racism undisturbed. Thus, we need more trans people of color not just as tech company employees, but as trans tech creators—with all of the power and *agency to design* that many white trans tech creators enjoy. These multiply marginalized creators could then design based on their own needs and desires and those of their communities.

But is this really a solution? Technology design cannot solve problems like systemic racism, transphobia, poverty, and ableism. What we really need is social change (Benjamin 2019). Perhaps trans people's time would be better spent on activism and advocacy to fight against racist and transphobic policies and practices; this may be more impactful than spending time learning to code or working toward technology design.

Just as many people assumed that the early Internet was "raceless" when it in fact defaulted to whiteness (Nakamura 2002), trans technologies are often assumed to be race agnostic when in fact they are designed with white trans experiences at the forefront. Ultimately, however the changes are brought about, trans technologies need to move away from their whiteness-as-default orientations and toward a trans politics that forefronts trans people who are marginalized based on race, ethnicity, ability, socioeconomic status, and additional identity facets. This is how we can move away from a trans technology imagination that is steeped in whiteness. As we continue to work toward these changes, meaningfully involving diverse trans people and communities in design processes can help to reduce the limitations and privileges inherent in isolationist approaches to technology design, as I explore in the next chapter.

4   Involving Trans People and Communities in Trans Technology Design Processes

The ride-hailing app Uber recently implemented a process to increase rider safety and confidence, requiring potential drivers to verify their identity by uploading a current photo of their face for comparison to the picture on their drivers' license. However, this system actively excludes some trans people because it assumes that people's faces stay the same over time, an assumption that is clearly untrue for many trans people. (It is equally untrue for people who merely change their appearance by growing a beard or wearing glasses—but facial recognition systems more easily accept those types of changes.) Uber's system flagged many trans people attempting to sign up to drive as fraudulent, which prevented them from beginning work—a blatant case of employment discrimination (Hussain 2021).

Identity verification systems like Uber's are often harmful for trans people because they are grounded in rigid expectations for appearance, name, and gender, which often change during gender transition. In the Uber example, harms could have been mitigated by involving users, including trans people, in the design process to ensure that the system works as it is supposed to and does not exclude marginalized populations. What we call human-centered design or user-centered design are processes grounded in the idea that the people who will use a technology should be involved throughout the design process. A human-centered approach is important because each person's experience is limited and no one can anticipate all aspects of how people

Parts of this chapter were previously published as an article: Haimson, Oliver L., Kai Nham, Hibby Thach, and Aloe DeGuia. 2023. "How Transgender People and Communities Were Involved in Trans Technology Design Processes." In *Proceedings of the 2023 CHI Conference on Human Factors in Computing Systems*, 1–16. CHI '23. New York: Association for Computing Machinery. https://doi.org/10.1145/3544548.3580972.

will use a technological system.[1] Probably, most Uber designers and engineers are cisgender, and it would not have occurred to them that their system would discriminate against trans people. It is only by involving people and having them interact with technology that we can see what we might have missed and how to design better to meet a wider range of users' needs (Nielsen 1993). While trans tech designers are generally much more mindful of inclusive design than mainstream technology designers, this chapter shows that human-centered design processes are important even when technology designers are themselves part of marginalized groups.

Traditionally, technology has been designed with minimal user input, and design was considered a logical and objective means of problem-solving (Norman 2005). But it matters who chooses the problems to solve and what solutions are seen as viable (Huppatz 2015). In a user-centered or human-centered approach, the design process moves away from one-size-fits-all design approaches (Ritter, Baxter, and Churchill 2014) to include user testing, ideation with users, and iteration (Norman and Draper 1986). Human-computer interaction scholars often describe this approach as "design thinking," a user-centric problem-solving design approach that involves ideation, generating many alternative solutions, and iteration (Gibbons 2016; Zimmerman, Forlizzi, and Evenson 2007), with designers adjusting the design after encounters with users.

Users are brought into design processes in several phases. First, designers conduct initial research with potential users to build a greater understanding of their needs, identities, and use contexts (Sharp, Preece, and Rogers 2019). This requirements gathering phase involves methods like interviews, surveys, and sometimes participatory design sessions with intended users. Second, during the testing phase, designers present their prototype to users and gather feedback through methods like task analysis (Nielsen 1993; Sharp, Preece, and Rogers 2019). Testing can involve user testing or play testing (for games)—any activity that puts the user in front of the technology, allowing the designer to see what works and what does not. Ideally, testing is iterative: users interact with different prototype versions, and designers improve each

---

1. Further, people's actions and interactions in computing systems emerge through use over time and often diverge from designers' intended or expected uses (Dourish 2001; Suchman 2007). By studying users' embodied interactions, we can learn how to design technologies better (Dourish 2001).

in response to feedback. Human-centered design is not a binary but a spectrum, ranging from no user involvement to user involvement in every step of the process, along with all possibilities in between.

In participatory design, community members are not just research participants but collaborators in the design process (Simonsen and Robertson 2013). Participatory design "is driven by social interaction as users and designers learn together to create, develop, express and evaluate their ideas and visions" (Simonsen and Robertson 2013). Participatory approaches are especially important when designing technology for marginalized populations, because designers often bring assumptions and goals into the design that may not align with the community's goals (Erete, Israni, and Dillahunt 2018; Harrington, Erete, and Piper 2019). Engaging marginalized groups in the design process helps designers to critically interrogate their assumptions, but it requires substantial time to develop trust with communities (Erete, Israni, and Dillahunt 2018; Harrington, Erete, and Piper 2019). Designers must also be intentional, taking into account tensions such as the historical context of the research environment and any potential harms of the collaboration (Harrington, Erete, and Piper 2019).

The design justice approach, described by Sasha Costanza-Chock (2020) in their book *Design Justice*, provides a way to think critically about design and consider how design can more equitably distribute technology's potential benefits and harms. The Design Justice Network advocates for a community-centered design approach that aims to work with marginalized communities without further burdening them. Design justice involves asking three key questions throughout the design process: "Who participated in the design process? Who benefited from the design? Who was harmed by the design?" (Costanza-Chock 2020). Design justice extends beyond design thinking. It does not simply innovate or improve designs but ensures that technological innovations benefit marginalized communities. Design justice is thus an especially relevant approach for trans technology design. In this chapter I detail how trans individuals and communities sometimes participated in and potentially benefited from trans technology design.

Many designers working with trans communities are themselves trans; in my research, 80 percent of designers were trans and/or nonbinary. This shared identity with the people a technology is aimed at can be a great advantage—after all, the designer knows the trans experience intimately and often feels like an expert in navigating the needs the technology is designed to address.

On the other hand, no one trans designer (or small group of designers) can possibly embody or understand the full range of trans experiences that must be accounted for in design. This is especially true for users with multiple marginalized identities. Thus, even when a designer is trans or a design team includes trans people, it is still vital to include trans communities in design processes. In my research, about 19 percent of the technologies meaningfully followed a human-centered design approach by involving trans people and communities throughout the design process; an additional 39 percent involved some aspects of human-centered design but did not involve community members throughout.

These numbers are more promising than those documented in other studies, possibly because so many creators in my study were trans themselves. In a previous study examining technological interventions for trans communities, only 23 percent of the technologies surveyed involved trans people in the consultation or development process, and then primarily as part of focus groups or advisory boards (Wong et al. 2022). Only 13 percent of technologies surveyed in that study directly involved trans people in design or development processes, signaling a severe lack of trans inclusion in trans technology design (Wong et al. 2022). Use of human-centered design processes is even more scarce in mainstream (non-trans-specific) technology development (Carthy, Cormican, and Sampaio 2021).

This chapter describes trans technology design processes to show how, and to what extent, marginalized users are involved in design processes. Here, I go beyond considering how design processes *should* work to illuminate how design processes actually *do* work in this context. I begin by describing several projects that involved community members in participatory roles throughout the entire design process. Then I discuss trans technology projects that involved community members only at certain stages—usually by gathering feedback from users or conducting user testing. This chapter helps us to understand how trans technologies are designed and developed, how these processes can bring in trans communities, and how trans tech designers' own identities interplay with their technology creation. I argue that trans technologies best address trans needs and most meaningfully practice technological trans care when their design involves community members; involving trans perspectives and lived experiences helps designers to rework and rethink technology design to benefit trans people. I then highlight a frequent disconnect that happens with trans technology between design and deployment: when trans people and communities were involved in design processes (which occurred more often in academic settings), the technologies were often not fully deployed, never reaching the people who needed them most.

Technological trans care is pervasive in the design processes I describe in this chapter. By meaningfully involving trans people and communities in design processes, trans tech creators show how deeply they care about trans communities and meeting their needs. Human-centered design shifts the focus from the creator's own needs toward technological care work for a broader set of trans people. This brings up another ambivalence that trans tech creators experience: when design processes are deeply personal, often connected to their own identity, creators vacillate between design for self and design for community, between design in isolation and design with community members. Sometimes trans tech creators lean into both ways of designing at different points in the process, typically moving from individual to more community-based: a design that starts with an individual need receives feedback indicating that it addresses a need for the larger trans communities, and thus a design process that started in isolation may expand to include community input. This ambivalence between self and other often remains, as trans tech creators try out different design approaches that involve community members to varying extents.

This Is Not Just a Me Thing: Human-Centered and Participatory Design Processes

Some trans tech creators stuck closely to a human-centered and participatory design process, with community members involved at all stages: ideation, design, testing, and iteration. For example, Guilherme Colucci Pereira and his collaborators used participatory design methods over a period of more than six months to create LGBTrust, an app to help increase safety for trans and queer people in Brazil.[2] The process consisted of a series of workshops that involved participants in design from "the beginning, from having the idea and discussion of what this app would be, until the prototyping and until the evaluation, the first usages. This group of people participated in

---

2. For more detail on Pereira's design process and the LGBTrust app, please see his publications (Pereira and Baranauskas 2017, 2018).

everything." Design activities included storytelling, picture cards, brainwriting, discussion, and prototype evaluation (Pereira and Baranauskas 2018). Pereira began the project without having a clear sense of what he and the design workshop participants would be creating. He said that in early design sessions, "I tried to make it very clear that I had no idea about what kind of application we would end up with. I had no idea of what kind of topics we would face and we would embrace."

Throughout the design workshops, the focus on safety emerged: "This is very deeply related to all these concerns about violence in Brazil. So it was natural to talk about and to think about safety: how to create safe spaces . . . to share about what places you should be careful, where you should not go. . . . But it was not given by me—it was not my choice at the beginning. It was just the natural development of the project." In this human-centered design process, Pereira learned along with participants that safety was a primary concern and that the technology design should focus on safety. Listening to participants and focusing on their primary needs was a way of practicing technological trans care. When I asked Pereira what he found to be the most exciting part of the LGBTrust design process, he answered, "I think this surprise, because it validated the choice for the participatory approach, because for sure I couldn't do this by myself. And to see this meeting by meeting, exercise by exercise, growing, and always being meaningful . . . it was very rewarding." The participatory approach enabled the technology design to go in unexpected directions, ensuring that the design focused on the topics most salient for the workshop participants and likely for trans and queer people in Brazil more broadly: safety. A deployed, working LGBTrust app could make trans people substantially safer—though as I discuss later in this chapter, unfortunately, the app was never fully deployed.

In Barcelona, Saúl Baeza Argüello and colleagues used a similarly participatory human-centered approach to develop a series of prosthetic facial devices that enabled people to present several different digital identities via Apple Face ID.[3] These prostheses were partly practical, in that presenting multiple digital identities can help trans people separate their past, current, and future selves during gender transition, and also help wearers

---

3. For more detail on Baeza Argüello's design process and the prosthetics for Apple Face ID, please see Baeza Argüello et al. 2021.

avoid surveillance in public spaces (which has the potential to "out" people as trans before they are ready to disclose). Yet the prostheses were also a conceptual art project that allowed people to think critically about identity, explore identity fluidity and multiplicity, and practice obfuscation with mainstream technologies like Apple Face ID and surveillance systems more broadly. Baeza Argüello explicitly considered this tool to be a trans technology because it enables "identity ambiguity, multiplicity, and fluidity," aligning with my previously published definition of trans technologies (Baeza Argüello et al. 2021; Haimson et al. 2019a). While this project's design process was not quite as open-ended as Pereira's, the design team wanted to determine "all the outcomes that are possible with this technology," so they organized design workshops that would "mix a lot of different perspectives, personal positions, and so on." Describing the process, Baeza Argüello said, "We're not [explicitly] saying the specific uses of what we're developing. Our aim is to really open [up] that conversation, put those tools [out] there and see how people can express a lot of different values. That's why it was super important for us to get all those different opinions." Baeza Argüello's design process thrived because it left the technology's values and uses open-ended, and the designers learned from community members how the technology could be used and understood.

At the workshops, designers and participants worked together to push the range of possibilities for the facial prostheses. Workshop participants used scissors to design and adjust facial prostheses and then experimented with their own iPhones and Apple Face ID to see how the prostheses impacted their identity verification (Baeza Argüello et al. 2021). The research team ensured that the workshops were accessible to people with little technical knowledge and that they were playful rather than serious, inviting people to express and communicate their identities, allowing people to explore hybrid physical and digital identities with facial prostheses. Baeza Argüello described this as a "super interesting approach and experience between all the people involved," primarily because of the trust and care that the participants and researchers developed with each other throughout the process. However, Baeza Argüello said that the process was quite "difficult and stressful in the beginning": it required actively learning how to incorporate a group of people into the design process, involve everyone, and represent each participant's unique narrative in the technology. This was a process of learning how to demonstrate trans care via collaborative technology design.

Alex Ahmed, codesigner of Project Spectra, a voice app for trans people, described her design work with a group of community members, done as part of her PhD dissertation research:

> People joined in and over the course of a year and a half . . . we worked on this. I was trying to involve people in different capacities. There were folks who were interested in doing software development, or algorithm design, or resonant frequencies, the various parameters of the voice that you could pick up using their computer and a microphone. They were working on that for their own purposes; they were wanting to develop these tools out of their own interest. . . . We had people working on the visual design, people working on the code, people working on algorithms, meeting informally and just talking on Discord.

Ahmed brought together a loose coalition of people, each of whom was motivated to work on the app by their own experiences, needs, and desire to use their skills toward the project. Ahmed had many complex feelings about the extractive nature of participatory design research in academic settings, such as her university's tendency to involve communities in research that primarily benefits the researchers rather than community members, and she was concerned about the potential for unintentional harm (Ahmed et al. 2021; Harrington, Erete, and Piper 2019). She took a community-based approach to offset some of these issues.

Two trans technology projects were produced as part of the University of Michigan master's-level course Introduction to Interaction Design, taught by human-computer interaction (HCI) scholar Tawanna Dillahunt and grounded in a human-centered approach to design.[4] One of these projects, Flux, was a transition and community-building app designed by a team of students in Dillahunt's class. The designers took an explicitly human-centered design approach, involving trans people of color in design workshops to envision and design the app. The other trans tech project from that class was Denny Starks's U-Signal, a wearable technology and app to increase safety for trans people of color (Starks, Dillahunt, and Haimson 2019). "The most important part of the design process for me is always talking to the users, getting their opinions," said Starks, "and [Dillahunt] made sure that we did that every step of the way. . . . Always talking to users, and just going to them and being like, 'Okay, what do you think now?'" Because the class was only one semester long, students

---

4. I teach the undergraduate version of this class, but none of the students in my class have designed explicitly trans technologies. In 2023, one team designed a queer app called Mosaic.

did not have enough time to conduct participatory design sessions, though they did learn about the method. Starks plans to iterate on U-Signal using participatory design sessions: "I want to take a more participatory approach, and this time really, really work with [community members] side by side. . . . I really want to give them more control and let them know, 'Hey, this is for us, by us. This is not just a me thing.' And that was part of checking myself in the design process, of having to take my own feelings and opinion out of it." Starks here describes centering community members' perspectives; participatory approaches are one way of implementing technological trans care in trans technology design processes. While Flux and U-Signal were the only two trans technologies in my dataset that were designed in courses, I suspect many others have been and will be produced by students. Technologies like LGBTrust, U-Signal, and the others in this section show how community involvement in design allows technologies to evolve to meet community needs, rather than simply fulfilling the designer's predetermined goals.

Switching the Approach: Requirements Gathering and Initial Research

The majority of trans tech creators I spoke with incorporated elements of human-centered design at certain points in their processes but did not use the approach throughout. Many creators conducted initial research to understand more about the people and communities who would use their technology. In human-centered design, this is known as "requirements gathering" (Sharp, Preece, and Rogers 2019). For instance, at the HackOut LGBTQ+ Hackathon, in the early stages of designing the Euphoria suite of transition apps, Robbi Katherine Anthony (who also goes by RKA) surveyed many trans people: "During that weekend, we started with the survey asking users what was keeping them stuck in transition, because in my personal experience, that's the worst place for someone to be. And our . . . survey respondents identified a few different things, but primarily, it was a lack of accurate and reliable information, the financial means to be able to afford it, and the safety, and the community aspect. And those became our three [sic] pillars for all the different apps we would design." This initial research allowed the Euphoria team to identify user needs that they could address with their technology.[5]

---

5. Yet note that RKA listed four themes, and Euphoria's apps (Solace and Bliss) only address the first two, as I discussed further in chapter 3.

Other creators did more involved initial research with communities. For example, Rob Eagle, creator of the *Through the Wardrobe* augmented reality (AR) exhibition, described their immersive ethnographic work with local trans and queer communities: "So it became a field site, but it was also my home. And so those boundaries as well, between insider/outsider, between ethnographer and 'supposed to be the professional person' and the nonprofessional person, a lot of those blur, I think, particularly within a long-term ethnography in which you are really embedded within a community and where you become a part of that community, the community becomes part of you." Though Eagle was a researcher, they were also a community member, and *Through the Wardrobe* was more than simply a trans technology; Eagle had recently moved to Bristol, and so collaborative technology design was also a way for them to connect to the local community there on a personal level. This embedded approach strengthened the project, as it enabled Eagle to combine their own experiences and the community's experiences.

Sometimes, conducting initial research entirely changed important elements of the project or its direction. Denny Starks had initially envisioned U-Signal, their safety app prototype for trans people of color, as a standalone wearable technology: "I really wanted to focus on wearable technology. But then when I started to work with participants, they were like, 'Oh, we would like to have a smartphone app.' So it is also a smartphone app that comes with . . . a smart watch." A similar tension faced micha cárdenas in her project Autonets, a series of technological garments that used wireless transmitters to alert people in one's network if they were unsafe. She describes the design process in her book (cárdenas 2022) and also discussed it in our interview:

> I had been an artist working with GPS technology for years on the Transborder Immigrant Tool. When I took that to communities to think about trans safety, a lot of the communities were like, "No thanks." So, then I switched the approach to being not about GPS, but just about detecting proximity with signal strength [the Autonets project]. Even then, when I started working internationally with groups in Colombia and Brazil, they were like, "That's cool that you can make a $100 hoodie, but if we had $100, we would buy smartphones." Real cost-prohibitive news for the communities that I wanted to work with. So, I changed the approach, and I think about that as part of the design process. I've been really inspired by the Design Justice Network: Sasha Costanza-Chock's work and Una Lee's work. Thinking about design as a process that could center affected communities instead of just centering the designer.

Eventually, cárdenas changed her project's focus entirely, shifting instead toward nondigital communication networks, thus bringing the project into alignment with the community's feedback and making it more accessible for low-income community members (cárdenas 2022; Chen 2019). As these stories indicate, though a designer might have a particular form factor (such as wearable technology) in mind, designing for community needs means understanding what would work best for the community and changing anything that would keep them from actually using the technology. In the case of these safety technologies, communities expressed clear preferences for technologies different than what the designers had initially envisioned. These examples demonstrate how trans community involvement in the early requirements gathering phase of design can help ensure that the resulting technologies meet the community's needs.

What Is Your Opinion on This? Gathering and Incorporating Feedback from Users

Creators who did not fully commit to a human-centered design approach still often solicited and incorporated feedback from trans people during the design process. Gathering feedback took many different forms, including having informal conversations with users, circulating surveys and feedback forms, reading user reviews, and receiving feedback at public exhibitions.

Several trans tech creators described gathering feedback via informal conversations with community members, in person or via phone or email. Rob Eagle, creator of the AR identity exploration experience *Through the Wardrobe*, took a community-based approach to gathering feedback with "a couple of groups here in Bristol, young, queer, trans groups." Eagle gathered feedback from these groups via "discussions, and . . . I was demoing the headset with [them] and getting their reflections. So the design process was led very much by feedback." In Eagle's project, feedback was combined with user testing sessions in community settings to make sure that the technology worked well for trans and queer audiences. Listening to and incorporating community feedback was a way for creators to embed trans care into their technologies. Similarly, Taylor Chiang from TranZap described consistently reaching out for feedback to people in their personal networks within the trans community: "This whole project I feel like I've been really leveraging the folks in my life that I know either in real life or online who are part of the LGBTQ+ community, saying like, 'Hey, I'm working on this project . . . what is your opinion on this?' And while it's only one person's opinion and things can change, it's been really helpful to at least have people to ask questions." These approaches are important to Chiang and improve TranZap because, in their words, "I'm only one person. I can have a great idea; it can also probably suck."

Feedback from trans community members sometimes helped trans tech creators avoid causing harm to trans users by uncovering important issues during testing. For example, RKA from the transition resource app Solace gathered feedback from users via a survey and found that the app was missing a very basic functionality for trans users: "So on all of our surveys we have multiple open-form questions for people to be able to say 'What do you wish Solace could do that the app can't?' . . . One of the biggest complaints we got was that there's no way to change your name in the app itself, which is an incredibly glaring design decision on our end. But that was one of those points that we're able to say, 'Okay, how do we actually design around this,' because this problem probably reflects more than 51 percent of this . . . population." User feedback uncovered an issue that trans people typically face in mainstream software but would not expect to encounter in a trans-designed app—one that RKA herself had not noticed, though she is also trans.

Similarly, Wayne Temple discovered through user feedback that one of his design decisions in his True Self browser extension, which replaces one's prior name with one's chosen name, had a potential design flaw that would not meet the needs of the entire trans community. He had designed the extension to be persistent, so that "once you put it in, every time you open your browser it's there," but as he pointed out, this could "obviously have drawbacks for people in shared scenarios who maybe can accidentally get outed." In user reviews, the feedback on this feature was split: some users really liked the extension's persistence, while others expressed frustration at potentially being outed. Temple considered a solution that might satisfy both camps: "Maybe I should figure out a way in another iteration where I can maybe allow the user to turn that off so that it doesn't persist." A toggle switch for persistence could be a simple yet elegant solution. As these examples show, trans tech creators can reduce harm to their users by gathering and acting on user feedback.

Another approach to incorporating user feedback involved researching similar existing technologies and designing to address their limitations. Before developing PRYDE Voice & Speech Therapy App, creator Eryn Gitelis read through feedback from users of existing voice and speech apps to inform her design: "So I read through those reviews, what people didn't like, and then tried to stay away from that, and what they wanted more of and tried to add more of that in mine." Reading user reviews of existing technology is a clever approach to gathering user feedback, and I expected that it would come up in more interviews, but Gitelis was the only person to mention this technique.

For art and game-based projects, creators received feedback from audience members when displaying their work in a public setting. This feedback tended to be primarily positive, which was validating for creators but did not often offer actionable suggestions for improvement—somewhat of a moot point, since once artists and game creators reach the exhibition stage, they are fairly far along in the development process and are usually not looking to significantly revise their work. Sandy Stone described the blandly positive audience feedback that she and her team received when launching their *Public Genitals Project*, a 2000 art project in which people placed screens displaying strangers' genitals over their crotch area. "The audience members were . . . I mean, they're not articulate in the way that you might think. They said, 'Oh, I love it.' Or 'Isn't that interesting?' I don't remember anyone asking questions about, 'How did you put it together? What questions did you ask?' . . . No one said, 'Tell me more about the aesthetic details of this.' People just said, 'Oh, I like that.' So there you have it." Interestingly, Stone focused on the limitations of both what people did say and what they did not say. This indicates the drawbacks of involving people only at the tail end of design processes, when a project is complete or nearly so. If audience members had been involved earlier in the design process, they could have potentially influenced both the project's aesthetic details or guiding questions—the things Stone seems to wish they would have asked about. This project faced another challenge: though the *Public Genitals Project* technology can be read as trans, its design team was primarily cisgender, and it was exhibited in Texas in the year 2000. Likely, there were few trans people at the exhibit, and it would have been difficult for Stone to involve more trans people in the design process, given the time and location. This example demonstrates some of the difficulties of involving trans people in design processes.

Like Stone, game creator Ryan Rose Aceae sounded somewhat unexcited about the highly positive feedback they received when exhibiting their games: "It's very overwhelmingly positive sometimes, like embarrassingly so. I get very overwhelmed. A lot of people will say stuff like that it's the first time they've really seen themselves represented in a game. That's a big one. That it provoked them to think about their own identity in a different way." Trans representation in both games and game creation can be particularly powerful, and exhibitions are a way for creators to hear that from their audiences. But at exhibitions, Aceae also sometimes received feedback they were not interested in acting on: "Heather [Flowers, Aceae's collaborator] and I were showing *GenderWrecked* at the Smithsonian arcade. We had a parent come over with a kid and played the game, and they were like, 'Oh, you should make a game like this about trans stuff for kids.' And I was like, 'Someone should do that. But my work, I think, is very adult oriented.' And I love kids. But I'm not very interested in telling kid-friendly stories. . . . It's very far from what I'm interested in." Here, we see that feedback is not always helpful, especially when it is unsolicited and implies that the work should move in an entirely new direction. Art and game creation can be very personal modes of creative expression, and sometimes audience feedback can run counter to the creator's own vision. Fortunately, creators can choose what to do with any feedback they receive: move forward with it, file it for later, or simply ignore it.

Instagram DMs and Discord Servers: Technological Means of Gathering and Incorporating User Feedback

The way user feedback is gathered matters, especially for technology aimed at marginalized groups. Many creators gather feedback from users via technological means, such as social media platforms or in-app feedback platforms. Eryn Gitelis, creator of PRYDE Voice & Speech Therapy App, described users sending feedback on how the app could improve via direct messages on Instagram instead of via public reviews: "So that's how I was getting the negative feedback, which is awesome that nobody reviewed it poorly." This interactive gathering of feedback via Instagram messages allowed Gitelis to improve her app without negative feedback being posted publicly. It also enabled her to get to know her users via casual messages, which gave her direct lines of communication to people who often had important suggestions for design adjustments.

A number of other creators used social media networks to gather feedback throughout the design process. Greyson Simon from Trans Language Primer, a language guide about gender terms, described their approach: "My friend group on Facebook, I've spent a lot of time curating and building that group of people. The original project had gone through so many of them in terms of making sure that we were user friendly, and making sure that it was legible. Cis people [were] making sure that it was legible to the older people, like my mom." Similarly, when creating a tool for people to specify nipple placement prior to top surgery (Blasdel et al. 2020), Gaines Blasdel reached out to his Facebook network: "I just posted this on my Facebook and was like, 'Which [nipple placement] would you choose?' just to have a first round of thoughts. And people were clustered here [points to his chest]. Which means in order for it to be useful . . . we need to move [the nipple placement] in. And probably provide an option that's even more medial than this." Taylor Chiang from the health care resource app TranZap frequently used their social media following to get feedback, posting screenshots of the app prototype on their Instagram story and requesting feedback from their followers. These examples show how social media worked as a lightweight approach to gathering feedback, enabling creators to potentially hear from a wide range of people (i.e., both trans and cisgender audiences and people of different ages) who were easy to reach and likely to respond.

Trans tech creators also created new online communities on platforms like Discord and Slack; these were often formed so that users could connect and form a community, but they also allowed users to provide feedback about the technology. Podcast host Tuck Woodstock described *Gender Reveal*'s Slack community as one mechanism out of many where he can receive feedback from his audience: "We have a Slack community that I get feedback from, we have a newsletter where people can send messages, we have contact forms on our website that people use. We have Twitter and Instagram. We're pretty much constantly in contact with people. And we also have a mailbox and people have sent us just letters and cards and feedback that way as well, which has been really cute and fun. So there's all sorts of different ways that people talk to us all the time." The use of multiple platforms and sources was common, for it allowed users to communicate in the format most convenient for them. As TransTech Social Enterprises put it in an announcement in July 2022: "Discord has been widely suggested and requested! And with true TransTech fashion; you asked and we made it happen. With feedback from all of you about ways we can connect together better, communicate AND have voice channels to network with one another and us; we have created our very own Discord server." TransTech originally used Slack to communicate with users, but in response to this user feedback, it switched over to Discord. Technologically mediated user communities were especially useful, because they gave users a direct way to communicate with trans tech creators while at the same time fostering community.

Some apps, including transition-tracking apps like Transcapsule and TRACE, gathered user feedback in-app. During the beta phases, both apps used Testflight, a beta testing platform that enables users to provide feedback directly through the app. After officially launching, TRACE continued to regularly gather user feedback using an online platform called Canny. TRACE posted in the app's feed, inviting users to provide feedback (see figure 4.1). In these posts, TRACE positioned itself as different from other apps, saying that they "would actually listen" to community feedback because "we aren't just 'an app,' we are a part of this community." TRACE was founded by a highly visible trans man, Aydian Dowling, who most TRACE users would recognize as indeed being a member of the trans community.

This Is Our Garden: Trans People and Communities Involved in Design Processes

Some trans tech creators who did not use a fully human-centered or participatory design process still involved trans people and communities in the design process in significant ways: through collective governance, intentional community-building, involving trans people as collaborators, involving trans online communities, incorporating the community's ideas and values into the project, and through trans advisory boards.

Trans Peer Network, an online trans support community hosted on Discord, involved community members in an ongoing way in the design process: it is nonhierarchical, and through collaborative decision-making, users and creators cocreate the online space. Laur Bereznai, its founder, described the importance of "continuously regenerating and reshaping the community as a space that it supports and empowers its members by limiting . . . hierarchical structures and centering the margins. So it's very much not a 'We are building a service that you use,' it's a, 'This is our garden and we all tend it together, and we make it what we need it to be as a community.' That's

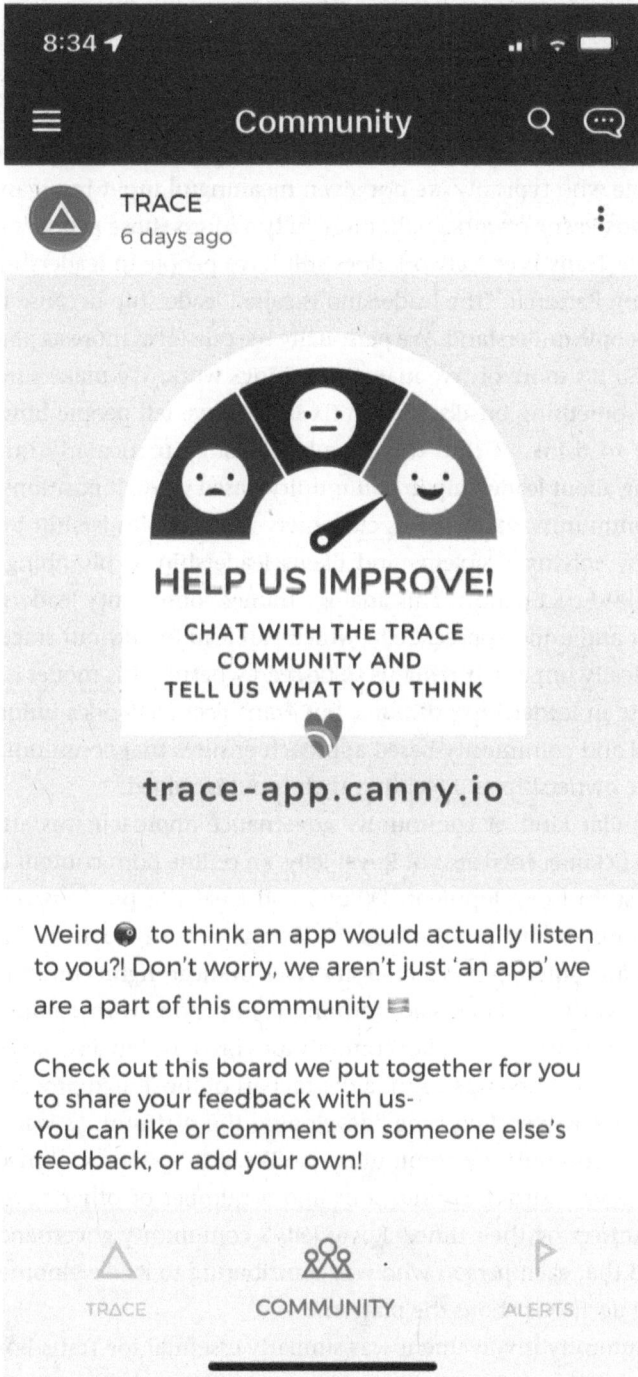

Figure 4.1
"We aren't just 'an app.'" Transition and social app TRACE's efforts to gather user feedback after launching. Screenshot by the author, 2022.

been really important for us as a core principle." According to Bereznai, it was important to offer decision-making power and leadership opportunities to people who typically are not given meaningful input in organizations, so that Trans Peer Network could more fully address those people's needs.

While Trans Peer Network does still have people in leadership positions, including Bereznai, "the leadership is called leadership because that's something people understand. We personally see ourselves more as plumbers than CEOs. So it's more of 'We make sure things work. We make sure things are safe. If something breaks, we can fix it.' Less we tell people how to behave, or how to think." I find this plumber analogy particularly interesting for thinking about leadership in community-based work. It positions nonleadership community members as customers who hire leadership to meet their needs by solving problems and likens leadership to plumbing—an often-stigmatized occupation. This analogy frames community leadership roles as difficult and underappreciated—which can lead to burnout since these roles are typically unpaid. It remains to be seen whether this model is sustainable for those in leadership positions, but Trans Peer Network's unique nonhierarchical and community-based approach ensures that community members can take ownership and feel that their input is valued.

A similar kind of community governance approach was articulated by Delilah D'Lune, cocreator of Royal Jelly, an online porn content creation site that is still in development. D'Lune had created a previous trans technology, a trans-specific social media site that never really took off—a failure that D'Lune attributed in part to the site's lack of meaningful community buy-in. To address this, D'Lune said, forming connections with community members (in porn and sex worker communities broadly, but also specifically with trans porn creators) was a fundamental part of the design process with Royal Jelly; she was spending time "developing the platform, as well as developing connections in the community, unlike with [prior social media site]. . . . We have very strong connections and a number of other developers who are volunteering their time." Royal Jelly's community governance approach ensured that each person who was contributing to its development also had a say in decisions about the platform.

Community involvement was similarly essential for Trans Boxing. While the organization was run in a more top-down fashion, with Nolan Hanson making decisions, the group of trainers and trainees regularly working together created a community atmosphere in which trainees felt ownership

Figure 4.2
Images from the *Creative Futures* project's film showing trans young people's VR creations (Paré and Windsor 2018). Screenshots by the author.

as well. Hanson said, "The ways in which community members and participants of the project are brought into the project is kind of just organic, relational stuff. I have personal relationships with everybody I train, and I talk to people a lot. And I just make myself available as their coach or their friend or just somebody in their lives. I just listen and talk to people about things. 'What do you think about this?' Or 'What do you think about that?'" By forging meaningful relationships with community members, Nolan transformed the organization into something more than just a boxing club: it became a community in which people supported each other and contributed their ideas. By making themselves available as a friend as well as a coach, Nolan demonstrated trans care for their members.

Some trans technologies involved trans people on a more creative level. Dylan Paré described their *Creative Futures* project (a collaboration with Scout Windsor) (Paré and Windsor 2018). They worked with three trans youths to create virtual reality (VR) art for immersive storytelling that eventually became two films (see figure 4.2). According to Paré, "The linear film would tell the story of how these youth came up with their ideas of what stories they wanted to tell, and what they were hoping people would learn from their projects. The 360 [film] was where you actually can go into the art with them, and they tell you about their art that they've created, and what that means to them." The process was time-limited due to funding constraints, so all the work happened within a single weekend. "That was the time we had with them to teach them how to make the art and have them turn around and actually have made something. It was really, really intense, but they also did an incredible job. That was also really rewarding in that way to see what they could do in such a short period of time." The project enabled Paré to tell diverse trans stories using an innovative medium, and it was also a way to teach VR skills to young people. This substantial level of involvement meant that the young people involved also became trans tech creators, since each of them had created their own virtual world.

Chitra Gopalakrishnan's AR installation *We Are All Made of Starstuff* did similar work to tell trans stories. The project was made with and for a trans organization called The House of Resilience, founded by Achi Vasquez. The organization spans San Diego, California, and Tijuana, Mexico, focusing on safety and housing for trans women of color in those cities. To create the project, Gopalakrishnan, a cisgender woman, "did a lot of interviews of trans women of color in our community for this piece. Their voices were overlaid on the animations. So the pieces were not my story in any way, it was entirely informed by my conversations with them, including their actual voices in the piece." Gopalakrishnan involved trans people in the design process by incorporating trans women's stories and voices into the exhibit, enabling their stories to reach a wider audience. The trans women involved in the project were enthusiastic about the end result, sharing it themselves on their websites and social media accounts.

Other trans tech creators worked to involve community in the process of building trans resources. "We felt like it was really important for it to be community-driven and to be both a community resource and a community project," said Riley Johnson, creator of the trans health care resource site RAD Remedy. RAD Remedy regularly hosted workshops where trans people gathered to compile resources, and many trans community members wanted to be involved as volunteers. To ensure that their work was meaningful, RAD Remedy would ask potential volunteers several guiding questions: "'What do you like to do? What are you good at? How much time do you have?' Those guiding questions, we did it for everything," said Johnson. Similarly, the Trans in the South health resource guide involves trans community members across the southern US by hiring "translators" to translate their local community knowledge of trans resources to a larger trans audience online. These translators enable Trans in the South to create a much more thorough resource than they otherwise could. Creator Ivy Hill noted that this approach "lifts up local knowledge, because I believe that nobody knows their communities like local leaders who are on the ground there." This type of community input is essential for building trans resources, because spreading knowledge to the wider trans population necessitates people contributing their local expertise as patients or customers of particular providers or businesses.

Some trans tech creators involved online trans communities in their processes. Keaton Kash described his approach in the design of Mod Club, a surgery site for trans men and transmasculine people:

> One thing that I actually spent most of today doing was gathering post-op surgical supplies that can go on the site. . . . I noticed in the groups [online communities where trans people discuss surgery] that guys are swapping information around about the best scar cream when you're fresh out of surgery. They're like, "Oh, I tried Medihoney, but I just got this new one and it helped my wounds close up way faster." So, it's like, cool, let's go find that one and put it on the site just so it's in there, so whoever doesn't happen to see that guy's post that day isn't going to miss out on that. . . . I've been combing the groups and really paying attention to when people drop products that are really working for them. . . . I'm just making a note and then trying to go find it later to add to the shop.

Kash was able to quietly crowdsource transition supplies from trans community members via his own membership in trans online communities and then provide those resources to a larger audience. Similarly, when creating Transpedia (an online encyclopedia of trans topics), Clair Kronk sought out collaborators from the Trans PhD Network Facebook group, an online community for trans academics. "I went to Trans PhD Network, I was like, 'Is anybody interested? I found all this cool stuff, do you wanna come help?'" Yet ultimately, people did not become meaningfully engaged with the project. "People would pop on for a day or two and then never access again. So that was kind of disheartening." These two examples represent different approaches to engaging trans online communities in trans technologies: Kash relied on passive community involvement, collecting information that other community members were already sharing, while Kronk sought (unsuccessfully) to draw community members into active involvement with Transpedia. Kronk wanted to integrate trans community members into the structure of her project, as other trans tech creators like Bereznai had successfully done, but she was unable to find people with enough time and interest to become an ongoing part of the work.

A number of creators engaged with trans people and communities both online and off throughout the design process to ensure that their technology was built on community values, though this involvement did not rise to the level of full participatory development. For example, Guerrilla Davis, a creator of Arm the Girls (the self-defense kit for trans women of color described in chapter 2), discussed the idea with community members in person and on social media during the design process: "We were doing a lot of events around . . . art and social justice, and it was at these events we were talking about . . . 'What do you think about this idea of Arm the Girls?' . . . These conversations that we had with people, [and] having conversations on our social media platforms, really informed how Arm the Girls came about." Davis and their collaborators sought out the local trans community's opinions every step of the way to ensure that the project expressed community values. Similarly, when creating Jailbreak the Binary, creator Dev[6] was heavily influenced by their trans community on Tumblr when making design decisions. When creators are deeply involved in trans communities, their community's values inform their creations from the beginning, helping to ensure that their projects meet community needs.

Other trans technologies like trans support groups on Zoom also involved community members in key decisions about how to design the technology to best meet user needs. For example, T. Michael Trimm, Executive Director

---

6. Github creator d3v-null.

of Services & Administration at Transgender Resource Center of New Mexico (TGRCNM), described how the organization determined which specific online support groups to host:

> All the different support groups that we have, we just listen to what people want. That's why we have a DD [developmental disabilities] waiver group. Because folks that were utilizing the DD waiver for developmental disabilities, they wanted their own group. So we said, "Okay, let's get you a facilitator." And they have their own group, the end. We now have a Black and brown trans, gender nonconforming, and intersex group, because people said, "Transmasc be so white," or "Transfem be so white. I want a group that's just for us." So we made it happen. So really just listening to the community and just paying attention to their needs, right? That really informs how we operate.

While creating support groups as part of transgender resource centers is far from what would typically be considered a technology design process, this is an example of how designers of technological services like support groups can involve trans people in the design process by centering the needs communicated by communities and designing the technological approach to address those needs explicitly. In TGRCNM's case, involving trans people in designing online support groups enabled the organization to form support groups that would meet the needs of people with several intersecting marginalized identities, such as trans people of color.

A similar bottom-up, community-led ethos was at play in other trans technology projects too. For some trans tech creators, it was important to ensure that the project was community-driven rather than driven by academics. For instance, AJ Lewis described the NYC Trans Oral History Project's approach that centered community, rather than "just credentialed researchers extracting repositories of experience from trans people." Given that many of the trans technologies in this research were envisioned and created in academic contexts, it is especially important that nonacademic trans community members be brought into design processes to ensure that a wide range of viewpoints is represented; because many creators were trans academics, they often had some types of privilege (e.g., educational, social, economic) that most trans people do not.

Some trans technology projects from academic contexts sought insight and influence from broader trans communities by creating trans community advisory boards. This is the approach taken by Laura Horak and her cocreator Evie Ruddy of Transgender Media Portal, an online directory of films made by trans people. Horak and Ruddy are both white and Horak is cisgender, so having a trans community advisory board helps to ensure that BIPOC (Black, Indigenous, and People of Color) trans communities' priorities and values are emphasized in the project.[7] Horak said, "We have an advisory board that's all trans scholars and artists. There's one Black person and one Indigenous person out of six people there, but we're going to reconstitute it majority BIPOC, and also pay the advisory board members." A similar community advisory board was used by Trans Women Connected, a technological intervention that used social aspects to increase trans women's knowledge about HIV. The team worked to ensure that the advisory board included racial minorities and also representation from many different US regions, building the network mostly through word of mouth. B.A. Laris, who coordinated various aspects of the project, described how the design team involved the board:

> Essentially, we had one meeting a month, and then they were asked to do one other contribution a month. We had a closed Facebook group where we would post certain things and get reactions, like to images or to content, or asking probing questions around for some of the stories that the [app's educational] activities were being built around. Or they were asked to do special projects, like, "Oh, could you review this, or could you have a one-on-one interview with one of us? We're stuck on this issue. Or could you . . ." So, basically, we asked them to have two engagement points a month and then for that, they got a hundred dollars a month.

By involving their community advisory board in some decision-making, Laris's team was able to reach beyond their own primarily cisgender thoughts and ideas. However, from what I could tell from our interview, it sounded like Trans Women Connected involved its advisory board primarily in smaller decisions (e.g., image choice) rather than larger or more contentious decisions that would substantially influence the project's direction.

Sometimes, communities were directly involved in project design and development, actually writing code—a task made more accessible by opensource software. Especially with browser extensions, where much of the code is borrowed from other extensions and then tweaked for a particular project, people from all across the world can easily help out with updates. Willow Hayward, creator of Deadname Remover, described, "It's a piece

---

7. Greater BIPOC involvement and leadership was also recommended by participants in Transgender Media Portal's usability tests (Chokly et al. 2020). The team's approach to meaningful community involvement is discussed further in Ruddy and Horak 2021.

of open-source technology. It's just been on the GitHub that whole time. Other people started to participate and help out and fix bugs and just make it better. . . . The last two releases, I haven't written a line of code, and it's much better than the original version." Basing trans technologies on open-source software is one way for trans community members to become directly involved in creating technology and influencing its development direction.

An Ever-Evolving Process: User Testing and Iteration

Iteration is crucial to technology design; nothing is perfect the first time around, and testing with users and communities allows designers to make important changes. In her book *Poetic Operations: Trans of Color Art in Digital Media*, micha cárdenas (2022) discusses how community-centered design projects shift and iterate after community input, bringing each version of the project into better alignment with community values. Many of the trans technologies in my research used iterative design processes, often involving user testing or playtesting with trans people and communities.

These user testing and iteration processes, whether formal or informal, were demonstrations of technological trans care. For example, Wayne Temple asked his son to test out True Self, the browser extension he had built to remove his son's pretransition name from websites. "I had him use it on the home machine. . . . I had him give me feedback. He was maybe eight by that point. So it was more like, 'Oh cool . . .' We put it on all the machines I had here in the house. So anytime he was working on our stuff, we could be assured that he wasn't going to see his old name." Temple's son was not a formal tester and did not have detailed design feedback for his dad, but this informal testing—the fact that the extension worked well in their home setting—was enough for Temple. By creating and implementing the extension, Temple demonstrated technological trans care for his son by helping him avoid seeing his previous name online.

In other cases, the trans care element remained visible even in more formal user testing situations. For example, the creators of the trans voice-training app Christella VoiceUp told me about their iterative user testing processes with different stakeholders: "So it went through different testing stages, and then changed at different stages, depending on the feedback. The design process is ongoing . . . they have to be updated, they have to be renewed, they have to be changed, depending on patient feedback." Similarly, Trans Tape creators noted that designing the product will "always be an ever-evolving process. We want it to be like we've included everybody." User testing helped RKA, designer of the transition app Solace, to understand tradeoffs in the user interface, such as how much structure versus unstructured exploration to build into the app: "'Do you need explicit instructions? When and where do you need that? And where is more comfortable just to explore?' So it's having that balance between inviting people to come in, explore, have fun, but also having them feel supported, held, and not just like they're in a world of chaos. So the user testing helped with understanding that balance between fun, exploration, and also structure." Technological trans care is apparent in RKA's description of user testing as a process involving support, comfort, and even being "held" and in Trans Tape's efforts to "include everybody."

Rob Eagle described the community-based user testing they employed when creating *Through the Wardrobe*. Eagle spent substantial time with the four people whose voices and experiences were featured in the exhibition, both during and outside of user testing, and said, "It brought me much closer to those four people. It challenged all of us to question ourselves, our assumptions about our identity and everything else. But also made me question, What is good design? What is obvious design? How do you signpost certain things? So I learned a lot in that process." In Eagle's design process, user testing went beyond just an impersonal testing procedure, becoming instead an intimate collaboration with community members.

The product designer for a prominent queer social networking and dating app, who wished to remain anonymous, described many different ways that the app incorporated user ideas and feedback into their design. This user feedback enabled the design team to innovate features in ways that they may not otherwise have considered:

> I'm thinking of this specific feature recently that a user suggested in testing. They were like, "It would be really nice to have an optional tag on a profile if someone is a person of color, or you can break it down even further, you can mark yourself as Black or Asian, your very specific race." And I thought that was an interesting idea. . . . There's having specific filters, so if you just want to search for trans people and you just want more trans people in your life, having some sort of filter system. However, these tags could also be used to abuse. I am curious how to explore a feature like that responsibly. We have to strike a balance between providing our users with an easy way of finding people they have things in common with while also keeping them safe.

The product designer saw involving users in design processes as inviting changes in the technology's direction: "I think design is literally all about going in ways that you don't expect it to happen. So, I'll do something and I think it's a fantastic idea, and we'll test it with a couple of people and we're like, 'We have to start over.'" Listening to users enables the app designers to innovate in inclusive ways. And in the case of this app, the trans care seems to run both ways. The product designer stated, "I feel like we have just the most helpful users ever. If something doesn't work, we'll know it doesn't work and people will tell us. I used to kind of take offense to that, but now I just realized it's because people really care and value this space and they want to make it better." Users who are invested in a technology's design can make that design better in ways that designers may not have considered. The above is an example of a successfully deployed app that takes user testing and feedback seriously and works together with its users in an environment where both care deeply about each other.

Several trans game designers described what it was like to have people playtest their games. The process often highlighted shared meaning and shared experiences between creators and players. Ryan Rose Aceae said,

> The first time I have someone playtest the full version of the game, especially if it's someone who's never seen it before, if it's a close friend who was the kind of person I had in mind for making the game, it's terrifying, but also exhilarating. And I almost don't want to watch, but also I need to watch, I want to watch. But I think just the experience of seeing someone enjoy the game and have fun with it, and . . . seeing the way that people light up when they play a game that's not something that they've really experienced before.

Aceae's quote speaks to how transformative it is for a person to experience technology designed specifically for someone like them for the first time. Similarly, when Logan Timmins playtested his table-top role-playing game with both game designers and trans people, he learned that "it really resonated with a lot of people, especially queer folks, who found it quite a moving experience." In early stages of design, playtesting sometimes leads to further iteration, but in later stages it can serve to validate a shared sense of meaning between the creator and trans users.

When trans people playtest trans games, they generally find it more moving than cisgender testers do. Jess Rowan Marcotte described their experience playtesting their game *TRACES* with both groups:

> Mostly the response from both categories of folk were generally quite positive about the experience, but I think the difference was that for trans folk, they noted . . . that there was joy and love in the stories that were being told, but also a fair bit of pain. And a fair bit of experiences that I think are common to trans

folk, and easily understood, but that point more toward pain. When I had trans folk play it, some of them really loved it, but some of them were like, "This is kind of a sad game in a lot of ways." And what they wanted to share, and something that stuck with me, is that trans experience is not sad and miserable because trans people are trans, but because of transphobia. That's embedded in the culture.

Trans users' playtesting brought out unique insights about the nature of transphobia and the ways that games can illuminate the complex and ambivalent nature of trans experiences—joy and playfulness mixed in with pain and marginalization. Creating technology that allows trans people to share these ambivalent experiences, and an outlet to work through them, is an important way of practicing technological trans care.

This Was Built by Trans Folks: Trans Technology Created by Trans People

One way of incorporating trans perspectives into trans technology design is by trans people doing the creating. Many trans tech creators are trans people working with other trans people to create their technology. For instance, Tuck Woodstock described *Gender Reveal* as "a podcast made by trans people about trans people, primarily for trans people," and Taylor Chiang stated how they "really want[ed TranZap], what it's driven by, the input, the building of it, really making that trans focused. I like that aspect. I like being able to say that this was built by trans folks." Ivy Hill, creator of the trans health care resource site Trans in the South, said, "Well, I'm also trans, so I think it is important that it was built by trans people for trans people. A lot of resources are not. So, that has been central to the whole process I think." Of the people I interviewed, 80 percent were trans and/or nonbinary themselves. The rest were either cisgender allies or people who were actively questioning their own genders. When trans people are the creators, the technologies they produce are inherently trans-centered—designed by and for trans people.

Several trans tech creators emphasized the importance of trans technology being created by and for trans people. Alice Barker from Trans Lifeline (a trans community support helpline) said, "We don't have an explicit policy that says that we must hire only trans folks, but we do have a pretty stringent hiring process when it comes to folks understanding language and experience, and that ends up usually being trans folks." For similar reasons, the trans telehealth platform Plume prioritizes hiring trans people, particularly trans people with multiple marginalized identities. As Dr. Jerrica Kirkley described, "I think that's something we've really put a lot of initiative into is as much as we can, having our employee base feel representative of the community that we're serving." Sam Martin from QueerViBE, an online resource site with empowering content for trans youth, said of the site, "It was something built for trans people, with trans people, through and containing trans people. It was started by a trans person. So it's very trans-centered. It was centered around trans experiences." According to Martin, this is one reason that QueerViBE connected with the trans young people it served. In each of these cases, we see how creators' own identities make their trans technologies trans-centered and meaningfully express technological trans care. But these creators cannot represent all facets of the trans population, and it is still important for trans creators to involve a diverse group of trans people in their design processes to truly address the needs of the broader trans community.

Halfway There: Successful Design Processes versus Successful Deployments

One characteristic ambivalence I uncovered in my interviews was a tension between *process* and *deployment*. I observed that many of the technologies that implemented human-centered design processes (often those developed in academic settings) were never actually deployed—and, conversely, the technologies that were actually deployed were often not designed with a human-centered approach. This tension was articulated by Pereira, an academic researcher who cocreated LGBTrust, the Brazilian trans and queer safety app that grew out of a classic human-centered design process. Pereira noted that he only "kind of" deployed the app: "It was like a prototype deployment. I had most of these functionalities working so people could ask for help, people could post things, it would appear in the map, and people could ask for any other kind of support and this kind of stuff." But Pereira simply did not have the resources to fully deploy LGBTrust. He said, "I think that in the end, and this is something that really frustrated me at the time, for you to be able to [deploy an app] you need a lot of money, and you need a lot of people working with you." Pereira knew that people would need to trust the app to keep them safe in dangerous situations, and that it must work properly to be released. He said, "And I just couldn't do it by myself. So I couldn't release the app, like in a store for a lot of people to download it . . . it was kind of halfway there." Pereira noted that the participants in the study who participated in the human-centered design process were also disappointed: "They were kind of frustrated as well, that it didn't go full live. They couldn't really use it in a daily basis. Because it was like a baby from all of us, and I felt that they had a kind of emotional attachment to the project in the end."

Baeza Argüello's facial prostheses for exploring multiple Apple ID identities, also created in an academic setting, was another project that did not fully deploy to a large public audience. However, the research team was able to deploy the prototypes with a small group of three people who had participated in the design workshops. "Those three [people really wanted to] keep developing it to have [their] own, properly designed ones [for themselves]. They came to the studio weeks later after the project, and we did the prosthetics for them. They keep using them. Actually, one of them uses it in the place that they work, they have that facial recognition system, and [they] use [it in] that exact [scenario] that [we discussed]"—that is, to evade the workplace security system. For a small group, the prototype prostheses were a success, but deploying on a larger scale was outside of the scope of the project.

Project Spectra, Alex Ahmed's voice-training app, has also not been deployed on a large scale. The code is available on GitHub, so anyone could technically compile, install, and use the app, if they were tech-savvy enough. However, no compiled, installable version of Project Spectra has been placed in the Apple or Android app stores for broad audiences to download.

As these examples show, technologies created in academic contexts often have plenty of support during the ideation stages, which are exploratory and can more easily "count" as research, but academics are much less likely to have the time and resources to build, deploy, support, and maintain technologies in the long term. Academics are much more likely to prioritize answering research questions over achieving the social justice aims that could come with technology deployment and long-term maintenance. These limitations are disappointing for both designers and community members, for unreleased technology does not help the communities who invested time and effort into helping design it.

In contrast, many of the technologies in this study whose creators did not employ a human-centered design process have been successfully deployed and are being used by hundreds or even thousands of users. In the Apple app store, one can find Solace, Tser, and Patch Day, none of which were developed with a human-centered approach. In the Chrome Web Store, one can find True Self, NameBlock, Gender Neutralize, and Jailbreak the Binary, all of which were created within a few hours or days with very little user involvement or feedback. The trans technologies that I see as having the most potential to address the challenges that trans people face are those that meaningfully involve trans community members throughout the design process—yet unfortunately, these technologies often never make it to deployment.

Conclusion

In this chapter I described trans tech creators' many different approaches to involving trans people in design processes. Some creators used a full human-centered design process including participatory design sessions; some incorporated feedback from users as part of an iterative design process; and some simply brought their own trans experiences to the design process. At whatever level they were incorporated, human-centered approaches helped make trans technologies usable for a wider range of trans people.

Trans technologies can be most impactful when they involve community members in the design process, because community involvement enables technology to address trans needs and challenges and practice technological trans care. When trans people are not included in design processes, designers risk creating systems that either miss the mark in helping improve trans people's lives or even harm trans people, such as when Uber's identity verification policy led to employment discrimination. Researchers and designers can use this chapter's results to understand why and how they should include marginalized communities in technology design processes to make the most impact. To sum up, I recommend substantial community involvement in design processes, particularly when the technology in question is aimed at marginalized groups; this will ensure that resulting technologies truly address community needs and challenges.

Human-centered design has typically been applied and studied in mainstream contexts (Bosch-Sijtsema and Bosch 2015; Carthy, Cormican, and Sampaio 2021; Ozcelik et al. 2011) rather than focusing on marginalization, equity, or justice (Rêgo et al. 2022). However, recent research has documented participatory and community-engaged approaches aligned with marginalized groups and social justice (Erete, Israni, and Dillahunt 2018; Harrington, Erete, and Piper 2019). HCI scholars have discussed how design processes work in the contexts of individual studies: examples include Christina Harrington et al.'s (2019) study with Black older adults, Calvin Liang et al.'s (2020) study with gender-diverse young people, and Brad Morse et al.'s (2023) work designing a health information app with and for trans and gender-diverse people. Here, I extend this work by focusing on a particular marginalized population and showing how users were brought into technology design processes in a wide range of ways.

Critiques of human-centered design have often been leveraged against mainstream technologies; for example, Silvia Lindtner (2020) critiqued human-centered designers' "often short-term engagements" that, rather than fostering social change, "function as powerful portfolio pieces" for the designers. Probably few technology designers would consider social justice a goal; most are likely content to develop portfolios and usable, profitable technologies. But in the case of trans technology, designers' investments were very different. Because trans tech creators are often trans themselves and embedded in trans communities, their efforts to create technology that helps to address their own and their community's needs are less extractive, less self-serving, and more focused on addressing community needs than mainstream technology designers'. When trans technologies were not deployed, it was usually because of a lack of resources, time, and sometimes skill needed to take the next step, not because the designer moved on to something more lucrative. In cases where the technology did not create substantive change, it was because the changes needed to address trans discrimination and inequality are massive and systemic. Large-scale social change was infeasible and outside of the scope of these projects. Like many of the participants in this study, I know that technology cannot solve the systemic problems that trans people face, but technology can make small inroads and make trans lives more livable.

The design processes that I described in this chapter differ in two major ways from traditional design processes, in which designers are outsiders to a community and may recruit community insiders to provide input on technology design. First, communities are extremely important in trans people's lives (Haimson et al. 2020b; Malatino 2020), and trans tech creators were often part of trans communities; interestingly, many trans tech creators were also in community with each other, creating technology to address different needs across the trans technology ecosystem. Second, trans technology design is inherently imaginative and future-focused, for it requires us to envision new possibilities for technology. If trans people's needs were being met by existing technologies, trans tech creators would not need to create technologies to meet these needs. Trans technology design processes thus highlight the ways that trans tech creators, often in collaboration with community members, question the underlying designs of mainstream technologies and rework them to benefit trans people.

Although trans technology has empowering and liberatory potential, this potential does not always materialize. Many of the technologies that used exemplary human-centered design processes were never actually deployed. What does this mean for HCI and interaction design? In this study, the tried-and-true methods of technology design that we teach were followed most closely in classroom and academic settings, used to create technologies that never reached users. It may be harmful and extractive to include marginalized people in design processes when the technologies that are envisioned and designed are never deployed (Harrington, Erete, and Piper 2019). It can be frustrating and disappointing for trans communities to invest time and care in helping design technologies to address their needs but never get the opportunity to use those technologies in practice.

At the same time, many of the technologies that we do see deployed are not built with human-centered approaches at all (Norman 2005). Perhaps our human-centered methods are not always practical or necessary, especially when people are drawing from their own personal experience. The True Self browser extension is a good example of this. Creator Wayne Temple knew that his son needed this extension and knew how it should be designed; his son thought it was "cool" and used it regularly. End of story. A complicated human-centered design approach, with Temple soliciting feedback from his son or other community members at every step, might not have substantially changed the end result—or it could have introduced so many complexities and new ideas that it stalled development entirely. Sometimes people ask for things far beyond the original scope of the project, such as when the parent suggested that Aceae make a kids' version of their trans game *GenderWrecked*.

But we must not forget that designing without community input risks the types of privilege and exclusion that I described in chapter 3. That is, True Self works well for a white middle-class trans kid in the Chicago suburbs with computers at home. Would it also work for a low-income Black trans kid in urban Chicago, who primarily uses computers at the public library? And if a tool like True Self were to scale up to try to reach wider audiences, where would Temple find funding, time, and resources for the extra work? Financial considerations touch almost every aspect of trans technology creation. The tensions between individualist and community-based trans technology design approaches become even more heightened when we consider how funding choices—such as pursuing investment funding or relying on one's own unpaid labor—come into play, as I discuss next.

5   Monetizing Trans Technologies: Trans Capitalism, Investment Funding, Mutual Aid, and Anticapitalist Approaches

"We've been waiting for months to share this with y'all!" began a tweet from Euphoria,[1] the company behind a suite of gender transition-focused apps that includes the transition-tracking and resource app Solace and the trans banking app Bliss. "We are beyond grateful to @ChelseaClinton, @GaingelsVC, & the rest of our cohort of investors for the trust and confidence they've placed in us to continue to build more trans tech. #HowItGetsBetter." The tweet included a link to a news article titled "Meet Euphoria, a New Trans-Focused App Backed by Chelsea Clinton, Others" (see figure 5.1).

Euphoria's tweet got, as they say, "ratioed." "Getting ratioed" refers to cases when a tweet gets substantially more replies and quote tweets than likes or retweets, signaling widespread negative reaction to the tweet's content. In this case, Euphoria's tweet received (as of this writing) 562 quote tweets and 363 replies, but only 56 likes and 12 retweets without added commentary. The vocal trans community on Twitter was appalled at the fact that a trans app company was being supported by venture capital. Musician and editor Janus Rose tweeted, "i am once again asking you to give trans people money instead of building a VC-funded app that mines us for profit,"[2] and trans studies scholar Jules Gill-Peterson responded to Euphoria's tweet with, "This is really sad—we don't need venture capital backed apps. Read the room."[3] Others called attention specifically to the disconnect between Euphoria's venture capitalist-backed funding priorities and many trans people's difficulty securing basic needs like health care and housing. For instance, YouTuber and

---

1. https://twitter.com/euphorialgbt/status/1362419707358363650
2. https://twitter.com/janusrose/status/1362854815957741572
3. https://twitter.com/gp_jls/status/1362766798945411073

Euphoria
@EuphoriaLGBT

We've been waiting for months to share this with y'all!

We are beyond grateful to @ChelseaClinton, @GaingelsVC, & the rest of our cohort of investors for the trust and confidence they've placed in us to continue to build more trans tech. #HowItGetsBetter

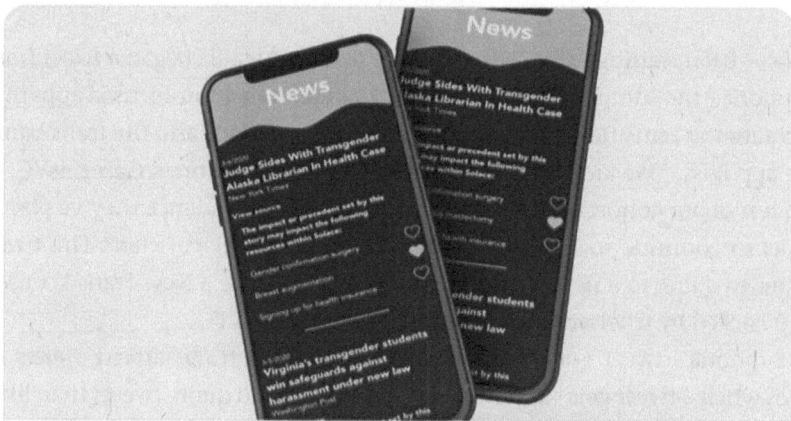

builtinaustin.com
Meet Euphoria, a New Trans-Focused App Backed by Chelsea Clinton, Other...
Euphoria aims to empower transgender people through every facet of their lives, providing tools for everything from financial planning to health tracking.

10:12 AM · Feb 18, 2021

12 Retweets   **562** Quotes   **56** Likes

Figure 5.1
"We've been waiting for months to share this with y'all!" Euphoria's tweet announcing venture capital funding, 2021. Screenshot by the author.

game developer Steph Wolf quoted Euphoria's tweet and said, "These kinds of products prey on vulnerable trans people who have limited resources. Creating a commercialized transition pipeline is predatory and gatekeepy. This is especially dangerous right now due to pandemic-driven resource and support scarcity."[4] Euphoria's venture capital funding clearly struck a negative chord among trans people who saw many more pressing priorities for trans-related funding and trans technology.

Commodifying queer identities is nothing new. Rainbow capitalism (also sometimes called pink capitalism)—the monetization of gay, lesbian, and queer identities through things like commercialized pride parades and companies marketing directly to queer consumers—has been prevalent since the 1970s (Branchik 2002; Drucker 2015; Roque Ramírez 2011) and has sometimes included marketing targeted to trans people under the LGBTQ+ umbrella (Dame-Griff 2023). Rainbow capitalists position the purchase of certain products as a path to queer authenticity, as with Nike's "Be True" campaign, which promoted LGBTQ+ inclusion in sports via rainbow-adorned Nike shoes and t-shirts (Brody 2023). A distinct but related formation is racial capitalism, which highlights the ways that racism is intertwined with capitalism: capitalism emerged and thrives in societies that supported slavery, genocide, and other forms of violence against people of color (Kelley 2017; Robinson 2005). As Catherine Knight Steele (2021) describes, the capitalistic nature of technology, via "ownership, bias, and platform design," restricts Black women's experiences while simultaneously commodifying them. Rainbow capitalism and racial capitalism are necessarily connected, for queer people of color experience overlapping forms of oppression and commodification.

Rainbow capitalism and racial capitalism have been named and chronicled for several decades now. A new sibling concept, *trans capitalism*, has emerged quite recently,[5] on the heels of 2014's "transgender tipping point" (Steinmetz 2014), which produced what Myrl Beam (2018) calls "trans mainstreaming." I define trans capitalism as the commodification and monetization of trans identities (rather than LGBTQ+ identities more broadly) and intentional

---

4. https://twitter.com/StephanieWolfie/status/1362948023689519104
5. However, trans activist Sylvia Rivera critiqued the capitalist, profit-driven nature of Pride and the mainstream gay rights movement throughout her life (Gleeson and O'Rourke 2021; Overskride 2021).

marketing to trans people.[6] Trans capitalism underpins the recent wave of investment-funded trans technologies: Euphoria, the trans health apps Plume and Folx Health, and the queer social apps Lex and Queer Spaces. According to Crunchbase.com in 2024, these companies have raised amounts ranging from $580 thousand (Euphoria) to $59.4 million (Folx Health). Trans capitalism brings with it trans representation in marketing and advertisements, such as a 2019 Gillette advertisement showing a trans man shaving for the first time (Durkin 2019), advertisements from Mastercard and Starbucks featuring trans storylines in 2020 (Dua 2021), and Bud Light's controversial 2023 partnership with trans influencer Dylan Mulvaney (Holpuch 2023).

While trans capitalism has increased trans visibility and directed investment funding to a handful of trans technologies, it has had little positive impact on trans people and communities more broadly. Gossett, Stanley, and Burton (2017) argue that trans visibility is a trap, for as trans visibility increases, so does antitrans violence—an argument that has been reinforced by the recent waves of antitrans legislation in the US and elsewhere. Certainly, apps like Solace help many trans people manage their transitions and find trans resources; according to cofounder Robbi Katherine Anthony (who also goes by RKA), "about one out of every fifty transgender individuals in the US use our tech, and that number is growing." Perhaps the most tangible positive impacts of trans capitalism come from Plume and Folx Health, which have increased trans health care access for many, especially those in rural areas and places where they otherwise could not have accessed trans health care. But most of the trans challenges that I listed in the introduction, such as lack of access to housing, employment, and safety, are not on trans capitalism's agenda.

In this chapter I examine how the landscape of trans technologies relates to capitalism and discuss the wide range of approaches toward capitalism and monetization taken by trans technologies. I begin with an overview of the different ways that trans technologies are funded. I then describe some of the material challenges that trans tech creators experience in their work, including lack of access to finances and resources and limited time. Next, I chronicle trans technologies that are grounded in capitalist systems and other trans tech creators' critiques of capitalist approaches. I then provide examples

---

6. I am not using the term "trans capitalism" from a social science, humanities, or labor studies perspective, which would require a deeper analysis of labor and capital.

of trans technologies that take anticapitalist approaches, including those that rely on mutual aid. I argue that trans tech creators' different orientations toward and access to financial sources and systems limit or amplify the potential impact of trans technologies: underresourced trans technologies typically have greater freedom to pursue their goals, but their scope is limited and their creators often suffer from exhaustion and lack of time, but trans technologies with financial resources can end up more aligned with funders' priorities than communities' (Beam 2018; INCITE! Women of Color Against Violence 2017).

This examination of how trans technologies are (or are not) monetized and funded highlights ambivalences that trans tech creators experience around money: capitalist and anticapitalist approaches, funders' values and community values, paid work and volunteer work, profit and mutual aid, and many others. While each of these pairs may seem like opposites, in reality they are closer than they seem. Trans technologies often involve both to some extent or at different times or oscillate between the two. For example, Transguy Supply takes an anticapitalist approach by setting their prices far below a profit-maximizing level, but at the same time, its creators are exploring investment funding (Davis 2022). I saw many examples of these ambivalent complexities in the trans technologies I studied.

The financial orientations of trans technology also reveal elements of trans care. First, underresourced trans technologies are often created on a volunteer basis in the creator's spare time, prioritized over free time, daily responsibilities, and paid work, because technological trans care work—helping other trans people meet their needs via trans technology—is often personally meaningful to creators in a way that their other, paid work is not. This care work is still work and should be recognized as such (Piepzna-Samarasinha 2018), but types of care that do not lead to profit are typically undervalued in capitalist systems (Care Collective et al. 2020). Next, many trans technologies practice technological trans care in the form of mutual aid efforts in which they redistribute resources to those who need them most. Dean Spade (2020) defines mutual aid as "collective coordination to meet each other's needs, usually from an awareness that the systems we have in place are not going to meet them." The mutual aid examples I describe in this chapter are both a form of trans care and a type of trans technology: mutual aid is a way that trans people and allies take care of each other when traditional systems do not, extending trans people's agency by addressing their most immediate needs.

There Is Always a Cost: How Trans Technologies Are Funded

The trans technologies in my dataset were funded in a number of different ways, including funding from grants, universities, donations, and crowd-funding; self-funding; and business- and investment-based funding. Each of these funding methods signals a different orientation toward seeking and accepting financial support, and together they convey the precarity involved in finding and securing funding for trans technologies.

The most common source of funding was grants. Funding sources included foundations, national research funding bodies, regional or topic-specific funds supporting social justice initiatives, or tech companies; thirty-six trans technologies were funded this way, including Transgender Media Portal (a collection of films made by trans people), Digital Transgender Archive (an online archive of historical trans materials), the Museum of Trans Hirstory & Art, and TransTech Social Enterprises. A related (and often overlapping) funding source was universities: twenty trans technologies were funded by universities in some way, whether via small internal grants, salary for faculty or students, or use of university resources to create the technology. However, grant funding for trans projects can be contentious in hostile political environments such as the US. Alex Ahmed, creator of the Project Spectra voice app, encountered this issue:

> I was advised by someone at the NIH [US National Institutes of Health] that I shouldn't talk about trans people at all in the most front-facing bits. This was 2017 or 2018. It was during Trump times. So, the person at NIH was trying to help me. He was like, "Oh you don't know who can see these things. So, if it goes by some staff member or member of Congress who's not into the idea of supporting trans research, then it's better to just not say it in the abstract. Just hide it somewhere else and say, 'This is for minorities' or something more innocuous." So, I did that.

Ahmed was able to use the NIH funding to create trans technology, but the app's goals were clearly misaligned with those of the funding body at the government level, and she had to obscure the trans focus of the project. Grant funding also often requires that recipients stick closely to the plan submitted in the research proposal. Ahmed described how in the grant proposal, "I said that I would build the app. . . . My advisor warned me that I shouldn't veer off track too much, because it looks bad if I do. So immediately, right there, there's no option to bail out if I didn't want to do this. It's problematic. So, I had to build the app, and had to evaluate its effectiveness." Although the federal research funding supported Project Spectra's creation, it also added constraints on Ahmed's work that eventually came into conflict with her community-based orientation (Ahmed et al. 2021). After conducting community-based design research, a designer sometimes realizes that the best design choice is *not* to design (Baumer and Silberman 2011); Ahmed did not have this choice, for she was obligated to build the app, regardless of the outcome of her initial research.

The next most common funding method was donation-based funding or crowdfunding. These funding sources supported twenty-three trans technologies in my dataset, including the Trans Language Primer (a language guide about gender terms), the *Gender Reveal* podcast, and many of the game designers I spoke with. Many of these creators used platforms like Patreon, Ko-fi, Kickstarter, GoFundMe, Venmo, Cash App, and PayPal to gather money from potential users or audiences. The reliance on these types of funding methods highlights the economic precarity of trans communities. "We're going to be doing another large crowdfunding thing," said Guerrilla Davis, discussing the Arm the Girls self-defense kit project:

> And something that we're thinking about next year is trying to figure out how to continue doing the work without having to crowdfund so much. Because one of the critiques that we've received, and also something that we've been thinking about, is our community is already poor, and we're crowdfunding money from a marginalized community to help more marginalized folks. But how can we get access to funds from institutions, or from people who have access to more money, and get money from them to distribute it to marginalized people? Instead of passing the same $20 in our own community.

Davis's quote identifies a common struggle in donation-funded trans technologies: those who donate are often the same people who need resources themselves. Affluent people and foundations are often far out of reach of the networks that community-based projects like Davis's can access.

Many trans technologies (twenty-three in my dataset) were self-funded—that is, the creator used their own money to fund the technology, at least in its beginning stages. Some examples include Mod Club (a surgery information-sharing site), Trans Reads (an online collection of trans literature), and many of the artists I interviewed. Self-funding their projects often put trans tech creators in a precarious economic position. Braxton Fleming maxed out his credit card to create the Stealth Bros & Co. supply company. Kai Jackson, founder of Trans Tape, said, "So I had actually left my job, I was actually collecting unemployment at the time. And I had to slowly squirrel away the money every week, $20 to set aside enough money so that I could purchase the first case of tape that we got." While both Stealth Bros and Trans Tape evolved into successful businesses, Fleming and Jackson each risked their individual financial well-being to build their companies.

For seventeen trans technologies in my dataset, creators stated that there was no funding and no cost attached to their project. This included technologies like Gender Affirming Surgery prototype app, Erin's Informed Consent HRT (Hormone Replacement Therapy) Map, Trans*Code Hackathon, and many of the browser extensions in the dataset, which were often created quicky in the creator's "spare time." Yet as I describe later in this chapter, there is always a cost: doing unpaid work in one's spare time can be draining and exhausting and necessarily involves an opportunity cost for creators.

Other trans technologies functioned as a business, collecting revenue from users or from some other mechanism, such as advertisements; sixteen trans technologies in my dataset were financially set up as businesses, including the Christella VoiceUp voice-training app, Trans Boxing, and Stealth Bros. Another six of the trans technologies in my dataset were funded by investors or venture capital funding, including the transition and resource app Solace and the gender-affirming health care app Plume. (I discuss investment-based approaches in more detail later in this chapter.) Finally, a small set of trans technologies were funded by other mechanisms, including paid exhibitions of the work, loans, or collectively pooling money. This wide range of trans technology funding models highlights both the creators' ingenuity and the precariousness of funding for technology to support trans needs.

Never Not Been Constrained by Funding: Lack of Financial Resources

When I asked creators to describe the biggest challenges they had faced in creating their trans technology, financial constraints was the number one answer. "That's a constant with art, is always, 'Who's going to pay for it? What strings might be attached to that?'" said artist Heather Dewey-Hagborg. For Dewey-Hagborg, who creates 3D art using DNA phenotyping, "trying to do work that is with cutting edge technology in a limited budget is just always hard." Similarly, game creator Jess Rowan Marcotte said, "Funding, money is always a big challenge. . . . Everything around trying to make a living from games is awful and terrible."

In general, trans technology is underresourced. As Laur Bereznai, creator of the online community Trans Peer Network, put it, "We as a community don't have the resources we need in order to have more technology that is actually for us. Usually, if we want to get money for them, we need to get money from cis people. Then suddenly they have their own thoughts about it, their own demands on how it's supposed to work. It makes the whole thing more complicated." Bereznai also noted that cisgender people cannot always be relied on to "actually show up" in providing tangible support. They continued, "I want to make sure that we're self-reliant and don't have to hope for that kind of support. But that means that there's a lot of patchworking, there's a lot of misusing things for what they're not actually meant to be used for. There's a lot of, 'Well, this kind of works, but it's not perfect.' Because we often don't have the resources to have something bespoke built for us." To address this resource scarcity, trans tech creators must find creative ways of adapting and combining existing technologies to meet their needs. While these "patchworked" technologies are often innovative and are surely a way of *transing* technology (as I described in chapter 1), the lack of resources means that trans technologies often cannot live up to their full potential.

Creators of trans technology projects that were not commercially viable or legible to mainstream audiences often struggled to find funding. Rob Eagle described that their *Through the Wardrobe* augmented reality (AR) project faced funding challenges "partly because it's not a commercial project. And I think it's very difficult for funders to see how this will turn into something that makes money. I'm using the HoloLens [AR/VR headset] in a different way, I think, in a way that I've not seen used before. So you could say that there's tech innovation in that sense. But there's no follow-on to where I could make money from this. That was never the goal, anyway." As Eagle says here, trans tech creators' goals and values (such as indifference to profit) are often misaligned with funders' expectations. And some trans technologies may come across as illegible or "weird" to funding bodies. Avery Dame-Griff described the Transgender Usenet Archive in this way: "Frankly, the Usenet archive and some of the other stuff I do, it's *weird*. . . . I'm absolutely sure there is great funding, and with the time and support, I could apply for it and get it and that would be amazing, but part of it is figuring out, how do I describe [the Transgender Usenet Archive]? . . . It's hard to make a particular argument toward funding for it." Like Eagle and Dame-Griff, many trans tech creators had little success finding funding because their visions did not align well with funding agencies' priorities. Marcotte's solution was to create a consulting company with trans game creator D. Squinkifer and Allison Kyran Cole; they consult on other companies' design projects, run educational workshops, and speak at events. This consulting work funds Marcotte and Squinkifer's game creation work.

In interviews, I heard a lot about what trans tech creators would do if they had more funding: expand the scope of their current work, increase access to their technology to a wider group of people, hire people (especially other trans and queer people), and involve trans communities more meaningfully in design processes. But it was difficult for some trans tech creators to imagine such possibilities. As Chris Vargas from Museum of Trans Hirstory & Art put it, "I've never not been constrained by funding or time." Dr. Jerrica Kirkley from the trans telehealth company Plume described her response to the ever-present financial constraints of trans tech creation:

> This is an opportunity to do all these different things, and in a way that hasn't been done before and is true, but at the end of the day, we have limited resources like anybody else. And trying not to get too overly ambitious and then limit the chances of doing the things we want to do. So, yeah, I think trying to push as much as we can and really radically redefine the system, which is our vision in transforming health care for every trans life. But being smart about it and being able to pace it accordingly so that we can do this a long time and really get to all those things we want to do. I'd say that's probably the hardest part for sure.

While Plume was one of the more well-resourced trans technologies in my dataset, it too faced financial barriers. These barriers created a wide gap between what Plume hoped to do—transform the trans health care system— and what it actually could do in the short term. This gap can be extrapolated to all trans technology, both existing and potential: financial precarity creates a chasm between what trans technology *is* doing and what it *could* do to transform trans lives and the systems that oppress them.

The Emotional Drain and the Time Drain: Limited Time, Spare Time, and Unpaid Labor

The vast majority of the trans technologies described in this book were passion projects—made in their creators' spare time, without compensation. Their work was often exhausting, requiring a larger time commitment than they had initially expected. In the gender-affirming hormone therapy

(GAHT)–tracking app Patch Day creator Juliya Smith's words, "It just took so much time to make this. I just wanted it to be a simple little utility app that's awesome. But it took way more investment than I imagined." For Tobey McKinley, cocreator of the transition-tracking app Transcapsule, trans technology became an "ongoing, drawn-out side hustle." McKinley continued, "So with that, I think comes an ebb and flow of just energy to put toward it, and whether or not the time is available." Most creators worked full-time jobs on top of their trans technology work. When time was not available (and it often was not), many creators reported that progress on their technology slowed and sometimes stalled entirely.

Jaylin Bowers took time off from her Silicon Valley programming job to build Trans Family Network, the app that connects people in states with anti-trans legislation with those able to provide support. Bowers's collaborators, a group of primarily financially stable trans women and transfeminine programmers, also took time off work to get Trans Family Network running. After the tool was functional, they used their spare time to continue refining and maintaining it. Bowers discussed the difficulties she faced in balancing this labor of love with the rest of her life:

> Biggest challenges . . . not overworking myself. So, stopping doing this and doing everything that I need to do to live, survive, and be a real human, like go outside, pet my dog. Just because the pull is so strong, too: "If I just get this one thing done, then I might be able to help one more person." Or we might be able to connect one more person, or we might be able to reach one more person, or what have you. If I just spend ten more minutes on this, that equals one more person. So, it's very hard to go, "Oh, I think I'm gonna go outside with the dog. . . ." It's hard to stop.

As Bowers described, trans technology can improve people's lives in tangible ways and is therefore often meaningful in a way that creators' day jobs are not. It can be hard for them to balance their time between work, day-to-day life responsibilities, and their projects. Many said that their more personally rewarding trans technology work took priority. "I actually also took a pretty big step back from my client work these last six months so I could focus more time on Mod Club," said Keaton Kash, describing his work on the trans surgery information-sharing site. "Mod Club was bringing me happiness to work on just as a fun personal project. I made the decision to allow my income to take a bit of a hit so that I could work on something that gave me joy." Because it was meaningful labor that could help others through technological trans care, creators found their trans technology work an especially compelling way to spend their time, even at the expense of paid work.

Many creators treated their trans technology projects as long-term side projects, working on them regularly as part of their workday. For instance, Erin Reed described spending five to ten hours each week on her Informed Consent HRT (Hormone Replacement Therapy) Map: managing direct messages from people on Twitter recommending resources, vetting those resources, and adding them to the map. Anna-Jayne Metcalfe, who created and maintains a Transgender Day of Remembrance (TDoR) website, spends an hour or more each day curating news reports about murders of trans people worldwide. For Metcalfe, this labor takes an emotional toll. "In the morning, I've got a choice," said Metcalfe. "I could get up first thing, and I could do some yoga, which is great . . . but then I'll have to leave all the TDoR stuff for later to get around to it. Then it piles up really fast. There's the self-care, and the time management issue." Again, we see that balancing work on trans technology with paid work and leisure time can be exhausting and difficult for trans tech creators. This is especially true for those who work on trans technology projects long term and those who work on emotionally challenging projects. These creators have become what Hil Malatino (by way of trans activist Rupert Raj) calls "voluntary gender workers:" people extremely committed to trans activism and advocacy work and, as a result, highly likely to experience burnout, especially when doing this difficult work without pay (Greene 2021; Malatino 2022).

Working on trans technology can be especially precarious for creators without financial stability or stable employment, but job stability limits time for trans technology creation. Game creator Ryan Rose Aceae talked about the difficulties of doing unpaid, creative labor while lacking basic resources like employment and housing: "During periods in the past where I've been unemployed, the stress and pressures of not being in a stable financial, or . . . a stable housing situation, really very much impede my creative flow and my ability to want to create games that are anything other than super, super depressing. . . . Then during times when I am more stable, like right now I'm a graduate student, it's impossible to find the time to work and becomes increasingly more difficult to prioritize making creative work." Sophie Debs (creator of the browser extension Gender Neutralize, which replaces unnecessarily gendered terms) had a different experience, writing much of her trans technology code during a time of financial and housing precarity: "I had pretty much nothing. I had no connections, I had no money, I had no place to go, I had no home. . . . I guess I got started coding extensions because it was something that I could do with literally nothing but a laptop." When I interviewed her, though, she was stably employed as a software engineer, and she said, "I haven't actually been doing a lot of personal coding projects lately, because I code all day at my job. And I suppose I'm a little tired of coding." These creators' experiences point to a difficult balancing act between paid work and unpaid trans technology work.

Finding time and energy to work on trans technology projects is especially difficult now, during a moment of deep political hostility toward trans people. Especially for those creating social justice–oriented and community-focused technologies, the dual personal/political nature of their work can be emotionally taxing and exhausting, leading to burnout. As Trans Formations (an antitrans legislation tracker) creator Alexander Petrovnia noted, "There's only so much you can ask of people. There's only so much you can ask of a marginalized community." Similarly, Juniper Porter expressed the emotional strain that their work on Tear It Up, a trans activism and protest-finding site, created: "We've got all the resources, it's just the emotional drain and the time drain. It for sure digs up old traumas that I forget I have every day. Our system is solid, it's just keeping the fuel on the fire." Keeping the "fuel on the fire" is a major challenge when trans people's "fuel" is so often used up just trying to make it through the day in a hostile and discriminatory society.

Many trans technologies, including Trans Formations and Trans Peer Network, rely on volunteers. Laur Bereznai, creator of the Trans Peer Network online community, explained how volunteers were also being affected by the hostile political climate. "Right now, for the last two years, everything has been shit; and then right now specifically in the US, for trans people, it's been extra shit. So it's really hard, because everybody's at their limit. And most people have jobs. So it's often hard to get volunteers to invest the time that they need to in order to make these things work. Because everybody's really struggling with their own mental health right now. I'm really seeing this lately when it comes to how quickly things are being taken care of." Those in leadership positions, like Petrovnia and Bereznai, can sometimes carry on and work through distress and hard times, but they recognize that volunteers cannot necessarily contribute at the same level, especially at the expense of their mental health. In these cases, demonstrating trans care means eliminating some of those volunteers' burdens, even when it slows down the pace of developing and maintaining the trans technology.

For some creators, the burden of maintaining their trans technology became too much, and they had to step back to prioritize other aspects of their lives. While there were many different reasons for the sunsetting of the health resource site RAD Remedy, cocreator Riley Johnson described disengaging after his life changed: "Once we moved, it was the combination of real life happening. . . . It became 'What do we do when the thing that you've created and the thing that you really want to happen, you can't live it out how you want to anymore?' I didn't want it to negatively impact my marriage or negatively make my kids be neglected or whatever. I felt like it was really important for it to be a thing I do, but not necessarily something that negatively is like an albatross." For many trans tech creators, there is a fine line between a trans technology being "a thing I do" and an "albatross"—an overwhelming burden hung about their neck, negatively affecting their life. When trans technology work becomes too burdensome, creators must make difficult decisions about what to prioritize, which contributes to trans technology's often precarious nature.

Cut Me a Check: Trans Access to Investment Funding

When discussing the economic precarity of trans technology creation—the lack of time and money that hindered their work—some interviewees contended that the answer was getting trans people more access to money and power. Often, this was brought up in relation to investment funding.

Many trans tech creators saw investment funding as an answer to problems. For Aydian Dowling, creator of the transition app and social network TRACE, it was exciting to be one of the only trans companies to raise money from investors and to bring positive trans representation into investment spaces:

> I think the exciting part is we step into a lot of spaces where trans people have never been. So, whether that's meeting with a potential investor or entering an accelerator program that there's never been a trans company before, or sitting down at a lunch and learn and everyone's goes around and tells what their apps are and we share what ours are. You could tell there's people in there who've never seen a trans person in real life. . . . It's like, now, everyone here will go home and be like, "Oh, trans people are making things."

Yet positive trans representation does not necessarily translate to funding, and antitrans discrimination could have hindered TRACE's funding efforts; Dowling did not comment on this issue.

Other trans tech creators who had not yet received investment funding would be happy to take it in the future from a funding source aligned with their values. For instance, Kai Jackson from the supply company Trans Tape said, "I mean, it would be great to have funding for sure, depending on where it's coming from, and what their values are and what they want as a stake in our business. Yeah, it would be wonderful for us to have more funding so that we can help more people." Because many trans technologies are so fundamentally focused on helping trans people to address their needs and challenges, capitalistic approaches like venture capital are often viewed favorably, because they can help trans tech creators achieve their goal of helping the community more quickly and at a larger scale.

However, trans entrepreneurs often face substantial barriers to receiving investment capital. Generally, funders lack understanding of trans people's "market potential," and there is likely also some underlying discrimination and transphobia (Davis 2022). This became clear at a session at the 2022 TransTech Summit (a conference I describe in more detail in the next section), titled "How to Raise Venture Capital for TGNC [transgender and gender nonconforming] Folx." At this session, serial tech entrepreneur and trans woman Natalie Egan described her journey. Before transitioning at age thirty-eight, she was a white man who enjoyed substantial success in the venture capital world: "It was almost like people were throwing money at me."[7] After her transition, people in her networks treated her very differently. For the first time, she experienced potential funders canceling meetings, ignoring communications, and deciding not to fund her projects. In Egan's words, she kept "hitting a brick wall." Egan used these experiences of discrimination and stigma as a trans woman to inform her design of Translator, a technology platform for diversity, equity, and inclusion training and analytics. "All the businesses I've ever started, I'm trying to solve my own problem," said Egan, echoing many of the trans tech creators I interviewed. She advised audience members to do the same.

---

7. The quotes included in this section and the next related to the TransTech Summit are taken directly from what presenters said at the Summit sessions; I did not interview these creators.

Egan's copresenter at this session was Brad Zapp, cofounder and CFO at Connetic Ventures, an AI-powered venture capital firm. Connetic's goal was to help tech entrepreneurs like Egan by "removing bias from venture capital." Zapp described Connetic's process: entrepreneurs submit their pitch in text to Connetic, where it is then inputted into the firm's AI technology, which is trained to predict whether the pitch will be successful (I assume the prediction is based on a training set of previous successful pitches). The algorithm produces a score. If the pitch is rated above a certain threshold, it is then passed along to humans to assess and potentially fund. By relying on algorithms and data to make the first cut, rather than networks and "gut," Zapp changed who gets funded: at Connetic, he said, "we fund women and minority founders at a rate eight times higher than the VC [venture capital] industry average." Entrepreneurs like Egan, who were outside of networks of privilege, could secure funding from Connetic based solely on their pitch's content.

What could go wrong with AI-powered VC funding? My concern here is that those projects that an algorithm will deem likely to succeed are projects that are similar to those that have been successful in the past—which were produced out of the networks and biases that arise when pitching audiences are primarily rich white cisgender men. Creators and founders still must have the privilege to know what ideas VC funders find attractive and how to write in the style expected for pitches. This know-how is much more likely to come easily for someone like Egan, who spent many years as a rich white man before transitioning, than for instance, trans people of color without Egan's race and class privilege.

Jaylin Bowers, cocreator of Trans Family Network, also spoke at length about the need to increase trans access to capital. Because Trans Family Network appears to be solidly a mutual aid trans technology, Bowers's statements provide an interesting juxtaposition, as mutual aid and investment funding embody different values. "I feel like there's a lot of really talented people in the trans community," Bowers said, "but it's really hard to network without money, power, and labor." She described the trans community, many of whom are in precarious financial positions, as "gutted of our economic engines," which gives trans people limited agency to create technology. As someone with experience in Silicon Valley, she was well versed in the disparities between sources of funding available to trans people versus those available to well-connected cisgender technology creators, echoing some of Egan's comments:

Now, as a white cis man in Silicon Valley with two startups behind me that have been funded, and one successful exit, I can walk up to anybody and say, "Cut me a check, I get all rights." And they're like, "I'm in for the ride." As a trans woman who said the same thing, nobody's gonna write you a check without having full ownership and control over your company. . . . That power dynamic needs to shift. You need to have people in the trans and broader LGBTQ societies have this power. . . . We just need to be able to make the same deals as white cis people.

As Bowers pointed out, many trans people are already working in the tech industry and "contribute, build, and own a lot of that capital; personal, monetary, networking, and labor." Bowers wanted to see wealthy trans people recognize their financial power and apply it toward funding trans projects. Additionally, she spoke of the need for trans projects to "generate income and revenue from outside sources." She described working toward this goal herself: "I'm trying to use my connections to funnel VC money into stuff in the trans community. I'm trying to funnel startup networks, technological networks, and things that help people get involved and embedded in these communities that operate with almost unlimited budgets. . . . It's important that we get that in the trans community, especially in the trans tech community. Because we can build really cool fucking things." To be most impactful, Bowers said, "we have to be strategic and utilize all the capital that's available to us to magnify our presence and our power."

Trans Lifeline was one example of wealthy trans people's money being channeled into trans technologies. Trans Lifeline's former director of advocacy, Yana Calou, explained that the organization was funded in part by trans donors, most of whom could afford to donate because of their lucrative careers in tech. But as Calou pointed out, there are inherent limitations to relying on trans funding: trans people as a group have limited financial power, and trans-specific projects are thus chronically underfunded. Like Bowers, Calou hoped to see a future in which trans people have increased financial resources to fund trans projects: "Trans people being able to, in tech, having that earning power. Being able to build the stuff. Having the knowledge to build the stuff. Having the funds to be able to fund trans movement stuff." Zoe Nolan, creator of the To Be Real prototype trans crowdfunding platform, reasoned that wealthy trans people had an obligation to fund up-and-coming trans technologies to increase trans representation in business and technology: "Hopefully, that becomes a feedback loop and increases that population of people doing stuff," she said.

This cannot be the only answer; relying on the generosity of a small set of wealthy trans techies causes excessive precarity, and rich trans people's priorities do not always align with the broader community's needs—for example, trans billionaire philanthropist Jennifer Pritzker primarily funds trans-inclusive military initiatives (Beam 2018; Spade 2015). The limitations, constraints, and value clashes inherent in receiving funding from the wealthy, whether in the form of VC funding or philanthropy, lead many trans tech creators to look in other directions. This is why mutual aid approaches are so common for trans project funding (as I discuss later in this chapter) and why many trans technologies are (often by choice) small, underfunded operations (as I discussed in the preceding sections). At the same time, many trans technology organizations are actively working to increase the capital available to trans people and communities, either by gathering investment funding or by working to increase trans presence in tech careers, as I describe next.

Trans*preneurship: Capitalist Trans Technology Approaches

TransTech Social Enterprises is, according to its website, "an incubator for LGBTQ Talent with a focus on economically empowering the T, transgender people, in our community" and "a co-working, co-learning community" that helps trans people gain the skills necessary for careers in tech. In 2022 and 2023, I attended the TransTech Summit, an online conference that helps TransTech members with skill-building and networking by presenting workshops on topics ranging from "Trans*preneurship" to "How to Raise Venture Capital for TGNC Folx." Attending the TransTech Summit was fascinating and helped me to understand capitalist approaches to trans technology; I heard from a wide range of trans people interested in tech, many of whom were optimistic about, rather than critical of, capitalism and the mainstream tech industry.

In the Trans*preneurship panel, sponsored by the venture capital firm Gaingels, panelists talked about starting trans-focused businesses to address problems they themselves face. These panelists' journeys to entrepreneurship reflected the agency I discussed in chapter 2: trans entrepreneurs felt that they were well positioned to start a company to meet their and their community's needs and emphasized that the best way to found a business was simply to begin. "If you wanna do something, start it!" said Stoney Love, founder of the gender-inclusive clothing company Stuzo Clothing. Panelists also emphasized maintaining their personal authenticity while starting a business: the goal was to be *you* but to make money doing it. Panelists and audience members shared excitement and positivity around entrepreneurship by marginalized people. In the online chat, audience members responded to what panelists had to say with comments like "Right!" and "That's a great point."

The entrepreneurs on the panel discussed how for trans people, there were benefits to creating one's own business: they could escape traditional work environments, where many faced discrimination and misgendering, while moving out of financial precarity. People have to find power where they can, and especially for multiply marginalized populations like BIPOC (Black, Indigenous, and People of Color) trans people (a group many of the TransTech Summit speakers and attendees belonged to), entrepreneurship can be seen as offering access to economic resources that have historically been out of reach. But as activist and scholar Robert L. Allen (1969) points out, starting more Black-owned businesses entrenches Black people within existing exploitative capitalist systems rather than working to overturn those systems—rather than working toward liberation. In facing this dilemma, Allen (1969) says, it is crucial to maintain a community-based approach to Black entrepreneurship. This community approach is, in part, what TransTech aims to create. Building technology is expensive, and building a large-scale sustainable product requires substantial capital investments; only more privileged trans people (i.e., those with more financial means or generational wealth, who are more likely to be white) may be feasibly able to reject capitalist systems or deprioritize profit. This creates an important ambivalence for the Trans*preneurship panelists and other trans entrepreneurs of color: the positives of business, capital, and trans entrepreneurship exist in tandem with the understanding that capitalism can be harmful for trans and BIPOC people.

This ambivalence was epitomized by the fascinating figure "The Trans Capitalist." At the beginning of the Trans*preneurship panel, the moderator announced that one of the panelists was K. Kenneth Davis, known as The Trans Capitalist. Audience members expressed excitement about Davis's presence in the virtual room, typing things like "The Trans Capitalist in the house!!" and "So glad Trans Capitalist exists." I was surprised at first that Davis, a Black trans man, would embrace capitalism to the extent that he named his brand after it, but as I would learn, his orientation toward capitalism was complex. "Capitalism ain't going nowhere," said Davis during the panel, "so what's the best thing to do? Learn the rules to the game and beat it!" Davis's services, advertised on his website and promoted on his Instagram and YouTube accounts, seek to improve LGBTQ+ people's financial literacy to address the trans population's disproportionately low income and employment rates.

A year later, at the 2023 TransTech Summit, The Trans Capitalist had his own session, "Defenses Against Capitalism Through Financial Literacy." He began by outlining the ways capitalist systems harm trans people, including predatory credit cards and high interest rates. He then provided "defenses" against capitalism, such as making sure to save money. While the session was well attended, I did not note the same level of positivity and optimism among attendees as I had the year prior, and some commenters voiced critiques of capitalism in the online chat.

In this session, the complexity of Davis's orientation toward capitalism was apparent; for example, one of his slides stated that capitalism creates "systems in place that range from liberating to exploitation." I never learned exactly what Davis meant by liberating, but it was clear that he felt ambivalent towards capitalism. During the Q&A, I asked Davis whether he had initially had a more positive feeling about capitalism when he first started his business, and whether his thoughts about capitalism had changed over time. According to Davis, his alignment with capitalism had shifted over the years. At first, he said, "I was uninformed. I didn't know anything about capitalism." Now, he said, "I'm not for capitalism. If another economic system can work better for America, let's do it." But right now, capitalism is "what America is doing." According to him, "too many white cis hetero men are using capitalism to make millions of dollars," so Davis adopted an "if you can't beat 'em, join 'em" approach. After he became more financially literate, he saw an opportunity to help others in the community: "When I started learning the rules of the game, I decided to start sharing it with everyone that I know."

Jaylin Bowers from Trans Family Network described a similar ambivalence toward capitalism. "I noticed too, there's a negative view on capitalism within the trans community, rightly so," said Bowers. "I feel like we've been screwed by capitalism more so than a lot of different people. Capitalism has really taken aim at trans folks. . . . I get the noncapitalist streak that runs. I am not that way. I think that in an ideal society, in an ideal world, capitalism goes away. Ideally, yes, 100 percent. But we're in today's society where we currently exist." For both Bowers and Davis, capitalism is not an ideal system for trans thriving, but it is our current reality, and they therefore sought to help trans people survive under capitalism and reap its benefits to the extent possible.

TransTech Social Enterprises itself is an interesting case study in the role of capitalism in trans technology. TransTech is a nonprofit and thus not explicitly focused on capitalist endeavors; its aim is to increase trans people's skills and networks and to help them become hirable in the tech industry—one facet of trans capitalism. The organization frequently partners with large tech companies. Google financially supported the 2022 TransTech Summit and funds TransTech's G.R.O.W. career-readiness program, aimed primarily at trans people of color. Etsy has given presentations to TransTech's membership and has hired at least one TransTech member. JP Morgan Chase regularly holds networking events with TransTech and posts job listings to its members. "We have three years of funding through Google for [G.R.O.W.]," said TransTech executive director E. C. Pizarro III in our interview. "Having a tech giant like Google say, 'Hey, we're supporting this program,' really pushed us into the light where other technology organizations, other corporate partners, were reaching out to us like, 'How can we help? What can we do? How can we support?'" By aligning with companies like Google and Chase, TransTech receives much-needed financial support for its initiatives—at the cost of uncritically aligning itself with some of capitalism's biggest players.

While TransTech Social Enterprises remains a nonprofit, in 2022 its team launched TransTech Global Enterprises, a for-profit creative design agency, described by founder Angelica Ross as "our very own pipeline to employment." TransTech Global Enterprises will let TransTech directly hire some of the trans people whose training the organization supported. When Ross announced TransTech Global Enterprises at the 2022 TransTech Summit, attendees responded with excitement, posting positive comments in the online chat, such as "Yesssssssss empowering our people!" and "Super powerful!!!!! Love the growth!" One online comment from a TransTech member explicitly lauded the for-profit nature of TransTech's new arm: "Because we need to break out of only ever seeing our work as non-profits. We create value in the world and should be pioneering what mission driven *for profit* business for good looks like. Love love love this!" A year later at the 2023 TransTech Summit, Pizarro announced that TransTech Global Enterprises has secured its first contract and that it would soon be placing TransTech members in web development positions.

TransTech, its Summit, and its community of members (who have a thriving online community on Discord) exemplify the complexities of capitalism and its relationship to transness in the trans technology world. TransTech programs and members uniquely combine capitalist orientations with community-based mutual aid: TransTech is a community-based program that provides free resources for its members to gain skills necessary for employment, but TransTech members often fold themselves into capitalist systems, getting jobs at companies like Etsy and Chase or starting their own businesses. The for-profit TransTech Global Enterprises is a new way for TransTech to work alongside traditional capitalist systems and the mainstream tech industry but is also in some ways transformative in creating its own community-based system and pipeline for trans people working in technology—thus both upholding and challenging capitalism.

When we look at TransTech in direct comparison to Euphoria, the venture capital–funded suite of apps I described in this chapter's introduction, many differences become clear. While both embrace capitalist approaches, Trans-Tech is solidly community-based, while Euphoria is a small group of people working from an individualist orientation. I see substantial ambivalence in TransTech's version of capitalism, which simultaneously plays into the capitalist system and harnesses that system to support its community members and practice technological trans care. I do not see the same ambivalence in Euphoria's approach, which reads as a much more straightforward for-profit business; while it does provide a product that helps its users in tangible ways, Euphoria seems to be financially set up to prioritize profit for its owners and investors.

Resisting Fuzzy Bunny-fication: Critiques of Capitalist Trans Technology

Many trans tech creators expressed critiques of capitalist trans technology, speaking about the unexpected recent rise of trans capitalism and their frustrations and uncertainties surrounding it. For instance, Myrl Beam from the Tretter Transgender Oral History Project (and author of the excellent and relevant book *Gay, Inc.: The Nonprofitization of Queer Politics* [Beam 2018]) lamented the fact that "so much trans technology is being politicized and monetized." Alex Ahmed, creator of voice app Project Spectra, even referenced trans capitalism in her definition of trans technology: "Cynical answer is a trans technology is any technology that's marketed to trans people and sold to trans people. This could be a for-profit app to manage your gender, feelings, or whatever. It's selling a service, where trans people are the customers. Which I feel is becoming more and more prevalent. Where trans people are target markets." Trans studies pioneer and digital performance artist Sandy Stone spoke about the marketing of trans identities that accompanied the rise in trans visibility:

> I think trans visibility is only going to increase, but as with any kind of visibility increase, what happens is capitalism comes along, it expropriates what you're doing, turns it into a commodity, and then sells it. So, how we're going to be sold I'm not exactly sure. But it's going to turn us into this fuzzy bunny Peter Rabbit social acceptability in a very marketable way. . . . I don't think anybody saw that coming. Yeah. I think when you're in the midst of struggle, the one thing you don't think about is how capitalism is gonna fuck you up.

Stone's comments point to why trans capitalism's emergence was so unexpected and why it continues to feel so strange: in the midst of struggles for basic needs like trans health care, trans capitalism snuck up on us. If we are not careful, we will all be palatable, marketable, monetized fuzzy bunnies before we know it. Sophie Debs, creator of the browser extension Gender Neutralize, said something similar. Debs found the monetization of trans identity "very frustrating" and said, "It's like trans people are no longer considered a fringe minority and are now considered viable consumers in capitalist America. The normalization of transness, I think it's good and has concrete things for trans people in the society. [But] I think, being normalized in a society that is unjust and shitty is not necessarily what we should be hoping for in the future of transness and trans technology." That is, by turning trans people into just another "normal" group of consumers to be marketed to, the capitalist system that has harmed trans people in so many ways then erases the radicality of trans identity; it becomes less revolutionary, unique, and exciting to be trans but does not undo any of the harm. The trans tech creators quoted here encourage us to expect more and to not accept the concession of normality and consumerization in place of a more just society.

Tuck Woodstock, creator of the *Gender Reveal* podcast, described his skepticism toward products or companies that profit from providing trans services: "It just makes me so nervous when trans people are the product, or when people are trying to make money off of trans people not hating themselves, because regardless of what their intentions are . . . we as a community know how to show up for each other. And I think that sometimes these apps tend to try to profit off of what can also be done by just trans mutual aid and trans people being in meaningful community with each other." Like many trans tech creators, Woodstock could see the value in capitalist trans technologies that could help trans people, but he found trans capitalism disconcerting and odd, given the trans community's lack of access to financial resources: "So I'm like, what do you want from us? We don't have any money. What do you think is going on?"

A number of trans tech creators explicitly mentioned the Euphoria suite of apps and critiqued the company's approach as primarily focused on making money from trans people. Interviewees described Euphoria's suite of apps as "money-grabbing," "a blatant cash grab," and a "very corporate attempt." Laur Bereznai, creator of the Trans Peer Network online community, said of Euphoria, "It is an example of us going from a place of 'nobody's building anything for us' to 'people are trying to exploit us.' That also means that there's an actual market there, and there's an actual value there. As long as the right people work with that, it has the potential to be something positive as well." Stone expressed similar uncertainty around trans technology capitalism, asking, "How do you know which ones help and which ones are making money?" Many other interviewees voiced similar critiques of Euphoria. However, they were less critical of other trans technologies with much higher venture capital investments, such as Plume, Folx Health, and Lex. It may be that Euphoria's particular online personality, and the way it conveys the company's unapologetically capitalist orientation, is jarring to some. As Simone Skeen and Demetria Cain (2022) observe, Euphoria's "up-front emphasis on financial viability seem[s] to herald the appropriative, extractive ethos of neoliberalism."

Some trans tech creators did comment on Folx Health's and Plume's financial models, which require users to pay a monthly fee and only recently began to accept health insurance (and only in some states and with some plans). Beam critiqued these companies as capitalizing on the US's subpar health care system, saying, "It's so problematic. . . . A health care concierge that you pay $100 a month to be able to get, that's not actually a replacement for Medicaid paying for people's hormones." Beam said that he feared that Folx Health and Plume heralded a future of trans technology in which "the way people utilize various tools is being monetized and depoliticized."

Other creators brought up privacy fears around capitalist trans health technologies and trans people's health data. Avey, who worked on trans biohacking projects, noted that because trans health care is so expensive, "this has allowed telehealth companies [such as] Folx to spring up and end up creating a neoliberal, personalized experience around transition. I'm thinking in the American context, you're either providing a lot of data to insurance companies, health companies, or venture capital companies. And it can look like a personalized experience, but at the end of the day, where's that data going?" While Plume and Folx Health certainly increase health care access for many trans people (and even provide a "queer" user experience [Beare and Stone 2021]), they do so squarely within capitalist approaches, as their venture capital funding requires, rather than working toward new forms of trans health care that are financially accessible to all trans people.

Donut Emojis and Stream Teams: Mutual Aid Trans Technology Approaches

Many trans tech creators who criticized capitalist approaches walked the walk, using alternative approaches to funding, such as mutual aid. In mutual aid, people collectively help to address the needs of fellow community members, since mainstream systems do not meet those needs (Spade 2020). Mutual aid is an important way to prioritize community and distribute resources to those who most need it. In fact, mutual aid can be considered a type of trans technology, in that it extends trans people's agency and addresses trans people's needs. Game creator Sasha Winter summed up trans technological mutual aid as follows: "The radical act of redistributing wealth, skills, and labor. Realizing that everyone has something that they can give to their community, and everyone has something that their community can give to them. Mutual aid has been a big part of my [online gaming] communities that I've been cultivating. . . . I think that technology doesn't mean anything unless it makes things more approachable and accessible to the people who are most in need." In this section, I describe some of the trans technology mutual aid projects I encountered in this research and the ways that mutual aid's community-centric approach is entwined with trans technology.

One explicitly mutual aid trans technology is Gender Federation, a "stream team" (a group of live streamers on a platform like Twitch) formed to raise money to help trans people get gender-affirming surgeries. Creator

GenderMeowster (they/them) described, "It's direct mutual aid, which means we will never touch the money. It will go directly to the people. And we're not going to gatekeep and say, 'Prove to us in a thousand ways that you're having the surgery for real' or whatever." While many Twitch streams are focused on gaming, GenderMeowster made clear that "we're not just there to play games . . . we're there to raise money for trans people." This kind of mutual aid can be life-changing for people, helping them clear one (large) hurdle to surgery. Gender Federation member Lee Hulme explained:

> We know how hard it can be to get anywhere with surgeries and treatment that you need. And even me being in the UK, treatment didn't cost me, but everything else did, including emotionally and mentally, just to get there. Gatekeeping and everything else. And to get through all of that stuff to a point where you can have the surgery or have the treatment that you need, but not be able to afford it, is a horrible cliff to be hanging off. And finding a way to work together, to help more of us get over that and get to the other side of that, that's one of the ways in which we keep people alive.

Trans technology mutual aid efforts like Gender Federation cannot address the systemic issues that keep trans people from accessing surgeries, but they can help with the tangible financial aspects. Gender Federation's mutual aid efforts use technology to help people move forward with life-saving trans medical care.

Another important trans technology mutual aid is We Are the Ones We've Been Waiting For, the Bay Area mutual aid initiative that created the Arm the Girls self-defense kit project I described in chapter 2. Creator Guerrilla Davis discussed the organization's mutual aid focus: "So we work primarily with queer and trans people, a lot of folks have mental illness or are in sex work, and can't make money. . . . Some people can't get a job, or experience discrimination . . . or just experience a lot of barriers to health care, and just making money, or making a living. So, a lot of the fundraising efforts that we did supported this specific part of our community." The group tries to help those trans and queer people who most need help, holding emergency fundraising events for community members who had been evicted and for trans and queer artists and DJs who lost their income sources during the Covid-19 pandemic. Their fundraising for trans and queer community members is a form of trans care that extends the agency of the local community and ensures that community members take care of each other. Davis summed up their views of mutual aid:

None of this work would be possible if it wasn't for community, and for having a team of people, and this idea of mutual aid. Because when we think about mutual aid work, it's essentially the opposite of capitalism. Because capitalism relies so much on greed, and relies so much on individuality, capitalism has created this culture of being cutthroat, doing what you need to reach the top, no matter who you have to harm, no matter who you have to cut down. What we're doing is an example of mutual aid that exists, in a way, outside of capitalism, where power is shared and it's horizontal. Where we're pooling our resources together. If we don't have the resources, we're going to find out who has them, and they're going to donate the resources to us so that we can share it for the greater good.

Davis and We Are the Ones must exist within capitalist systems just as everyone else does, but their use of mutual aid to support their community challenges and provides vital alternatives to the individualist nature of capitalism. Because they raise funding as needed to support the community's emerging needs rather than relying on mainstream funding models or applying for grants, We Are the Ones maintains substantial agency to direct money and community resources where they are most needed.

Trans Family Network, which I described earlier in this chapter and also in chapter 2, is another example of trans technological mutual aid. With Trans Family Network, people who need support can be connected with people who can provide support in six different categories: legal assistance, housing, transportation, emotional support, financial support, and local support. Matching people manually would be tedious and difficult at the scale they operate on—thousands of help offers and requests. Trans Family Network demonstrates how a technological system can support trans mutual aid in a wide-reaching way. Like We Are the Ones, Trans Family Network does not rely on formal funding (it is fully volunteer run, though I am unsure how it meets nonpersonnel expenses). It thus maintains substantial agency to help people redistribute resources to each other: it is a form of trans technology that enables people to practice trans care toward each other.

Many trans technologies did not have mutual aid as their primary goal but ran mutual aid initiatives in addition to their main function. For example, at the time of our conversation in 2022, Tuck Woodstock and his *Gender Reveal* podcast had raised and distributed $223,000 in mutual aid and grants for trans community members. Stealth Bros & Co. supply company provides a mutual aid fund that helps trans people to be able to afford transition-related supplies and work toward funding their surgeries. Trans Lifeline (a peer support crisis hotline) provides microgrants for trans migrants and for trans people in states where legally changing names and gender markers is prohibitively expensive. Yana Calou, Trans Lifeline's former Director of Advocacy, explained why mutual aid was an expression of Trans Lifeline's mission of supporting trans people in crisis: "Sometimes the best support that a trans person can receive is actually economic. It's not just emotional. We provide emotional and economic support as part of our core mission, and we put money directly in trans people's hands." Trans Lifeline used technologies like PayPal to transfer funds, but there were technological hurdles to distributing mutual aid to the most marginalized trans people, who may be homeless or unable to access financial infrastructures. As Trans Lifeline's director of technology Alice Barker put it, "This is a really tough thing that we're dealing with right now, is how do we . . . get them money in a way that they can easily access it and spend it without needing to have a bank account, a social security number, those kinds of things?" I heard from many interviewees that it was challenging to verify people's identities when distributing mutual aid funds; most were less concerned with verifying identities and more concerned with making sure that people who needed funds got them, despite barriers like those mentioned by Barker.

Some trans tech creators discussed the possibility of better technological ways to distribute mutual aid to community members. For instance, Tuck Woodstock from the *Gender Reveal* podcast ran a yearly "Trans Day of Staying in and Having a Nice Snack" mutual aid initiative, which donated $10 each to over a thousand trans people each year. This initiative was successful in raising and distributing lots of snack money, but the manual task of gathering and distributing the funds was, in Woodstock's words, "exhausting." Yet when he considered whether there was a way to automate sending out the snack payments on Venmo, Woodstock realized that "I don't want there to be." He valued the community and volunteer-based aspect of it too much. "One of the things that was really cool was that we had a bunch of people helping, and they would have long conversations with people about what their favorite snack is. And a person would be like, 'Hey, hope you have a good day (donut emoji)' because they like donuts, and that's part of it." Woodstock concluded that "you can't automate community. And so we're just doing a lot of extra work, because that element of it is really important to me. And that means that we're just doing more work. And that's really hard." While Woodstock saw community as, in a way, opposed to technological means of distributing mutual aid, the *Gender Reveal* volunteers were in fact still using technology, like donut emojis and Venmo, to distribute mutual aid funds. Given the barriers that trans people sometimes face in using mainstream payment platforms like PayPal and Venmo, it would be helpful if there were a trans technology payment system, built on values aligned with mutual aid, that had the ability to automate large numbers of payments.

Many people talked about trans mutual aid as a closed pool of funding: many trans people have relatively little money, and trans communities circulate the same small pool of money among themselves, rather than receiving donations from those outside the community with more access to wealth. Some interviewees viewed this cyclicality in a positive manner. For example, Denny Starks, creator of the prototype safety app U-Signal, said, "The queer community is just a cycle of us just helping each other. Even though we might be broke or whatever, when we got a little bit, we help the next person." Other creators sought to bring in financial resources from more privileged groups. For instance, Trans Boxing creator Nolan Hanson said, "If there can be cisgender participants that pay the asking rate, and enough of them, or trans folks that have the means to pay, then it makes it possible for me to offer trans people discounted sliding scale rates for training. And ideally, I'd really like to set something up where Trans Boxing could pay for a boxer's gym fees, or have a scholarship program or something." Starks described a similar potential approach for U-Signal, saying that the tool could be used by cisgender and/or white people on a paid basis, while trans BIPOC people could use it for free. In these ways, trans technologies can enable more privileged groups to support trans mutual aid.

The mutual aid efforts I have described in this section are not always fully technologically mediated, but they all meet the definition of technology I provided in the introduction, of extending one's agency. Some explicitly use digital technology to do so, while others use more traditional organizing and fundraising methods, but all are deeply community-based and demonstrate technological trans care.

I Don't Aspire to Profit: Anticapitalist Trans Technology Approaches

According to game creator Ryan Rose Aceae, "the biggest obstacle [to creating trans technology] is the crushing weight of capitalism"; as such, many trans tech creators found creative ways to resist capitalism in their work. Many interviewees refused to create technology simply for profit. Podcast creator

GenderMeowster (they/them) said, "The thing that I use to console myself that I'm not winning at capitalism is like, that was never the goal. The goal was to make a difference, and I do make a difference." Similarly, game creator D. Squinkifer remarked that their games are "a project I am doing more for myself and more for creative expression than something that I am going to aggressively market, or try to . . . make a lot of money out of. If people want to pay me money for it, that's wonderful." Keaton Kash, who created the surgery information sharing site Mod Club, described his changing approach to monetization: "I did experiment with charging a small membership fee in the beginning, but then I just felt like it was just . . . I don't want to say problematic, but it's just better to just let everybody in for free, and then try to find other ways to monetize . . . The focus is not 'How do we get this money?' It's 'How do we get this out, get people excited about it, provide value, and at least break even.'" In these quotes, we see that many trans tech creators prioritize goals like helping people and making a difference over profit.

Alex Ahmed of the Project Spectra voice app put it this way: "I don't feel like [profit is] what I aspire to. I don't aspire to trans people creating and profiting off the technologies marketed to trans people. I don't think that's a future that we should be striving for. That's just basically saying trans people should basically just become capitalists, and create our own shit to sell to ourselves. I mean, we can do it, and we'll probably do a better job than cis people would. That's fine, [but] we shouldn't call that revolutionary or anything." Ahmed noted that trans inclusion in capitalism does not improve matters for trans people more broadly: "Minority and oppressed groups have been incorporated into capitalism in all kinds of ways already. Has the world changed? No. A trans person being a homeowner doesn't really change anything for trans people who can't buy a house." In many ways, anticapitalist trans people are more closely aligned with cisgender people who are fighting class struggles than with trans capitalists (Spade 2015; Gleeson and O'Rourke 2021). Because capitalism has consistently harmed and excluded trans people, some trans tech creators chose to reject capitalist goals like profit rather than attempt to fit into a system they considered unjust.

Several of the trans technology small businesses I spoke with intentionally set their prices low enough that everyone who needed the product could afford it. Scout Rose from Transguy Supply said,

> It would be incredibly difficult to have a business for trans folks and not to be thinking about how to make it accessible financially, because the community is

strapped for resources. I get emails on a regular basis from people telling me that they're saving up for their first Mr. Limpy, which is a $13 product. You know that if folks are saving up to buy something that costs $13, that these aren't folks who have a ton of spending cash. What we've done is we have really tried to keep our margins as low as possible and still be able to pay ourselves and to sustain the business.

Trans Tape took a similar approach; its prices were low enough that demand outstripped supply and they struggled to keep products in stock. A capitalist approach would raise prices when demand is high, yet these companies set their prices as low as possible. Game creator Tabitha Nikolai took it farther, giving her creations away for free.

Creators in the health technology space often pointed out that capitalist systems are not good for meeting trans health care needs. Many of these creators deliberately rejected mainstream funding models so they could maintain control over their technology's direction and not have to compromise their values. For instance, Dr. Crystal Beal from the telehealth service QueerDoc described how their patient care goals may conflict with capitalist funding models: "I did not want investor funding, because part of the joy of having left traditional health care jobs is that I don't have to answer to someone else's pocketbook on how I take care of my patients. And if you take investors' money, that part is still there. I think one of the biggest, quickest parts that burned me out in traditional health care jobs was that I chronically felt administrators were making patient care decisions based on money and not on what patients actually needed." For similar reasons, Gaines Blasdel was resistant to accepting funding for Healthy Trans, a site providing health resources for trans people. Instead of selling advertisements from surgeons, a monetization approach that some of his colleagues running similar sites have taken, Blasdel chose not to monetize at all.

Another anticapitalist approach taken by trans tech creators was to channel profit or redistribute grant funding and extra resources back into community efforts—an approach that aligned well with the ethos of mutual aid. As Scout Rose from Transguy Supply shared, "I was a political anarchist who's now running an e-commerce business, so there's some tension there. . . . If Transguy Supply became massively financially successful, we know that we want to commit a huge percentage of those resources back into the community for growth, for change, and maybe not even just our own communities, but into things that we believe in and things that we want to see, changes we want to see in the world." Along the same lines, AJ Lewis from the NYC Trans

Oral History Project said that if they had the resources, they would use them to pay trans community members to contribute to the project:

> We've decided as an organizing principle that whenever we come into funds, the mandate is downward distribution of material resources, not the elaboration or further institutionalization of the project itself. We don't want to hire staff, we don't want to hire development workers, we're really just about: get funds to trans communities. . . . For instance, half of the ballroom scene is underrepresented in the [NYC Trans Oral History Project] archive. There are tons of amazing folks who could contribute their testimonies. We don't think that it would be equitable to ask them to do that without being able to pay them for it. We have a number of target communities that we would like to have stronger showings that we would throw money at.

Because the NYC Trans Oral History Project did not hire staff, it was less reliant on funding mechanisms like donors and grants and could target smaller pots of funding that could be redistributed to community members—an approach much more aligned with the project's values. Game creator Tabitha Nikolai described a similar tactic: "I really try to make a point when I'm getting grants to really be distributing those funds to people to help make stuff. Try to let people access [my] multimedia space . . . for free or no money to just come and have space or tools to work on stuff." These creators' values align much more with mutual aid than with capitalism: they aim to help their community rather than keeping profits, grant funding, or other resources for themselves.

Other creators distributed nonfinancial resources. For example, Trans Reads is a site that provides PDFs of trans-related articles and books for free. Many of these would otherwise be behind a paywall, inaccessible to many community members. According to Trans Reads' creator, the site's primary value was that that literature and information should be available and accessible to anyone who wants to read it and that "copyright unethically withholds knowledge from our communities." Thus, she aimed to "subvert laws to commit these . . . acts of property and copyright theft and redistribute resources." This is an active form of resistance to capitalism: by distributing copyrighted materials for free on its site, Trans Reads siphons profits away from large publishing companies.

Still other organizations build anticapitalist tenets into their organizational structures and practices. RAD Remedy, the trans health resource aggregator site, structured their organization in anticapitalist ways. For example, many organizations' boards of directors are appointed to help raise funds for the organization via their affluent networks, but RAD Remedy chose board members not for their financial status but for their deep connections to the community. Further, the company's pay structure ensured that every employee earned a living wage and that the highest and lowest paid workers received raises at similar levels. Similarly, the Trans*Code Hackathon rejected capitalist structures and goals: it was not tied to financial incentives or entrepreneurship, like most hackathons, but instead focused on building community and trans technologies. "We were more a day-long community Hack Day, but hack and storytelling and community building day," said founder Naomi Ceder. "We didn't have any competitions. We didn't have any prizes. We didn't have any money. We just had a place to have the event, and they provided us with food as well. That's all we needed. We had a great time for a day. That's what Trans*Code has always been since then." Participants felt less pressure to produce technology products that were ready for market; instead, they made connections with and learned from other participants.

Anticapitalism can also be built into the structures of trans organizations or technologies in other, less material ways. Because marketing and advertising work better for identities and systems that are stable and predictable, an anticapitalist approach can involve creating systems and platforms that value ambiguity and change in relation to people's identities, as represented in databases or user interfaces. Transgender Usenet Archive creator Avery Dame-Griff called this characteristic "fuzziness," saying, "How can we develop systems that encourage fuzziness, or have the expectation of fuzziness built in? There are people [who] will change and that is okay. I think ultimately that means that these cannot be capitalist systems. These cannot be the same platforms that have been about 'How do we sell data for money?' because that is what it encourages." Dame-Griff's comments align with arguments he and I made in a previous coauthored paper, which examined Tumblr as an example of a trans technology that enabled users' ambiguity and change (Haimson et al. 2019a). As Dame-Griff stated in our interview, "[Tumblr] wasn't any good [as a capitalist company] because it doesn't make anybody money, because it's weird and fuzzy and messy." In the definition of trans technology that Dame-Griff and I and our coauthors came up with in 2019, a trans technology embraces ambiguity, flexibility, and change, and it therefore cannot also be a capitalist technology. "That's why I think trans technology, it cannot be this corporate system," Dame-Griff continued. "It has to be something different, because if you base it around [making] money when your identity's in flux, you can't sell someone something based on identity, unless you expect their costumes to be wearing blue, white, and pink" (i.e., based on the trans flag). Identity change—gender change in particular—cannot easily be captured in mainstream systems and is difficult for marketers to pin down. Trans identity and capitalism are simply not well aligned, and we can consider fuzziness—a form of transness in its ambiguity, multiplicity, and ambivalence, similar to my theoretical trans technology definition—an anticapitalist approach to creating technology.

I hope that these examples of anticapitalist approaches that trans tech creators took—from de-emphasizing profit to distributing resources to community members to building in fuzziness—will help to inspire future trans technologists who wish to create anticapitalist trans technology. But it is worth noting that even anticapitalists still need to earn a living and survive. As described earlier in this chapter, many trans tech creators work full-time jobs and create trans technology in their "free time," but this is often unsustainable, leading to burnout. Thus, we see people like Scout Rose, the former "political anarchist who's now running an e-commerce business"—people who find balance in their ambivalence, which allows them to maintain their political beliefs while still running a successful company. Ambivalence is key in combining trans technology creation with survival in a capitalist society.

Conclusion

In *Normal Life: Administrative Violence, Critical Trans Politics, and the Limits of Law*, Dean Spade (2015) describes a growing divide between two facets of the trans population, one focused on trans visibility, trans equality, and trans inclusion in mainstream institutions (similar to the technological inclusionist approach I described in the introduction) and another that works toward social justice and transformative change by challenging and critiquing those mainstream institutions for the harm they cause trans people and other marginalized groups (a more justice-based approach, and similar to what I call technological separatism). We can see this same divide in the ways trans tech creators approach their work: capitalist approaches align more with inclusion, and anticapitalist approaches align more with justice. While there is no clean line between the two camps, and many trans technologies demonstrated ambivalence around capitalism, most trans tech creators expressed values and described funding models that aligned more prominently with one or the other. For example, companies like Euphoria, with its VC funding and Bliss trans banking app, and The Trans Capitalist, who teaches trans people how to play the game of capitalism, align with the inclusionist approach, which aims to provide trans people equal opportunity in existing capitalist systems like banks, stock markets, and venture capital funds—systems that harm trans people by exposing their past identity (Mackenzie 2017) or perpetuating income inequality. Other trans technologies align much more with a justice approach; these include groups like We Are the Ones We've Been Waiting For, which prioritizes mutual aid and support for trans people (especially those who are people of color, financially insecure, and/or immigrants), and Trans Reads, which distributes copyrighted trans material online for free and challenges mainstream publishing institutions.

Another way to think about trans technologies' funding approaches is through Paul Kivel's (2017) conception of the difference between social service work and social change work. Social *service* work directly addresses individual people's needs after they have been negatively impacted by violence or harmful institutional systems. For example, services that support domestic violence survivors would be considered social service work. Social *change* work, on the other hand, addresses the root causes of violence and harmful institutional systems. For instance, services that work with domestic violence perpetrators to help them unlearn generational cycles of violence perform social change work. Kivel argues that we need both types of work in political movements: social service work helps people who desperately need support in the moment, and social change work seeks to transform the world into one that we want. In Kivel's (2017) view, when too much of the work is focused on social services rather than social change, it hinders transformation and liberation.

We can think about trans technologies using this social service versus social change designation. Many of the capitalist trans technologies I discussed in this chapter take a social service approach. For instance, venture capital–funded trans health technologies like Plume and Folx Health are engaging in social service work, helping to tangibly address the barriers that trans people in many geographies face in accessing trans-inclusive health care (Everhart, Ferguson, and Wilson 2023). Yet despite Plume founder Dr. Kirkley's goal to "really radically redefine the system" and "transform health care for every trans life" (a transformative goal of social change), what these companies currently provide is a "market-based solution to social problems" (Beare and

Stone 2021) that does not challenge the core issues in the health care system that affect marginalized groups, such as lack of access to care for people who cannot afford it and the need for insurance reform. Some anticapitalist trans technologies also engage in social service work, like creating apps and supplies to help people adjust their appearance and survive in a transphobic world. However, they also do social change work—potentially transformative work that challenges existing financial systems, such as refusing to make profit and redistributing money and resources back to community members.

Certain types of funding can hinder social justice movements: when organizations rely on grant funding from foundations and donations from wealthy individuals, wealthy people end up having substantial control over which types of organizations can exist and thrive (INCITE! Women of Color Against Violence 2017). The same is true for investment funding. As Silvia Lindtner (2020) observes, when companies pitch a new technology product, the primary audience is potential investors, not users. But deciding against accepting donations, grant funding, and investment funding brings its own problems: trans technologies that refuse these types of funding are often perpetually underfunded or unfunded, which necessarily limits their impact.

The majority of the trans technologies in this research were funded by grants and donations—funding sources that sometimes limited the technologies' transformative or liberatory approaches and their work toward achieving social change. However, many of the donation-funded trans technologies in my dataset were funded not by a few wealthy donors but by a large group of community members, each donating small amounts. This crowdfunding approach is much more aligned with mutual aid and community-centeredness. Community-based political work, particularly work that takes an anticapitalist approach, is more likely to make meaningful change that is rooted in the community's values (INCITE! Women of Color Against Violence 2017; Spade 2015). As Spade (2015) suggests, political work "should build the capacity of directly impacted people to work together and push for change that will significantly improve their lives," and transformative change can only occur when led and organized by those most impacted. This is one reason why trans technologies that involve trans communities in design processes are more likely to address the community's most salient needs and challenges, as I discussed in chapter 4.

Spade (2015) argues for a critical trans politics, defined as a trans political orientation that goes beyond visibility, equality, and inclusion to instead work toward social justice and transformative change to institutions that harm trans people. A critical trans politics "imagines a world in which people have what they need and govern themselves in ways that value collectivity, interdependence, and difference" (Spade 2015). With the recent mainstreaming of trans identity, Spade claims, a more individual-based inclusion approach has predominated. This approach works best for those who are most privileged, and laws and policy changes have thus tended not to be based on what multiply marginalized trans people need most (Spade 2015). I see many of these same issues playing out with trans technologies, particularly those that perpetuate trans capitalism. Capitalist trans technologies often eschew community-based and need-based approaches and instead create money-making technology products that are palatable and pitchable to investors and wealthy donors.

In this chapter, I have argued that if trans technologies hope to impact society in ways that align with their creators' and communities' values, it matters what type of funding model they choose, for their funding model affects their goals, impact, and sustainability. Many trans technologies are underfunded or unfunded, which limits their impact and requires sometimes exhausting amounts of unpaid work, but their financial independence also allows them the freedom to choose their goals; trans technologies that receive grants and donations are less financially precarious, but there are often strings attached that shift the work's focus (Beam 2018). After all, as Beam (2018) argues, it is impossible to critique or challenge capitalist systems if an organization is funded by and must appeal to wealthy donors who have benefited from capitalism. Funding also impacts trans technologies' sustainability and longevity. Trans technologies with thousands or millions of dollars in VC funding, who can pay themselves and their staff and access the resources they need, have a better chance of long-term survival, even if their work can only create limited social change. At the other end of the spectrum, underresourced trans technologies reliant on unpaid work have the potential to make more substantial social change, but creator exhaustion may lead to burnout before that radical change is achieved.

As transness becomes increasingly more mainstream and visible, it is important to keep an eye on the rise of trans capitalism and where it may be taking us. While few trans technologies are actively harmful, many do not have nearly the impact that they could, because they are not properly aligned with the community's needs and challenges, particularly the challenges faced by the most marginalized trans people. Other trans technologies may be well aligned with community needs but are so underfunded that they are limited in their ability to positively impact the community and make transformative change. Within capitalist systems, disconnects between trans community needs and trans technology funding are inevitable, and this problem will not be easily solved. Some trans tech creators are playing the game of capitalism, and others are playing a different game on the periphery of capitalist systems. None are really quite winning for trans people—yet. In the next chapter I turn to the future of trans technology and what we might expect and hope to see as time moves forward.

6 Trans Technological Futures

I think the future of trans technologies is more, better, more complicated, and more in your face.
—trans studies founder Sandy Stone

Hi Oliver, Unfortunately I will be unable to participate as I am 16 years old.
—response to my request for a research interview from a creator of a browser extension that removes one's deadname from webpages

While I was not able to interview the trans tech creator quoted above because my study required participants to be eighteen or older, I was excited to learn that some trans tech creators were as young as sixteen and that young people like this one were skilled and motivated enough to create trans technologies as teenagers. Several others in my study were over eighteen at the time of our interview but described trans technologies that they had worked on as teenagers or preteens, some beginning as young as eight years old (like Mia, described in chapter 2). Young people's involvement signals a thriving future for trans technologies. As these creators grow and continue creating innovative technologies, they will in turn attract more young people to start creating their own trans technologies.

As another signal of trans technology's flourishing future, during my year of interviews with trans tech creators (July 2021 through June 2022), countless new trans technologies sprang up. Some of the up-and-coming trans tech creators I spoke with in spring 2022 had not even envisioned their trans technologies, or yet had the skills to create them, when I began this study in 2021. As I mentioned in the introduction, I had once (naively) thought it would be possible to request interviews with all existing trans tech creators.

Once I understood how rapidly new trans technologies were being created, I realized that this quest would be impossible. As one indicator, at the time of this writing, the "transgender" tag on itch.io brings up over 1,300 games—and I am sure this number will grow over time.[1]

Many interviewees talked about the burgeoning future of trans technologies. "I think the future of trans technologies are, they're going to be all around us," said game creator Tabitha Nikolai. Similarly, Christella Antoni, cocreator of the trans voice app Christella VoiceUp, noted that "we're nowhere near having enough trans technologies" and saw an upward trajectory in the future. Augmented reality (AR) trans tech creator Chitra Gopalakrishnan said, "I really think that there are a lot of engaging and bold content creators from the trans community that are making their voices known these days—the younger generation, so to speak. I'm very excited to see how, with more equity of access of these softwares and the wide availability of devices and softwares you can build things on . . . I think it will only get more and more experimental and engaging." TRACE transition app creator Aydian Dowling also spoke to the flowering of trans technology creation, which parallels trans people's agency to create: "I mean, we're growing . . . it seems like everywhere I turn there's another trans company of something. . . . So, I think as we evolve as a community, we're going to get more people who feel like they can actually do things, and then those people are going to go do stuff. So, it's going to grow exponentially over the next years. I'm sure of it."

As new trans technologies continue to spring up rapidly, some older ones fade away. Many of the trans technologies that I wrote about in this book are no longer active. Some of them, such as the transition and social app Flux and the safety app LGBTrust, were never fully deployed in the first place. Others, such as the health resource site RAD Remedy and the wiki encyclopedia of trans topics Transpedia, have been quietly sunsetted. Yet new trans technology creation seems to be outpacing old trans technologies' departures, replacing those that are abandoned or obsolete. Some address the same needs in similar ways and some in new ways (Everhart, Gamarel, and Haimson 2024); some address new and different challenges altogether. For instance, in recent years many trans technologies emerged that help to document and fight back against antitrans legislation, as I discuss further later in this chapter.

---

1. https://itch.io/games/tag-transgender

But it is not enough to simply have *more* trans technologies; I also heard from interviewees that it matters *who* is creating the trans technologies of the future. That is, they hoped to see more trans people, and more diverse groups of trans people, creating trans technologies. Justin Bantuelle, creator of Gender Infinity Resource Locator, discussed the positive impacts of having more trans creators of technology: "I'm becoming more and more aware of talented trans developers. And I think the more that they're integrated in the space, the more that they'll be able to shape technologies moving forward, possibly create their own companies to produce technologies that would really benefit [trans people]." On a similar note, Dr. Nabeel Shakir, a cisgender gender-affirming surgeon, remarked on the need for more trans surgeons to become leaders in the gender-affirming surgery space:

> More and more trans and nonbinary folks are becoming doctors, becoming surgeons, and I think really should be the leaders of the next generation of surgeons. Historically this has been a field where cisgender folks have been the leaders and dictated what surgery ought to look like. The future ought to be more representative and ought to be driven by innovators and leaders from the community. I'm excited because there are some future leaders in the pipeline, that are training in this space, and are already establishing a name for themselves. I think that really, the future belongs to them.

With more trans people leading trans technological innovation, technology can go in directions that could not be imagined by cisgender creators—and as more multiply marginalized trans creators come to the table, trans technologies can push in directions that white, highly educated trans people have not yet imagined. "The more diverse people that are pushing technology forward, the more exciting things that we're going to see that we can't imagine right now," said B.A. Laris, cocreator of the health resource and social media app Trans Women Connected. Diversifying the pool of trans tech creators will expand the creative directions trans technology takes and help to address some of the limitations I discussed in chapter 3—that trans needs, and especially multiply marginalized trans people's needs, are not always met by trans technologies, because trans tech creators often hold more privileged identities.

Trans technologies of the future also will, I hope, truly address the most pernicious trans needs and challenges, "hopefully with the actual goal of uplifting or improving the life chances of trans people," in the words of Avery Everhart, creator of a spatial database of trans health care facilities.

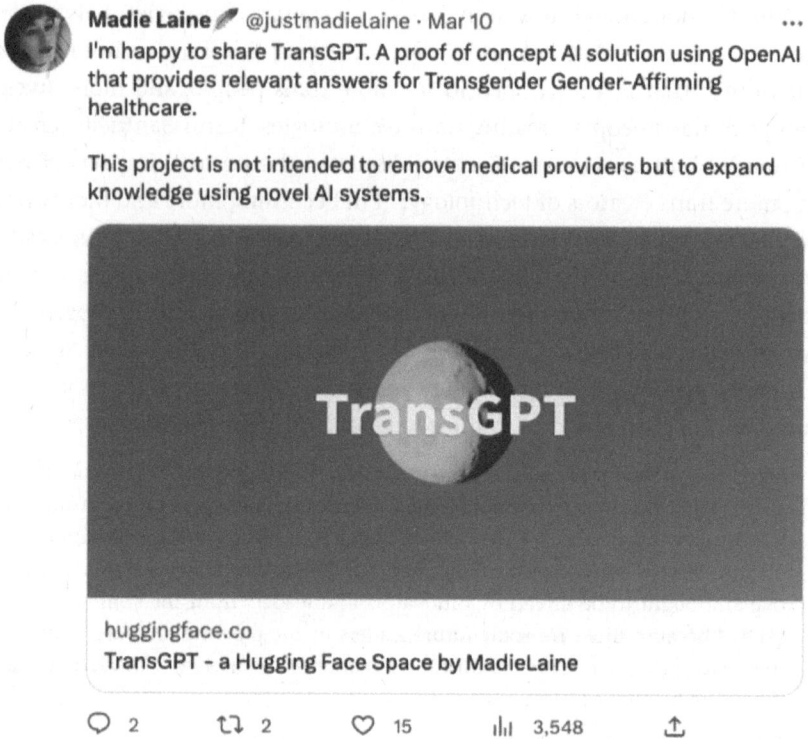

Madie Laine 🖋 @justmadielaine · Mar 10   •••
I'm happy to share TransGPT. A proof of concept AI solution using OpenAI that provides relevant answers for Transgender Gender-Affirming healthcare.

This project is not intended to remove medical providers but to expand knowledge using novel AI systems.

huggingface.co
TransGPT – a Hugging Face Space by MadieLaine

💬 2   🔁 2   ♡ 15   ᵢₗᵢ 3,548   ⬆

Figure 6.1
"Expand[ing] knowledge using novel AI systems." Madie Laine's tweet announcing the AI tool TransGPT, 2023. Screenshot by the author.

Willow Hayward from the browser extension Deadname Remover similarly stated that she "would hope that we start seeing more things which are just designed to make trans people's lives a bit easier." These hopeful takes speak to the need to prioritize aligning trans technology creation with the real challenges trans people and communities face.

Yet trans technologies might simply follow the technological trends of the moment. A salient example is TransGPT, created by AI researcher Madie Laine. This is a chat application using OpenAI to answer questions about trans health care, drawing from the WPATH (World Association for Transgender Health) Gender Affirming Standards of Care (Laine 2023) (see figure 6.1).[2] For instance, if you ask TransGPT "How does estrogen help transgender

---

2. https://twitter.com/justmadielaine/status/1634199812131241984

women?," the tool gives an accurate five-sentence response, starting with "Estrogen helps transgender women by inducing physical changes such as breast development, redistribution of body fat, and decreased body hair growth" (Laine 2023). Along similar lines, a group of researchers created an AI chatbot named "Amanda Selfie," "conceived as a Black transgender woman and . . . a virtual peer educator" to help increase uptake of HIV prevention medicine pre-exposure prophylaxis (PrEP) (Massa et al. 2023). TransGPT and Amanda Selfie very well might help some trans people, as access to trans health resources is a common need for trans people, and searching for accurate, unbiased medical information about gender transition and sexual health is often a difficult process (Augustaitis et al. 2021; Delmonaco and Haimson 2023). Yet Laine acknowledges that TransGPT is a proof of concept rather than a tested and validated tool, and there are concerns about AI large language models presenting false or misleading content (Weidinger et al. 2022); further, not all AI tools will be trained on trans-inclusive source materials as TransGPT is. This could pose real misinformation challenges to AI solutions for trans health information access. Perhaps the most optimistic AI trans technologies are those that help trans people envision themselves in affirming ways, such as with generative art portraits (Tao 2023) or by transforming childhood photos to align with one's posttransition gender.[3] So far, though, it seems that the recent acceleration of AI has caused more harm than benefit for trans people, such as with automatic gender recognition (Hamidi, Scheuerman, and Branham 2018) and gendered data surveillance (Shelton et al. 2021). I am certain we will continue to see an uptick in AI trans technologies[4] —which may or may not address trans needs.

When I asked trans tech creators about what they envisioned for the future of trans technology, not one of them mentioned a need or desire for AI, machine learning, or even algorithms. Instead, they talked about trans liberation and resistance against rights violations, imagining future possibilities for new trans worlds, utopian and dystopian visions of the future, community and connection, ways to facilitate access to trans health care and body changes, and much more. While some participants envisioned speculative technology that would enable futuristic trans worlds and trans

---

3. This is the goal of the Saved Memories Project (https://www.saved-memories.org/en/).
4. For example, see https://theresanaiforthat.com/s/transgender/.

liberation, others described dystopian futures where trans technology is increasingly commercialized. Trans technology futures may involve technology that further addresses trans needs and challenges, but some envision a future in which trans people integrate into mainstream society to such an extent that explicitly trans technology is no longer a useful distinction. This chapter provides a wide range of visions of what trans technology may look like in the future.

In looking to the future of trans technologies, I note several important ambivalences, each of which represents two potential paths that the future may take. First, some interviewees spoke about trans technology's potential to integrate into mainstream society to such an extent that trans-specific technologies are no longer needed; at the same time, interviewees also spoke about trans technology's potential to create inventive new trans worlds. These align with the two orientations for marginalized groups using technology that I described in the introduction: technological inclusionism (focused on improving existing mainstream technologies to be more inclusive) and technological separatism (focused on specific technologies for that group). Second, while many trans tech creators discussed the dystopian futures they feared, they also described the utopian futures they hoped for. Finally, in dystopian futures, capitalist approaches loomed large, while in utopian futures, mutual aid and trans care were prominent. Sometimes the same interviewee would discuss both sides of these supposedly conflicting visions, holding them simultaneously or wavering between them. While no one can predict the future, it seems most likely that for each of these ambivalences, our future reality will be a complex combination of the two, just as we currently see both negative and positive implications of technology existing at once.

Trans care is pervasive in some versions of trans technological futures—utopian futures, and futures that involve mutual aid and new ways to facilitate trans community and connection. Trans care will also be vital in some of the dystopian trans technological futures I describe in this chapter. In resisting trans capitalism and surveillance from large corporations, trans people will necessarily need to rely on and take care of each other, sharing obfuscation techniques and building alternatives to mainstream technologies that are not aligned with some trans communities' values.

In this chapter, I argue that while transness is inherently future-focused, both personally and politically, trans technologies enable us to augment our present experiences in the world, whether by adjusting our bodies or by working toward social change—toward the future that we want. Trans lives are hard, because the trans lives that we truly want—with bodies that align with our gender and with politics that align with our ability to survive—often feel out of reach. Creating and using trans technologies enables us to imagine and work toward those hopeful futures and avoid the futures we fear.

All Technologies Are Trans Technologies: Future Trans Technologies Integrate into Mainstream Technologies and Society

When I asked trans tech creators about the future of trans technology, many described a technological inclusionist future in which trans technology integrates into mainstream society. For some, this means that trans technologies will be incorporated into mainstream technologies or that mainstream technologies will become inclusive enough of trans identities that there will be less need for separate trans technologies. For others, trans technologies themselves, or the types of technology they are built on, will become pervasive in society.

Interviewees gave many examples of ways they could see trans technologies integrating into mainstream technologies. "I think one day, it'll just be another part of a voice app," said Eryn Gitelis, creator of the PRYDE Voice and Speech Therapy app, about trans voice training technology. Similarly, Willow Hayward described imagining the functionality from her Deadname Remover browser extension, which replaces trans people's previous names with their current names, being integrated into mainstream operating systems: "I would honestly be unsurprised if in ten years Windows launched with a version where it was like, 'Hey, if you're trans, here are some configuration settings to do that on everything.' Because at that level, it should be possible." Different software, databases, and web browsers across an operating system could integrate seamlessly to enable a trans person to change their name easily without their deadname showing through (as it currently does in many systems). Ash (a pseudonym for a creator who wished to remain anonymous), who cocreated a makeup support system for trans people, described how this type of system could be integrated into mainstream makeup technologies in the future. Ash did not see value in continuing to iterate and improve their trans-specific system, seeing their technology as having more impact and reaching more people if its functionality could be integrated into makeup technologies already in use.

Some trans tech creators stated that increased trans inclusion in mainstream technologies was one way for trans technologies to integrate into the mainstream. "I think you will see a lot of cis people putting more conscious effort into trans inclusivity," said Hayward. Tobey McKinley (cocreator of the transition app Transcapsule) gave the examples of dating apps and banking technologies: "The ultimate goal is for that trans tech to eventually phase out and just have that be an inclusive part of any dating app. Shouldn't need our own bank provider that's inclusive, everybody should just be inclusive." McKinley's statement directly contrasts with trans dating technologies like Tser and trans banking technologies like Bliss, which separate trans dating and banking away from mainstream dating and banking.[5] In the dating context, separation from mainstream dating apps can be important in the present, given safety and harassment concerns. I am more critical of trans banking being segregated from the mainstream, as it perpetuates trans capitalism. Trans Peer Network online community creator Laur Bereznai described a future with "more and more inclusion of trans technologies in cis technologies. When it comes to very basic and not really life changing things [like] Instagram allowing you to set your pronouns, that kind of stuff, small trans technologies come into the cis world more and more often. I think that's a good step forward. It allows us to have docking points between technologies, and that allows us to not be completely external." Bereznai's "docking points" analogy is an interesting way to understand how future trans technologies can hook into mainstream technologies, creating a point of connection without full integration.

At the same time, mainstream technologies can (and some already do) include trans-inclusive features, such as pronoun sharing. The future will likely see more trans inclusion in information systems. Dev, creator of the Jailbreak the Binary browser extension, discussed trans inclusion on social media sites. They described a period when the Facebook interface did not allow nonbinary genders, and some trans hackers figured out how to adjust the HTML code to create a third gender field. According to Dev, this practice "only stopped being necessary because they added nonbinary [options to Facebook] because everyone's hacking it in a way that probably actually

---

5. Though Bliss pivoted in 2024 to focus primarily on domestic violence survivors and, more broadly, "the most vulnerable souls," it was initially designed for trans people (https://bliss.lgbt/).

influenced their decision to add nonbinary genders. Theoretically, someone could have seen on the back end, 'Oh, there's a lot of people here who have entered in a null gender, that's probably because of this hack, we should probably just add it in as an option that people can pick.'" Dev sees a positive trajectory in which mainstream technologies evolve to be trans-inclusive by default so that such hacks are no longer needed. Another example in a different context came from QueerDoc creator Dr. Crystal Beal, who described how Alaska Airlines instituted a trans-inclusive policy and system change that allows people's legal names to be different from their chosen names and prompts employees to refer to passengers using their chosen names. This system and policy change takes "the emotional burden off of us explaining it to each individual we interact with," improving trans people's experiences at airports—traditionally a major site of technologically imposed stress for trans people (Beauchamp 2009; Costanza-Chock 2020). "I feel that's what technology is supposed to do, is supposed to decrease some of our labor," said Dr. Beal. "I guess that would be my wish and hope." As more and more technological systems become trans inclusive via features like additional gender options, pronouns, and increased flexibility in name changes, trans technology becomes more integrated into mainstream technology.

A number of interviewees described a future of trans technology in which "all technologies are trans technologies," in the words of Dr. Jerrica Kirkley, cocreator of the Plume trans health care technology. Dr. Kirkley continued, "I think that's truly my hope is that regardless of what the technology is—Is it health care? Is it financial? Is it . . . who knows, real estate or whatever? But [the trans] experience is taken into account and acknowledged in the use of whatever platform it might be." Similarly, To Be Real crowdfunding prototype cocreator Zoe Nolan envisioned a future in which "maybe every technology becomes a little bit of a trans technology, rather than being its own category. It just permeates to the general landscape." QueerMed (an online trans health service) creator Dr. Izzy Lowell described this concept in the realm of health care:

> I think and hope the future of trans technology looks more and more like the future of technology. Where . . . there doesn't have to be a special . . . I'll use this big comparison from medicine. I think there's trans medicine right now, which is treating transgender people. And it's very specialized. It's not complicated, it's not difficult. It's very safe. But still not a lot of people provide that care. And it should be primary care, but it's not. So it's got its own home, separate things. But we don't talk about

diabetes medicine like that's a whole separate special thing. That's just regular medicine. . . . The way that I think [trans] medicine will work [in the future] is no longer
a special "other"-ized thing. It's just something that you can get from any doctors
and from your local primary care doctor in a rural Alabama town. We're a bit of a
ways from that. But I hope that I would say the same for trans technology . . . in
terms of incorporating trans and nonbinary identities into technology. I would
hope that would just be all technology.

In Dr. Lowell's view, in a hopeful future world, trans identity would be destig-
matized enough that trans people could receive trans medical care from any
relevant provider. Currently, almost any endocrinologist will treat diabetics,
but few endocrinologists will treat trans people for gender-affirming hormone
therapy (GAHT), although both treatments fall under this medical specialty. In
the same way, perhaps we will not need separate trans technologies, because
all future technologies will be welcoming and inclusive of trans people.

Some interviewees thought that widespread trans inclusion in mainstream technology would phase out the need for trans technology and considered this a positive development. Dev said, "I mean, ideally, in the future,
the whole idea of needing anything special to make trans people lives easier
wouldn't be a thing. Because trans people would just be accepted in society
and not have any additional issues that are just because of being trans. So
ideally, the future of trans technology is it not existing anymore. In a perfect world." Karen, creator of the Safe Transgender Bathroom App, saw trans
inclusion as signaling a potential endpoint to the technology she had created:
"It seems like there are a lot more bathrooms that are all-gender these days.
And maybe the app isn't as necessary as it used to be." It seems right now like
we are still a long way from universal restroom access for trans people, but if
trans-inclusive restrooms were pervasive enough, no one would need an app
to find the nearest one. As trans inclusion increases and trans stigmatization
decreases, trans technologies may become less necessary.

Others saw trans technologies as remaining trans-specific yet becoming
mainstream. For instance, Nikki Nguyen from Trans Defense Fund LA stated,
"I just hope more [trans] technology comes out and it just becomes big and
as mainstream as any other technology." Some interviewees anticipated certain types of technologies (such as extended reality) becoming more pervasive, which would enable trans technologies that incorporate those tools to
integrate more with everyday life. This was the future that Rob Eagle, creator
of the *Through the Wardrobe* interactive AR exhibit, saw for AR. "I think AR

will become even more pervasive. . . . I think the more that we have filters in every form of our screens, the more that we potentially might have AR glasses over the next five years. . . . We are augmenting our environment through screens and this is becoming increasingly pervasive. And I think it will become ubiquitous here very, very soon within the next generation." As AR becomes ubiquitous, trans technologies that use AR to help people explore trans identity or augment their surroundings to help them navigate the world as trans people will also become increasingly more accessible, usable, and mainstream.

While this section focused on technological inclusionist visions in which trans technologies integrate into the mainstream, the next section focuses on technological separatist approaches. Inventive trans technologies that envision new possibilities for technology will be unlikely to integrate well with mainstream technologies; they will instead require specifically trans ways of thinking about and implementing technology.

Robot Avatars and Other Transy Potentials: Future Trans Technologies Imagine New Possibilities and Create New Trans Worlds

Many interviewees saw future trans technologies not as assimilating into the existing mainstream but as pushing boundaries outward, creating room for new trans worlds and imagining radical new possibilities for technology, transness, and identity. This is a form of trans worldmaking (Rawson 2014a). In trans worldmaking, built from the concept of queer worldmaking (Muñoz 2013), trans people envision new worlds through developing community knowledge and engaging in activism (Rawson 2014a). Trans worldmaking is enabled by trans technology, which can both allow us to think about the world in new ways and help to bring about those new worlds, creating positive social change for trans people.

Trans game creator Sasha Winter saw herself and her online community members as leading the creation of new and futuristic trans worlds:

> I honestly think that my community represents the future. [When] you messaged me talking about trans tech, I immediately was like, "Yes, I know that my community is right there at the front of it!" What we're doing, this on the ground collaboration, the writing, and the art that we do—it's something that the corporations cannot take from us. They can't possibly do what we are doing. They will never be able to. We are experiencing a kind of art that is personal. It is bold and brave

in ways that corporate art can never be. That makes me feel very invigorated and excited for the future.

Winter's community involves trans gamers, streamers, artists, and writers using platforms like itch.io, Discord, Twitch, and Twitter to create and spread their creative visions in "bold and brave," independent, and anticorporate ways. From talking with Winter and exploring her community's exciting games, art, and online communities, I fully believed her: this community is on the bleeding edge of trans technology and represents its future.

AR is one particularly promising medium for trans technology to enable people to imagine and create new trans worlds. Rob Eagle, creator of the *Through the Wardrobe* AR experience, discussed how AR enables new "transy" possibilities: "The way for us to see ourselves differently, the way for us to see our environment differently, that, to me . . . is super transy and I think points to the trans potential of AR. And I think that will only grow. I don't see it diminishing anytime soon." By augmenting the physical world with interactive digital content, AR allows people to imagine and explore identity and their relationships to physical and digital worlds in new and exciting ways. Chris Vargas, creator of the Museum of Trans History & Art (MoTHA), also saw physical and digital hybrid spaces as key to the future of trans technology: "A kind of reversing out of only existing in physical space to technology that is more of a hybrid of a virtual space and physical space. Something that rides that line that makes both a little bit more habitable." AR, in its potential to straddle the line between digital and physical spaces, generates exciting potential for trans technological innovation and trans worldmaking.

Social media is another direction for new and inventive trans technology. Rather than attempting to forge trans communities within existing mainstream social media sites, trans communities could create new, "transy" online spaces specifically for trans people. In a previous research study, my research team and I studied this potential with the now-defunct social media site Trans Time, which supported online trans community-building and identity exploration through its unique privacy, safety, and content warning features (Haimson et al. 2020a). Up-and-coming trans social platforms like TRACE and more established queer social platforms like Lex have had some success creating new online worlds for trans people by reimagining not only site features, but also how people connect and represent themselves online.

Some trans tech creators imagined new possibilities for trans technological futures via futuristic digital self-presentations. "Will I get to be a cyborg in my lifetime? Will I get to be part wolf/part human in my lifetime? Who knows?" asked Winter, in considering the future of trans technology. LemmaEOF (who uses it/its pronouns), creator of the NameBlock browser extension, is also a VTuber, or live streamer who appears on their stream using a virtual avatar. LemmaEOF described its ideal future as follows: "I mean if I'm being hyper optimistic of the limits of what we can do, I want a robot body. I would like that a lot. Being able to switch out parts based on how I'm feeling, that would be trans tech to me. That's what I ultimately really want. Probably not going to get it for a long while. But that's what I want." For LemmaEOF, blurring human/machine boundaries is intertwined with traversing gender boundaries (Halberstam 1991). As a VTuber, it uses a robot avatar online, and it sent me an image of what this character looks like, including lights that change color, body parts that can disconnect and switch out for other parts, and animal-like features like hooves (see figure 6.2). LemmaEOF shared, "Being able to look however I want is one of the best parts of tech and the Internet for me, and I'm gonna fight like hell to make sure that sticks around." When I asked about the avatar's face, concerned about the potential racial implications of its black background color (LemmaEOF is white), it clarified that the face was black because it was a screen: "It can be used to display all different things. . . . I would love to have a screen for a face, just personally. Because it's all about externalizing expressions. I am autistic. That can make express-ing myself really difficult. So, if I could express myself with more than just standard facial expressions, that would be a huge help." Part of LemmaEOF's idealized self-presentation also involved its robot avatar's body type. "Yeah, I'm fat," it said. "There are not enough fat robots just out there, in general. There are not enough fat characters in general. I decided, I want my character to be very visibly fat, chubby not skinny. . . . There needs to just be more fat positivity. I want to do that."

In LemmaEOF's robot character, which it embodies anytime it presents itself publicly online, I see endless potential for creating new trans possi-bilities and customizing self-presentation in inventive new ways—cyborgian self-actualization in the future trans Internet. LemmaEOF can represent its multiple marginalized identities—trans, autistic, and fat—in the form of a robot, increasing representation for each of these identities and their inter-sections and helping it feel comfortable while streaming. Someone else's ava-tar character would look and operate completely differently. Each person's online avatar could enable imaginative new types of embodiment that are

Figure 6.2
LemmaEOF's robot avatar that it uses for VTube streaming. Art by Cura Sylfaen.
Reprinted with permission from LemmaEOF and Cura Sylfaen.

not possible in the physical world, demonstrating trans worldmaking's transformative potential for identity presentation.

Fighting for Existence: Future Trans Technologies Are for Liberation and Resistance

In recent years, many trans technologies emerged in response to widespread incursions on trans rights in a number of states across the US: trans health care was banned, legislation mandated that people use the restroom corresponding to the sex they were assigned at birth, and it was made illegal to even mention trans identities in classrooms (as just a few examples). In chapter 2, I described some of the technologies responding to these antitrans laws, including the Trans Formations Project online database of US state-level antitrans legislation and Trans Family Network, which connects those impacted by antitrans legislation who need support with those willing to provide support. Trans tech creators have also built multiple online map resources to track legislation and estimate the level of risk in each state. These include the State Legislation Tracker,[6] created by Equality Federation; LGBTQ+ Legislative Tracking,[7] a frequently updated Google spreadsheet created by Allison Chapman, Alejandra Caraballo, and Erin Reed; and the Anti-Trans Legislative Risk Map,[8] created and updated monthly by Erin Reed (see figure 6.3). On itch.io, user Rue (ilananight) put together a bundle of games called "TTRPGs [tabletop role-playing games] for Trans Rights in Florida"[9] as a fundraiser, which included over 500 games and raised almost $300,000. These technologies speak to a future in which trans technologies are built as forms of resistance, ways of fighting back against rights violations and discrimination—a future in which trans technologies work toward trans liberation.

While Reed had yet to create her Anti-Trans Legislative Risk Map when we spoke in March 2022, she spoke of the need for exactly this type of technology:

> I think that in the immediate future, a lot of trans technologies, and I hate to say this, but with all the attacks on trans people, I think that a lot of the near future for

6. https://www.equalityfederation.org/state-legislation
7. https://docs.google.com/spreadsheets/d/1fTxHLjBa86GA7WCT-V6AbEMGR
FPMJndnaVGoZZX4PMw/
8. https://www.erininthemorning.com/
9. https://itch.io/b/1753/ttrpgs-for-trans-rights-in-florida

Erin's 2024 Anti-Trans Legislative Risk Map

This map shows the 2-year risk for anti-trans laws and represents the final update of 2023 for the 2024 cycle. Both the risk to trans adults and trans youth are found in this report.

ERIN REED
DEC 30, 2023

♡ 214   💬 14   Share

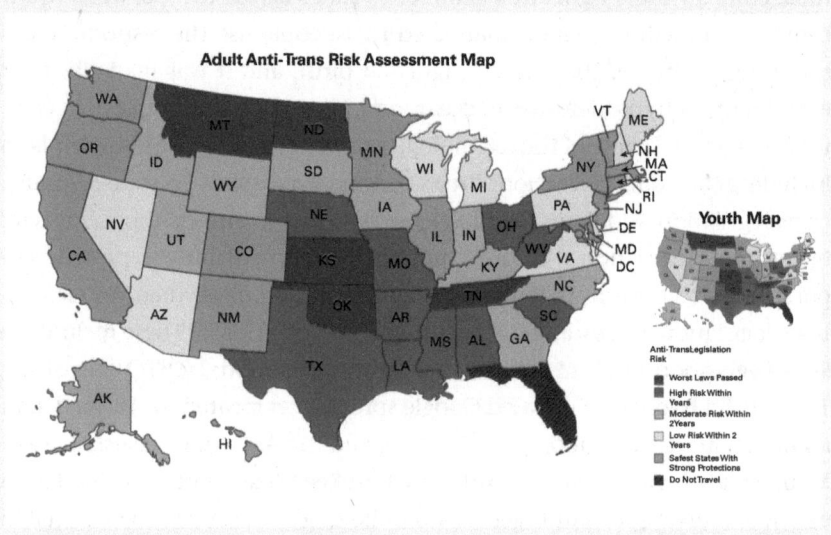

Figure 6.3
Erin Reed's frequently updated map of US antitrans legislative risk, 2023. Florida received a "Do Not Travel" advisory. Screenshot by the author.

trans technologies is going to be centered around mitigating those attacks. We're seeing the beginnings of it in places like Texas and Idaho and Florida. But as things get, in my opinion, a little tougher for trans people in the United States in coming years, trans technologies are going to be essential ways that we mitigate the damage that's caused, and that we do seek community . . . and that we even fight back.

Reed predicted this short-term future well. Currently, many trans technologies are focused on documenting, addressing, and fighting back against antitrans legislation. In the time since we spoke, she has dedicated substantial time and effort to activism and independent journalism documenting and spreading news about trans legislation, both on her website and on her Twitter account, which at the time of this writing has over 200,000 followers.

Some creators described a more radical view of future trans technologies and their potential for trans liberation and resistance. Game creator Jess Rowan Marcotte spoke about the future of trans technology as "a resistance to the status quo" and a way of "transforming it and imagining what else could be there instead," which involves "a resistance and a thorniness" rather than mainstream appeal or efforts to convey positive affect. In Marcotte's view, future trans technologies must embody resistance, not seek to make cisgender audiences comfortable. Alex Ahmed, creator of the voice app Project Spectra, also pointed to a radical trans technological future when she said, "The hope would lie in a trans technology created by and for trans people whose goal is the destruction of cis society." She gave a few examples, such as a technology to "fuck with TSA scanners," or a mechanism to expose people posting harmful alt-right content online. "I mean, I feel trans technology doesn't have to be geared to change our behavior, to provide a service even potentially useful to us as customers. A trans technology is just us using technology to fuck shit up. I feel like that's great." Ahmed's approach runs counter to trans capitalism and imagines trans resistance via technology in a more chaotic and revolutionary way. Radical approaches like these, if sustained and supported by many, may even lead to fundamental structural change.

Interviewees recognized that in the immediate future, trans technologies must fight for trans rights and liberation, but they hoped for a future in which we could move beyond that need. "I think we're still at a point where we're still fighting for existence," said Dylan Paré, creator of Queer Code virtual reality (VR) projects. "What I want to see as a future is where that fight no longer exists, and then see, what are those trans technologies that exist then?" It is exciting to consider the potentials for trans technology in a future world where trans people no longer have to fight for basic resources and rights. For some, this kind of hopeful future could be difficult to imagine. Sasha Winter described the complexities around dreaming of a better future for trans people: "It's hard to imagine a future. It's hard to imagine a better world, and that is important work that we need to be doing. Looking to the future and not being afraid of it." Winter approached this future vision by combining joy, anger, and art as forms of trans liberation. "I think that finding ways to express unfiltered trans joy and trans rage, and all of these things that we're told that we can't have, is very liberatory. There is a very artistic aspect to the concept of revolution, and to the struggle for liberation, because we have to be the ones who are imagining a better future." Because she considered art as activism, Winter could work on creating trans games, coordinating game jams, and facilitating online communities around art and games as a form of trans liberation. Charlotte Danielle from The Transverse media network saw a similarly optimistic future for trans technology, despite the current struggles: "We're in the middle of a revolution. It's just beginning. What it's going to look like is unknown, but with what's going on with all of these Discord platforms, community groups and everything, that's just under the layer, under the first layer of soil, if you will. There's a lot incubating, and I think the future is incredibly bright." In the face of oppression, trans people are seeds, and trans technology can help those seeds grow toward trans liberation.

Bodies by Apple and Binders from Target: Dystopian Trans Technology Futures

Many trans tech creators had a less than rosy view of the future of trans technology. Avey, creator of a trans biohacking project, saw the trans technological future as "quite exhausting and grim," and artist Myra Day said, "It looks pretty dystopian right now. If I'm being honest, shit looks pretty bad." The most common examples of dystopian trans technological futures were capitalist, with technologies designed specifically to make profit from trans populations. Game creator D. Squinkifer worried about "capitalists taking on the language of trans liberation and selling it back to us." Laura Horak, cocreator of Transgender Media Portal (a transgender film directory website), feared trans communities being monetized like gay communities, who have often been viewed as a target audience for marketers: "I think certainly . . . there'll be this very neoliberal version of trans technologies that's similar to the way gay men became this demographic that, 'Well, oh they have income, so now we want to make some random shit for them. . . .' I would love for trans people to have lots of disposable income too, but I feel like there is a very circumscribed version of trans technologies that we'll see." Clarissa Diaz from the design education community QTBIPOC Design also worried about exploitative, profit-based trans technologies, especially those that could help trans people but would exclude those who could not afford the cost. These capitalist dystopian views align with the concerns about trans capitalism I raised in chapter 5.

A capitalist trans technological future might create more products that trans people can use or expand access to existing products, but this would divert money out of trans communities, coming at the expense of more creative, exciting, and liberatory trans technologies. As Alex Ahmed described, "I think, realistically, the future is going to be more startups by trans CEOs. More . . . products geared to trans people, [more] for-profit technologies geared to trans people. For a variety of things. I've seen transition support, I've seen voice apps, of course . . . and I think it's unfortunate, I think that there's so much more that we can do." Scout Rose from Transguy Supply discussed their ambivalence around capitalist trans futures in which trans technologies become more mainstream:

> Larger corporations have started to understand, at least from a financial perspective, that they can make money off of trans people; that they *can* ignore it, but that they could make money if they didn't ignore that market. Is that a good thing? Is it a bad thing? I don't know. I mean, I've heard that Nike is working on a gender-expansive clothing line. I've heard that Adidas is working on binders.[10] On the one hand, I think it could be incredible for companies that have these resources and access to technologies that Auston [Transguy Supply cofounder] and I don't, certain types of proprietary technical fabrics, for example, and then also to own their own manufacturing. They can create a product that is probably way better than what we can produce, and they can probably produce it for less, and they can charge people less for it, and that is something that the community absolutely needs. At the same time, what is Adidas going to do with those profits? Yes, they can make money off the community. Where does that money go? Is it just an extractive . . . Is it going to go back into the community? Is it going to be uplifting the community? I don't know. I mean, I think we will see more and more larger brands start to flirt with trans consumers.

Rose here expresses an ambivalence toward trans capitalism that echoes many of this book's themes: trans capitalism increases access to products that trans people really need, but it is extractive and exploitative, ignores the needs of the most marginalized, and is vulnerable to political pushback from antitrans lobbies. For example, it is hopeful to think that trans people in rural areas could buy binders and other trans supplies at stores like Target (Rude 2022). But in 2023, antitrans activists launched a viral campaign, based partly based on misinformation, targeting Target's Pride Month displays. The campaign resulted in Target employees being harassed and the company

---

10. Binders are constricting fabric for chest-flattening used by many transmasculine and nonbinary people and trans men.

eventually removing some Pride products from some of their stores (Mey-ersohn 2023). Whether trans capitalism would improve trans access to sup-plies depends on how Target ultimately responds to the controversy and how other companies respond to potential antitrans pushback that we may see in the future. We must remain skeptical of a future in which trans technology is increasingly monetized, viewing trans people as a market to tap rather than a community to support. And unlike small, trans-run businesses like Transguy Supply, large, cisgender-run corporations like Target and Adidas do not use their profits to benefit trans people. Does a capitalist trans technology future offer meaningful progress?

Deliliah D'Lune, creator of the trans-inclusive porn site Royal Jelly, also worried about "technologies specifically trying to profit off of us and poten-tially exploit us for whatever reason." She gave the example of a recent medi-cal procedure she had undergone:

> I was noticing . . . that the veins on the back of my hand were really prominent. And I got very self-conscious about this. I actually went and had them surgically removed. They injected a poison into the back of my hand. And now, the backs of my hands are really not very veiny anymore. Afterwards, the surgeon asked me, he said something to the effect of, "How can I market to trans people, because I see a real need in your demographic for this kind of service." My first thought was like, "Oh, my God, I don't want you marketing to trans people. That is going to create this idea that we need this thing," where it's like, if people don't feel like they need it, they don't need it. I would be really worried about . . . trans technologies in the future that are creating needs in people that will get them more entangled in the medical industrial complex, or whatever else it might be that people could take advantage of.

Trans medical innovation is generally considered positive, but as D'Lune notes, it can also create opportunities for medical professionals to profit from trans needs that otherwise would not have existed, forming new (and expen-sive) appearance standards and insecurities for trans people. The same is true of any future trans technologies that are driven by profit. Companies that see trans people as consumers will actually *create* needs and markets, instead of addressing the real, existing, pressing needs faced by trans communities, which may be less profitable.

Several trans tech creators detailed dystopian technological scenarios in which trans people lose control of their data and even their bodily auton-omy. "I think we're gonna see more of these for-pay apps that are selling your information about your transitions to people for a number of different reasons. I think that's probably where we are headed," said Transpedia creator Clair Kronk. "The data is profitable," said game creator Tabitha Nikolai, "and people will want that. And people want to control identities to make them purchase things." Greyson Simon, creator of the education resource site Trans Language Primer, engaged in dystopian trans worldbuilding. Drawing from the science fiction role-playing game *Eclipse Phase*, Simon gave the example of a planned obsolescence future in which large corporations like Apple manufacture and update parts of people's bodies, making people reliant on that corporation for updates. "Kind of like how Apple makes the iPhone slow," Simon described. "When the new models and bodies come out, suddenly you're walking slow, you're having digestive issues, you've got to update your mental [health]." While trans cyborgian futures are often portrayed in a positive light (cárdenas 2011; Halberstam 1991; Nelson 2020; Stone 1995), such as in LemmaEOF's robot avatar described earlier in this chapter, Simon's dystopian example shows how reliance on technology for body changes may result in harm. Squinkifer brought up a similar concern about decreased trans autonomy: "One of my fears . . . is technology becoming more of these walled gardens that are under the control of huge corporations. . . . I worry about people creating new tools and new tech that is impossible to repair by yourself. Making it impossible to hack, impossible to have any autonomy around what you do, and just increased surveillance. What if the only way you can access this technology is to have all of your data being mined and owned, just to sell you more stuff, or prevent you from pursuing actual liberation?" Fear of data mining and increased surveillance, both of which are often sources of profit, are legitimate and pressing concerns that we must contend with in a future where trans technology is entwined with capitalism and corporate interests.

Creative Cultural Endeavors: Utopian Trans Technology Futures

As much as trans tech creators worried about dystopian trans technological futures, they were also often optimistic, with the same people also describing utopian futures of trans technology, sometimes in the same conversations. "I mean, I think there's gonna be bad and also good, right? That's how technology is," said Tuck Woodstock, creator of the *Gender Reveal* podcast.

In a utopian future world where trans people struggle less for life chances, resources, and basic rights, trans technologies can address a wider range of goals. A future in which trans people can focus less on survival allows for trans media that covers a wider range of trans stories—"not just about coming out, not just about violence, not just about horror," as trans games creator Jess Rowan Marcotte said. With less pressure and need to take up quintessentially trans experiences like disclosure and violence, trans media like games and art could focus more on a broader set of topics and experiences, including joy. "I hope we can get to a point where the development of trans technologies can be fun," said Hacking Biopolitics creator Avey. "I feel there's just a lot of things that are in the way. I hope [disparities in] access to health care [are] eliminated. So that people can feel more comfortable exploring gender options, but also just having the care they need. In order for the future of trans technology to be utopian, the structural barriers need to be taken apart first." Some scholars assert that technology design for marginalized communities should center joy and "flourishing," rather than needs and challenges (To et al. 2023). But for some creators, it may not be possible to design for joy and flourishing when their community's rights and basic needs are under attack. While many trans tech creators could imagine a utopian future that allows more room for enjoyable rather than need-based trans technologies, they recognized that serious structural oppressions must be dismantled first.

Interviewees described how trans technologies might be able to help with the work of reaching these utopian futures, by working to reduce issues like transphobia and racism and ensure equal access to life chances for trans people: "Maybe there will be trans technology that's developed to help reduce the structural barriers to jobs, housing, health care, and other stuff," said Avey. Some trans technologies are helping to address these systemic issues, but in a utopian future world without transphobia and struggles for rights and basic resources, they would not need to exist. Jaylin Bowers discussed how the Trans Family Network team has "had conversations where we've said, 'I wish [Trans Family Network] wasn't required.' . . . That would be my endgame here."

Interviewees saw utopian trans technological futures as drawing from the unique aspects of trans experiences, such as prioritizing community, and as remaining in the hands of trans creators. Sophie Debs, creator of the Gender Neutralize browser extension, said, "I think that alternativeness, and the grassroots nature of trans tech is very exciting. It feels very community-centric, and very organic and powerful in ways that I like. And I don't think that the future of trans tech looks like Silicon Valley." Rather than aiming for profit and vying for investment funding, trans technologies could remain community-based, small scale, and grounded in an ethos of trans care. Marcotte described their hope and excitement for trans technologies made by trans people but noted, "I don't think that we'll always know if creators are trans or not, or they may not know yet either. It's kind of interesting to look at work before and after, or as people are in the process of discovering that aspect of themselves." In this utopian vision, creators have the time and space to explore their own identities as part of the trans technology creation process.

In contrast, Delilah D'Lune imagines a future where trans identity is less foregrounded and where trans people are just accepted as creators: "I really love it when I see a trans woman on Twitter posting about a videogame that she has written. . . . And her voice matters and it's not specifically because she's trans, but because she's a person who is engaged in this creative cultural endeavor. And so I guess, in essence, my utopian vision of trans technology in the future is that it doesn't matter, or something like that. But we are just able to exist amongst everyone else." D'Lune's vision aligns with Marcotte's in that both see trans media as able to focus on a larger set of topics beyond trans oppression; a game need not even be about transness, and its creator's trans identity need not be foregrounded. Trans people can create whatever they want to create, just like everyone else. In some ways, trans creators already have this freedom, but structural oppression and transphobia mean that trans people are often reduced to their trans identity, rather than having their work valued on its own merit. Utopian trans technological futures would give trans creators more autonomy to either explicitly make trans technology for trans communities or to design technology that does not center their trans identities at all.

Sex Change on Demand: Future Trans Technologies Facilitate Health Care, Body Changes, and Medical Transition

Many trans tech creators spoke about trans technological futures that gave trans people more agency over their health care, body changes, and aspects of medical transition, providing tools, resources, and services that give trans people agency over their physical changes with fewer barriers and less guesswork. In *Gender Reveal* podcast creator Tuck Woodstock's words, the future will involve "more specific and more successful trans medical care, where we have more control over what we're doing when we do little trans science experiments on our bodies."

Many creators talked specifically about increasing access to GAHT, which is sometimes difficult for trans people to get because of trans health gatekeeping, financial barriers, distribution restrictions, and frequent supply shortages. Rian Ciela Hammond, creator of Open Source Gendercodes, discussed ways of collectively creating do-it-yourself (DIY) hormones—an idea that is not currently possible but is an exciting area for future innovation. Trans technologists are currently practicing technological trans care by creating new online mechanisms for hormone distribution. For instance, in 2022, a service called Otokonoko Pharmaceuticals[11] stated on their website, "We work as a compounding pharmacy, just ask and we'll see if we can provide the product in the dosages that you want :3," and a site called DIYHRT.market was recently launched as "a community-driven project to provide accurate and up-to-date information to the trans DIY community about sourcing of hormones. In our view DIY is an unfortunate but inevitable consequence of a transphobic medical system that does not trust trans people know who they are."[12] Similarly, the creator (who wished to remain anonymous) of Trans Reads mentioned wanting to "find ways of distributing hormones through the digital sphere," which she viewed as similar to distributing trans literature online as she did with Trans Reads. "What I considered doing," she said, "was hosting an overseas-generated account through a web hosting service that doesn't give a shit and finding a way to link people with hormones to those who want to access it. Of course, very illegal—it would have to be very anonymized." In the meantime, she started a small-scale, informal hormone distribution system—a kind of GAHT mutual aid and trans care: "I always order twice the dose from my doctor that I'm supposed to have and then just keep the rest and give it away." These imagined futures and current practices speak to the deep need for better access to GAHT. Each of these approaches—collectively creating hormones, distributing hormones online, and redistributing one's hormone prescription—might be classified as biohacking, which Malatino (2017) defines as taking place outside of legal and official channels and involving collaborative rather than individualist approaches.

---

11. https://otkph.am/
12. https://diyhrt.market/about

Trans surgeries are another key area of trans medicine that, like GAHT, involve substantial barriers to access. Many interviewees spoke about how future trans technologies could help increase access to gender-affirmation surgeries: "I think the future is . . . better surgery and cheaper surgery," said Alice Barker from Trans Lifeline. Trans media scholar Cáel Keegan envisioned this future:

> Sex change on demand. For everybody. And not packaged as sex change. Just like, you want a dick, here's a dick, you want boobs, here are boobs, you want this level of hormone, go for it. Just all kinds of somatically shifting medical technologies that people can apply in any range of combinations based on their own comfort and health, completely driven through self-determinative praxis. . . . For me, the technological pathways should all move toward allowing people to use that science to create more livable lives for themselves around the concept of bodily autonomy and self-determination, choice.

Keegan detached gender-affirming surgeries from the dominant gender transition norms, instead imagining *a la carte* procedures that would enable everyone, not only trans people, to reconfigure their bodies as they wished. Such a future would necessarily require easier access to surgery.

Some interviewees considered futuristic ways of changing trans bodies, such as rapid body-swapping and body-changing technologies. According to Greyson Simon, "I think body swapping is probably, amongst my friends, the number one wish for our gay, socialist future selves." Denny Starks (creator of the safety app U-Signal) said, "That's something I always think about—when can we trade bodies?" Sophie Debs (creator of Gender Neutralize browser extension) described a "cyberpunk" future where "people go into a clinic and they change bodies at will." Many trans people's physical body realities are far from their ideals, and they envision a future with fewer logistical, financial, medical, and administrative barriers to changing one's body. While it may never be technologically feasible to change one's body parts easily and rapidly, speculative trans worldbuilding of this kind is helpful in understanding trans desires, which can be used to guide development of new procedures and health care systems.

Imagined utopian trans technological futures included innovations in the areas of prosthetics, surgical implants, and surgical techniques. Leo, from the prosthetics company TransFormaGear, referenced recent innovations around medical organ printing, which could lead to future innovations for trans prosthetic devices. "Better and better prosthetic solutions can exist," said

Leo. "They just don't yet. . . . We're still really just in the infancy of where things can be at, in terms of surgery, in terms of prosthetic solutions. . . . For me, the future is exciting and then I can only see things getting better and better in terms of what is available for trans people." In the surgery space, gender-affirming surgeon Dr. Mang Chen described future innovations that could improve on the current state-of-the-art phalloplasty techniques: "There's talk of penile transplant. There's talk of stem cells." Dr. Chen also discussed the possibility of trans-specific innovations to penile implants like the Coloplast Titan. Keaton Kash, creator of the trans surgery online community Mod Club, spent substantial time doing research and talking with gender-affirming surgeons to understand the existing landscape and areas for improvement. "My head is pretty firmly rooted in the bottom surgery stuff and how to improve those outcomes and those processes," Kash said. "I think that we have to advocate very loudly for our needs when it comes to pushing the health care industry forward to care about us at all." Kash described advocating for extending trans bottom surgery options for trans men and transmasculine people through innovations such as penile transplants or growing donor skin in a lab. Improving prostheses and surgical techniques is a form of technological trans care, as people like Leo, Dr. Chen, and Kash work to understand how technologies can improve to best augment trans people's bodies.

Trans agency over trans health care includes trans people's ability to pursue surgeries that do not meet cisgender standards of what bodies should look like. For many trans people, surgeries that go against cisgender bodily norms may involve additional barriers, such as insurance coverage and surgeon approval. Alice Barker from Trans Lifeline described wanting to see a future with "a wider understanding of the diversity of trans folks' bodies in the sense where . . . I have a lot of nonbinary friends who are interested in certain surgeries that are extremely difficult for insurance to understand when they don't conform to one norm or another." Not every trans person aims to transition into a body that looks like a cisgender person's, and they should have the ability to explore those options. For example, when creating their top surgery nipple placement tool, Gaines Blasdel and his cocreators enabled people to experiment with creative, nonstandard options in the simulation software, such as "the option to just add unlimited nipples" or adding trans pride colors onto one's torso (Blasdel et al. 2020) (see figure 6.4). While most people would likely not choose to actually pursue a body like this, some might

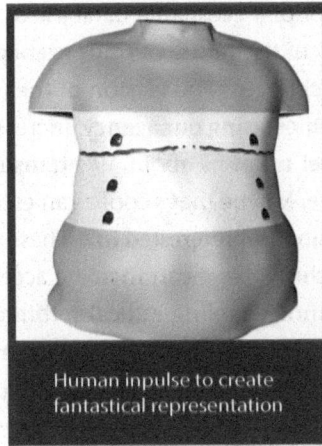

Figure 6.4
Gaines Blasdel and colleagues' example of a "fantastical representation" using their top surgery nipple placement tool (Blasdel et al. 2020). Image shows trans pride-colored stripes on the torso (blue, pink, and white), six nipples, and scars and nipples in shiny gold. Reprinted with permission from Gaines Blasdel.

choose creative or fantastical bodies if they were exposed to the wide range of possibilities beyond cisgender body standards. Blasdel described the importance of allowing for experimentation in tools like this: "I think being able to have 'this is just for fun' and 'no, really, this is what I want' [options] . . . being able to give people the option to say if they're serious or not, I think it's necessary in that context." A trans patient could spend some time using technology to experiment with different surgical options—some as creative, fantastical options and others as more serious surgical wishes—and then select which ones to send to their surgeon. Gender-affirming surgeon Dr. Nabeel Shakir also spoke to the need for more varied options for trans surgeries: "People should have the freedom to have options. . . . As more innovation happens in this space, [more surgical options are] the natural consequence of having people who are catering to [the trans] market." As the trans surgery field grows and evolves, a greater understanding of nonstandard procedures will emerge, giving trans people more agency to decide how their bodies will look and pursue those options more easily. Some surgical options may not be feasible, and others will involve new experimental surgical techniques, requiring surgeons and patients to have new kinds of collaborative conversations about feasibility and risk before moving forward.

Avery Everhart, creator of a geospatial database of trans health care facilities, had a different view of the future of trans agency over health, more oriented toward structural change: "The version of the future of trans tech that I'm invested in is one of increasing our agency, increasing our ability to make change at structural level and less about VR, transhumanist, totally body-modifying sex-doll future. Maybe that's cool as an escape, but I don't know. I don't think that's the vision I'm interested in." These two approaches are not necessarily mutually exclusive—we can increase access to basic trans health care while at the same time enabling radical rethinking of how bodies can look. I agree with Everhart that structural changes in health care access and agency are sorely needed, and there may be ways that trans technologies can help move us toward those structural changes; at the same time, imaginative speculative trans technological futures can work to realign people's thinking about the limits of trans body augmentation and change.

Robbi Katherine Anthony (who goes by RKA), creator of the transition-tracking and resource app Solace, saw trans technological futures in terms of creating personalized transition plans that enable people to efficiently meet their transition needs. "The future, at least in my belief, is specialized care and doing so in a way that is built and designed around the user itself," said RKA. "I do envision a future where someone comes out and they're able to get, for lack of a better word, a custom transition plan, and which it speaks to their needs and doesn't center their lives around being transgender and just centers it around, 'You've got this unique biological medical phenomenon, and this is how we're going to address it,' and then let you get back to the most important thing in this life, which is just being yourself." This future vision focuses on reducing how long it takes to transition—from an average of seven to ten years (RKA's estimation) to one to two years—by providing a customized transition plan and a set of resources to accomplish each step. RKA's to-do-list-esque vision is quite different from most trans tech creators' future visions, which tend to be less regimented and more about individual choice and agency. But many trans people might value a quicker path through gender transition's often difficult liminal stages.

These varying views of trans health technological futures share a commonality: the need to allow trans people more agency over their health care and body changes. The future we need for trans health care requires novel new trans technologies that reduce the obstacles between what people want and what people can get, and working toward and creating those technologies is a form of technological trans care.

Open Arms Become Wider: Future Trans Technologies Facilitate Trans Community and Connection

Many interviewees spoke about trans technological futures that enable trans connection, community, support, and safe spaces. Interviewees felt that in the future, online spaces and other technologies would emerge to help trans people gather, find a sense of community, and support each other—a continuation of the past and the present importance of trans online communities, where, as Juniper Porter of the protest-tracking site Tear It Up put it, "people can be comfortable, feel safe, and explore." "I think [trans technology] will continue to be a way for trans people to connect with each other safely," said Tuck Woodstock, "to keep each other alive. Especially when we look at all of these states who are trying to criminalize being trans. I think more than ever, trans technology becomes just safe ways to connect outside of government surveillance. And so I think that future ways to let trans people exist at all, despite the government trying to eradicate us, is kind of technology." For Woodstock, technologies like Signal and Venmo that enable trans connection and mutual aid are as vital to connecting trans people as online communities are. Trans community and technology-enabled mutual aid were also central for Kai McBride from *Stealth: Transmasculine Podcast*: "For some people, it's lifesaving, the connections people made and the humanity people show each other virtually. I see a lot of people that are having hard times, and they're getting GoFundMes, meal trains, or whatever it is to meet basic needs." By enabling trans people to connect with each other and fill social and financial gaps unaddressed by mainstream society, technological trans care, in the form of mutual aid and community support, will continue to be vital for trans futures. Until systems begin to meet trans people's basic needs, trans people will rely on each other and take care of each other, often via technologies like online communities and payment platforms. Mutual aid is not possible without community connections, so future trans technology must continue to facilitate both.

Future trans technology will also continue to connect isolated trans people with community and support. E. C. Pizarro III from TransTech Social

Enterprises said, "The future of trans technologies look like the trans person that's in middle America, or internationally, where being trans is illegal or even more dangerous—[future trans technologies will ensure] that they have access to support. Whatever that looks like." Similarly, Clair Kronk said, "Being able to find a community is a big deal, and it's hard sometimes for people who don't have access to technology, especially during the pandemic. Because so many people are online. A lot of people are immunocompromised who can't leave home." Trans people continue to face danger and decreased life chances, and the Covid-19 pandemic and other health hazards continue to spread; in the face of these real-world dangers, trans online communities will continue to allow people without local trans support networks to connect with similar others. Indeed, it is sometimes through communities that we understand ourselves; podcast creator GenderMeowster (they/them) said that in the future, "I hope that trans people will keep finding each other, and therefore finding themselves, because they realize it's possible." Technologies are and will remain crucial for trans connection, community, care, and identity exploration.

Several interviewees discussed future trans technologies bringing cisgender allies into the picture to help meet trans community needs. Lee Hulme from the mutual aid stream team Gender Federation imagined how some online spaces for trans community could also include cisgender allies, as long as some spaces remained that were for trans people only:

> I think [the future of trans technology is] going to be a widening of some of these spaces to include cis allies and straight allies and gender conforming allies that have shown up to try and help. In some ways it'll be after they've proven themselves, because letting just anybody in, the results are bad. We all know this. We've all been through it. But I think that there will be some spaces—not all, because we still need spaces that are safe for ourselves—but I think there'll be some spaces that are going to get opened up to the people that want to come in. Because [at] the end of the day, the people that want to come in with us are bigger in number than the people that want to get rid of us, and . . . that's starting to become obvious. And I think that whilst keeping our safe spaces that we really need, because of all of our trauma around cis people in particular, and around just the world, those are the spaces that are going to be needed for a long time to come. But I do think that the open arms will become a little bit wider, by those that are strong enough to overcome that trauma enough to let cis people in.

In trans online communities, cisgender allies could help to combat some of the transphobia and online harassment that trans people experience regularly and could provide support and technological trans care in ways that other trans people may not have the bandwidth or resources to provide. Across many participants, there remained a sense of optimism for the future of trans community and connection. "I am excited about us, those who are doing the work," said Denny Starks, creator of the U-Signal safety app. "I'm so excited to see us flourish and us help our community,"

Conclusion

While conducting research for this book, I was excitedly following Queer Spaces, a new "group chat platform for building queer communities," as an example of a platform with potential to form new online trans worlds. Queer Spaces presented itself as "the safest, least toxic platform for queer people." In March 2023 on Instagram, Queer Spaces posted a photo of a customized tote bag that placed the platform as an edgy new alternative to other social media platforms, reading "Fuck Facebook. Fuck Twitter. Fuck YouTube. Fuck Discord. Fuck TikTok. Fuck Instagram." with their website, queerspaces.com, underneath (see figure 6.5). This framing signaled that Queer Spaces hoped to provide a new, alternative online world for queer and trans people to gather outside of mainstream platforms. Yet five months later, Queer Spaces announced that it was shutting down after being repeatedly turned down for investment funding (though according to Crunchbase, the company raised a total of $1.1 million). Financing "has been exceedingly difficult, particularly in this current funding environment," said founder and CEO Christof Wittig.[13] This "underfunding . . . stifled the required growth to get the app to the next level."

Several other trans and queer technologies also said their public goodbyes in 2023, primarily due to financial concerns. A queer app called Out, which helped queer and trans people find LGBTQ+ people, events, and businesses, announced on Instagram in September 2023 that it was closing down, citing "the current economic landscape," which "has presented challenges beyond our control, making it impossible for us to continue providing the user experience you deserve." Shortly after this announcement, Out's website and its presence on Instagram and all other social platforms disappeared completely. Somewhere Good, a Black and queer-centric social platform and

---

13. https://www.instagram.com/p/CviJbxYO0vl/

Figure 6.5

(top) An Instagram post by the social app Queer Spaces, positioning itself as distinct from existing social platforms, March 2023. Screenshot by the author. (bottom) Queer Spaces says goodbye via its Instagram account, August 2023. Screenshot by the author.

physical community space in Brooklyn, also shut down in September 2023 after raising $3.8 million in investment funding in 2021, stating nothing more concrete than "sometimes good things come to an end, especially in a volatile and fraught economic market."[14] In late 2023, the trans crisis hotline Trans Lifeline announced it would cut back its hours starting in 2024 and would take a full pause during the 2023 holiday season, although demand for the hotline had reached unprecedented levels. Trans Lifeline had to reduce its operations because "corporate funders who had previously supported the crucial work of TLGBQ+ organizations like ours have now significantly dialed back their financial support"—perhaps connected to the rise of antitrans rhetoric.[15] The sometimes fleeting nature of trans technologies that I witnessed in 2023 builds on a longer history; Andre Cavalcante (2018) documented the "ephemeral and unstable nature" of now-long-gone trans technologies Safe 2 Pee and XX Boys in his 2018 book.

As much as Queer Spaces, Out, Somewhere Good, and Trans Lifeline struggled, other trans and queer technologies seem to be thriving, at least financially. The venture capital–funded queer app Lex raised a record $5.6 million in late 2023, bringing its total funding amount to $7.2 million. With this infusion of funds, Lex introduced a redesign that incorporated new features that many users criticized for de-emphasizing the app's prior focus on dating and sex and introduced a monetization model requiring users to pay to post more than six times per month (Weber 2023). For Them, a trans "gender tracking" app and binder company I had somehow never heard of, made waves when it acquired the queer feminist digital publication Autostraddle in August 2023 (The Editors 2023). The Autostraddle community voiced disapproval and anger about the merger, rooted in concerns over data privacy, the change in funding models (Autostraddle had relied on donation and community-based funding, but For Them was investment funded; according to Crunchbase, the company has raised $2.2 million as of 2024), and recent Autostraddle staff layoffs.

Two map technologies, both with grassroots funding approaches, are recent trans technology success stories, signaling exciting futures. Queering the Map is a crowdsourced digital map-based archive of queer and trans physical spaces, marking locations of personal stories of "coming out, encounters

---

14. https://www.instagram.com/p/CxLl-ycOO4J/
15. https://translifeline.org/navigating-change-for-long-term-resilience/

with violence, [and] moments of rapturous love" (LaRochelle 2020). For instance, in downtown Ann Arbor, a Queering the Map user posted, "Made out with another transgirl in this alley after putting up tags. The tags were covered by next year, but we are still together." Drawing from queer theorists like Sara Ahmed (2006) and José Esteban Muñoz (2009), the site queers Google Maps, enabling spaces of queer possibility; on Queering the Map, any place can become a queer space momentarily "through queer acts" (LaRochelle 2020). The map's intentionally queer design elements include anonymity, obfuscation, and opacity. For example, if the user scrolls out far enough, "the blurring of thousands of stories into opaque masses . . . obscure[s] borders and converge[s] individual narratives into collectivities," eventually completely covering most of the map and impeding the site's ability to load (LaRochelle 2020). Queer features also manifest in the intentional absence of many typical contemporary Web 2.0 features: no user profiles, data collection, algorithms, search, passive scrolling, likes, reactions, or comments. Queering the Map also incorporates collective technological trans care: in 2018, when Trump supporters attacked the site with spam and malicious popups, creator Lucas LaRochelle posted a call for help and quickly received it from many willing volunteer coders and moderators; they all worked together to rebuild and secure the site and set up a moderation system. Moderating the stories before they are posted "is at once incredibly gratifying and emotionally laborious" (LaRochelle 2020). Queering the Map currently documents over half a million queer places worldwide, and new submissions are added daily (Oung 2023).[16]

The second map is called Everywhere is Queer, and it focuses on queer-owned businesses (e.g., Queer Comics Peddler, a pop-up comic shop in Ypsilanti, Michigan) and local communities (e.g., The Queer Outdoors, a meetup for hiking and camping). It now displays over 7,500 businesses across the world. Everywhere is Queer is more commercial and less theoretically queer than Queering the Map, for it focuses on businesses instead of personal stories and elicits sponsored content partnerships, but it, too, is grounded in community. Both of these queer maps address important trans needs and seem sustainable; neither are investment-funded as of this writing.

---

16. As a spin-off to Queering the Map, its creator Lucas LaRochelle also created QT.bot (https://lucaslarochelle.com/qtbot/), an AI-powered tool trained on Queering the Map's data to "generate speculative queer and trans futures."

In these examples of both sunsetting and success, financial precarities arise when trans and queer technologies push toward mainstreaming and trans capitalism, such as by repeatedly applying for investment and venture capital funding. Even when technologies gain the funding they seek, it changes them. Making trans technologies palatable to investors requires creators to sell a vision that investors will support—which is unlikely to align with trans technologies' radical and justice-based potential. As Avery Dame-Griff (2023) argues, a central challenge for trans technology is "the need for safe spaces we own." That is, we need control not only of software and user interfaces but also of platforms' governance, hosting, and servers; we cannot rely on corporate companies for this. Dame-Griff notes that in the days of the early Internet, trans communities on BBSs and on Usenet did have this necessary control. As the Internet evolved, we lost control and gained precarity. Without control, trans online content could disappear without notice; in Dame-Griff's (2023) words, "So much trans knowledge and history appears to live on borrowed time." So far, trans and queer-owned and operated platforms have largely not been sustainable. In the future, I hope we find a way for trans technologies to be financially viable without relying on investment funding.

Gwendolyn Ann Smith is a trans technology pioneer who, in the 1990s, created the Transgender Community Forum (TCF) on AOL (America Online), one of the earliest trans online communities. She also founded the Transgender Day of Remembrance and the accompanying Remembering Our Dead website (Leveque 2017). When I asked her what the most exciting part of creating trans technology is, she said it was "seeing the ripples." With "ripples," Smith evoked a trans technological future spreading out, affecting larger and larger areas, as we see when an object disrupts water's surface:

> Seeing the people who were hanging out in the periphery of the TCF back in the day becoming well-known trans people or notable trans people. Seeing the things that we set out to do then affecting the world going forward. Seeing the Remembering Our Dead website that I was feeling nervous about and shouting into nothingness, become an event that is solid, honored around the world by countless people. I never ever imagined that happening. It still to this day feels incomprehensible. But really, [the most exciting part is] seeing that. It's seeing the pebble that I dropped, creating waves.

Smith could not have envisioned these waves at the time, just as the people creating trans technologies today cannot imagine how those technologies, and the people involved in making and using them, will shape the future. We cannot possibly predict how today's trans technology pebbles will manifest as future trans technology waves. We can, however, imagine exciting trans technological futures and hopeful worlds in which trans people are more safe and cared for. At the beginning of this book I mentioned how I discovered, years after transitioning, that I had been limited by lack of access to trans technologies—for instance, I did not have the tools I needed to effectively research my surgeon. Similar limits will become apparent when viewing *this* present from a later future: although today we seem to have a wealth of trans technologies to help trans people, one day we will look back and see how limited we were in the first quarter-century of this new millennium.

In thinking about trans technology design and our desires for the future, then, we must try to move past the constraints that bind the present. Queerness, says José Esteban Muñoz (2009) in *Cruising Utopia: The Then and There of Queer Futurity*, "is essentially about the rejection of a here and now." For marginalized people, "the present is not enough," for it is "impoverished and toxic;" queerness is future- and forward-focused, always on the horizon but "not quite here." Queerness thus requires that we imagine new possibilities for creating new worlds: "we must always be future bound in our desires and designs" (Muñoz 2009).

According to Muñoz, it is hope that allows us to consider utopian queer futures. Utopias, in his view, are "potential blueprints of a world not quite here, a horizon of possibility." By longing for these queer utopias, queer communities enable the "possibility for political transformation" to escape the current cruel world, insisting on a new world. LaVelle Ridley (2019) describes such hopeful futures as "imagining otherly" and shows how thinking outside of oppressive and limiting systems can enable Black trans women to actualize their own joys and desires. These types of queer and trans technological futures work similarly to prefigurative politics, in which groups of people cooperatively begin implementing and inhabiting aspects of the world they wish to see in the future (Leach 2013); they also draw from speculative design approaches in which communities imagine through design new possibilities for a better future (Dunne and Raby 2013). "From shared critical dissatisfaction," Muñoz (2009) writes, "we arrive at collective potentiality."

I argue that transness, like queerness, is also future-focused—on the horizon. For those in transition, the slow arc of physical, social, and legal gender changes means that transness always seems not quite here. And politically speaking, the present is not enough, especially during this era of trans rights struggles. In the present, trans people lack access to basic needs like health care, housing, and even restroom facilities (a lack that shuts them out from public life and sometimes even ends trans lives[17]). Trans people are villainized in both mainstream and social media. Equal access to life chances is a hope for the future, not a real possibility in the present. Trans people often feel both politically and personally stuck in a grim present, chasing after a hopeful vision of transness in the future. This is, I think, exactly why trans technologies are so powerful: they feel futuristic and sometimes speculative, and they allow us to glimpse and even experience new trans worlds that have not yet arrived. Trans technologies help us to feel hopeful about the future and its possibilities for transformative change, both personally and politically.

As new medical technologies like GAHT and surgeries emerged, they have had substantial impact on the ways that people could exist as trans in the world (Halberstam 2016). Trans technologies more broadly, such as the technological innovations I describe in this book, can also impact what transness means to people on an individual level and how they experience transness in the world. Jack Halberstam (2016) describes how being trans provides people with "radically new knowledge about the experience of being in a body" and enables them to see the world in new and different ways. This experience of being able to redesign one's body is exhilarating, as represented in a speculative fiction piece by Stelarc (1991) about a future in which humans can expand their body's capacity (e.g., adding a third hand) via technology. This changes everything: "It is no longer a matter of perpetuating the human species by *reproduction*, but of enhancing the individual by *redesigning*" (Stelarc 1991). Some types of technological enhancements may be purely speculative, but we can think about future trans technologies as enabling people to *redesign* their own bodies through improved and expanded surgical and hormone technologies, prostheses, online avatars, and AR. Some of these technologies are available now for trans use, and they will all continue to evolve to address trans needs better and more fully. Trans technologies, now and in the future, augment experiences of being in a body and in a world; they enable us to strive toward the trans future that we want to see.

---

17. Such as in the case of Oklahoma nonbinary teen Nex Benedict (Goodman and Sandoval 2024).

Trans futures are most precarious for multiply marginalized trans people, who are deeply vulnerable to violence, such as trans people of color; micha cárdenas (2022) writes that "the need for trans people of color to engage in creating their own futures by engaging with digital technologies is urgent." In response to this danger and urgency, trans of color communities envision unique survival strategies. As C. Riley Snorton (2017) points out, the intersections of Blackness and transness open up ways of "reviving and inventing strategies for inhabiting unlivable worlds." According to cárdenas (2022), the path forward to imagining futures for trans people of color runs through activism, community-based design, and trans of color poetics—her more artistic approach to Costanza-Chock's (2020) concept of design justice. To address trans futures for trans people of color, trans technology design *must* meaningfully include multiply marginalized trans people and communities in ideation and design processes. As we look to trans technological futures, the transness we see on the horizon must be intersectional.

As we continue to search for ways to emerge from the toxic climate that trans people are currently forced to inhabit, we can set our sights on trans technologies on the horizon and start to build those technologies that help us escape transphobic worlds. I personally tend toward a more optimistic, utopian view, and I hold out hope that we can resist the capitalist dystopian trans technological futures that some interviewees discussed (Duggan and Muñoz 2009). I have immense hope for those sixteen-year-olds, sitting in their bedrooms in their parents' houses, or in libraries, or in youth drop-in centers, hacking at their keyboards to create browser extensions; those vast armies of trans game creators channeling their rage and creativity into trans game jams; and all those people building new technologies to help address the challenges their community faces. Each of these creators are ripples, extending out from earlier trans technologies that have inspired them. At the same time, they are also new objects breaking the surface, and they will inspire waves of future trans technologies, spreading out across the water toward the horizon.

Conclusion

Technology and transness are inextricably linked. Trans people use technology to change: first to discover that gender transition is possible, then to find out how to do it, then to actually implement those social and physical changes, then to stick around and help others through the same process. Along the way, all kinds of trans technologies provide all kinds of help: there are online communities to receive and provide support, apps to track transition milestones, games to try out different embodiments and narratives. Trans people are often born via technology, exploring and presenting new identities in digital spaces and interacting with similar others in online communities. This regeneration can threaten outsiders; it can appear as though trans people are multiplying via technology—what some have called "rapid onset gender dysphoria," a debunked theory that transness is contagious for young people online. While technology does not and cannot infect cisgender people with transness, it does enable trans people to discover and embrace their trans identity in networked settings.[1] As Stone (1995) argues, transness is natural online, while physical spaces can feel unnatural. Technology is like water to us—we need it to survive; we can breathe here.

In this book, I have described the world of trans technology, in both the present and the future, and its importance in the lives of its creators. I have provided two definitions of trans technology: technology that helps to address the unique needs and challenges faced by trans people and communities (a practical definition) and technology that harnesses aspects of change and crossing to reimagine what technology is and can do (a theoretical definition). I described how trans technologies are designed and how

---

1. I am indebted to Cassius Adair, whose comments contributed to some of the ideas in this paragraph.

these design processes only sometimes include trans communities, highlighting their creators' relative privilege and potentially perpetuating exclusion of multiply marginalized trans people. I discussed how trans technology has recently become increasingly monetized and then showed how trans tech creators work within and against capitalism. Finally, I provided some visions of potential futures for trans technology, which are in different measures separatist, inclusionist, utopian, and dystopian.

This book illuminates how *technology helps us imagine new possibilities for trans people and communities, while at the same time, trans experiences help us imagine new possibilities for technology*. In the former, many trans technologies help trans people in new and unique ways, such as novel technological forms of connecting people with important support networks (e.g., ModClub, Trans Family Network). With the latter, transness opens up new technological possibilities like augmenting one's face to enable multiple digital identities or using DNA phenotyping to make visible the face of someone who cannot be physically seen. Transness and technology both exhibit Catherine Malabou's (2011) concept of plasticity: they are at once both malleable (can take form) and able to change their surroundings (can give form).

I have shown how trans technology design can often be empowering and exciting, because trans tech creators have the agency to create technologies that address challenges that they themselves face in the world. Yet when trans technologies are built using individualist rather than community-based approaches, they potentially exclude multiply marginalized trans people, such as trans people of color and those without access to financial resources and technical skills. Thus, I argue that trans technology design processes should include trans people besides their creator to close the gaps between which technologies could most help trans communities and which technologies are actually being designed.

I have also highlighted the practices of trans care involved in trans technology creation, which reflect the ways that trans people often turn to each other for support in times of need, when mainstream systems and technologies reject or exclude them (Malatino 2020). This caring labor is challenging and often undervalued but can at the same time often be enjoyable (Gleeson and O'Rourke 2021). Technological trans care is a way for trans people to fight against discriminatory and hostile systems and political environments, and it might help us to survive and flourish in the utopian trans futures we hope for.

Trans technologies are also wrapped up in ambivalence. Each chapter is organized around a particular type of ambivalence—a tension between competing goals and desires that trans tech creators often experienced simultaneously: technological separatism and technological inclusionism, individualist and community-based design methods, privileged and inclusive trans technology design, capitalist and anticapitalist approaches, and utopian and dystopian trans futures. In each of these cases, the ambivalence signals that these opposite ends of a pendulum's swing are not truly so far apart, and decisions between them are complex; a trans technology can swing back and forth between the two, and its creator might waver between them or hold both at once. These fluctuations can complicate and challenge trans technology design processes, partially explaining why the landscape of trans technologies that exist does not map perfectly onto the grid of trans challenges that technology might help address.

Trans technologies are a site where trans studies and human-computer interaction (HCI) come together. Trans studies allows us to see what happens when identities and bodies that change and transition are put at the center of analysis rather than considered difficult edge cases, and HCI has increasingly focused on marginalized technology users rather than attempting to design for an "average" user who may not truly exist. In recent years, HCI researchers and designers have increasingly valued designing for users who transition and change, rather than for static and unchanging identities (Haimson et al. 2019b). Connecting trans studies and HCI, as I have done in this book, helps us to understand how technology design can work best for people who are both marginalized and changing. This intersection between trans studies and HCI also makes visible complexities that occur when design processes are personally meaningful and when the designer is part of the user group. As scholars continue to examine marginality, change, gender, and design, a growing body of research on trans technology, with a focus on both building theory *and* documenting and improving trans people's material conditions, can thrive in trans studies, HCI, and their intersection—*trans technology studies*.

The connection between trans studies and HCI is also marked by ambivalence. Transing technology involves leaning into ambivalence and multiplicity rather than trying to simplify or choose one direction over another. HCI has often steered away from such complexities, particularly in its pragmatic problem-solving approach focused on user needs. User needs-based research is vital for trans technology to make the most impact in trans people's lives. Yet a new line of HCI scholarship argues for moving away from needs-based design to prioritize design for joy, flourishing, and desire (e.g., To et al. 2023). I find this flourish-based approach troubling, because when the basic needs of many marginalized populations are not being met, only the most privileged are able to flourish. But there is ambivalence here too: we cannot actually separate needs from desires, because so often both exist at the same time. For trans people, technology helps us stay alive, but it also helps us to dream, achieve and share meaningful moments, and celebrate the pleasures of being trans. Sometimes joy can exist in the need, such as in technologies that help people experiment with aspects of their physical appearance. Other times, real needs, such as facial feminization surgery or other "cosmetic" gender affirmation procedures, are seen by outsiders as merely desires.[2] Such interventions do bring joy, but that joy is also a need. Trans studies allows us to cross over the dichotomy between desires and needs, and queer theory enables us to disrupt it. Ambivalence is not often explored or embraced in HCI scholarship, but trans technologies show how it can be.[3] *Ambivalent HCI*—HCI that recognizes and studies how multiple seemingly conflicting truths can exist simultaneously—is a future direction I hope we lean into.

In the introduction, I presented a list of challenges faced by trans people and communities, which my research team compiled in collaboration with trans community members (Haimson et al. 2020b). Now I return to these challenges, looking at how current trans technologies are and are not addressing them, and consider ways future trans technologies might be designed to help address these challenges. In table C.1, column A shows some of the existing trans technologies that address trans challenges. For example, health care resource-finding technologies like Trans in the South and Erin's Informed Consent HRT (Hormone Replacement Therapy) Map are helping address challenges in the health care space, and trans online communities and social platforms like Trans Peer Network and TRACE are helping in the online identity category. However, several categories, including documents, gatekeeping,

---

2. As a result, trans people must often double down on the needs narrative, especially to medical providers, to gain access to medical care (shuster 2021).
3. This could add to existing HCI work that highlights the ambivalence inherent in domains such as technology for LGBTQ+ hate crime reporting (Gatehouse et al. 2018), contraception self-tracking technologies (Park et al. 2023), and smartphones (Yurman 2017).

housing, and lack of respect for one's identity, are not, to my knowledge, currently addressed by any trans technologies. Many of these gaps can be explained by column C, which lists the systemic issues at play that cannot be solved with technology: transphobia, racism, poverty, discrimination, and more. In each category, I considered some ways that trans technology could help to address, or further address, these challenges to some extent (column B). For instance, though we cannot solve trans housing discrimination with technology, we could design systems to help match trans people with affordable and inclusive housing (if and when it exists). Similarly, while technology will never eradicate police violence, systems could be designed to help trans people avoid police or report police harassment and violence.

With this table, I make visible some of the areas for trans technological innovation that respond to community needs, rather than a trans tech designer's own personal experiences and needs. Those trans people who are likely to have the skills and resources to create technology are not likely to also be those struggling to find housing and other resources and those most targeted for violence. Column B is populated only based on my own thoughts and ideas in response to each of these community needs (though influenced by my many years of research with trans people and communities). A better approach would be to brainstorm and sketch out potential technologies with diverse groups of trans people, especially those who are most impacted by these challenges. Only then can we know how to best move forward with the trans technologies most needed to support trans people and communities. This exercise can be a starting point for filling in some of those gaps in the trans technological landscape—those technologies that are so desperately needed to help improve trans people's life chances and make trans lives more livable. Addressing these gaps can help us depart from trans technological imagination and move toward a better reality.

While individualist approaches to trans technology design can be empowering and agentic for trans tech creators, these approaches do not always produce technology that significantly improves other trans people's life chances. This goal is less relevant in the context of game design, for video games, according to Anna Anthropy (2012), are "personal artifacts" that should be created by individuals to reflect their own values. Games are thus closer to an art form than a technology meant to address trans needs and challenges. However, game design approaches can usefully illuminate trans technology design more broadly.

Table C.1

Trans challenges (from Haimson et al. 2020b), current trans technological approaches, and potential future trans technological approaches

Type of challenge	Column A Types of trans technologies that currently address this challenge	Column B Ways trans technologies could help address this challenge to some extent	Column C Aspects not possible to fully address with technology (systemic issues)
Access to society	Restroom-finder apps	Make physical spaces safer and more inclusive	Transphobia
Document-related	None	Digital systems to change names and gender markers on identification documents	Policies, laws, and procedures that restrict name and gender changes on identification documents
Financial/employment	Trans banking apps (e.g., Bliss), trans-focused skill training (e.g., TransTech Social Enterprises)	Match people with jobs, make workplaces more inclusive	Financial disparities, hiring discrimination, workplace discrimination, poverty
Gatekeeping	None	Make spaces more welcoming, reduce pressure to disclose	Exclusionary behaviors, erasure, transphobia within LGB spaces
Health care	Health care resource-finding technologies (e.g., provider maps), health resource sites	Encourage and train providers, facilitate communication between trans patients and providers	Lack of trans-competent providers, access to insurance, addiction, HIV
Housing	None	Help trans people find affordable and inclusive housing	Housing discrimination, lack of affordable housing, homelessness
Lack of access to resources	Queer clothing exchange site	Resource-finding technologies (e.g., food, housing, education, clothing)	Poverty
Lack of respect for one's identity	None	Train and educate cisgender people about trans identities and how to respectfully interact with trans people, train designers and programmers on how to make systems more inclusive	Transphobia

Legal and police	Safety app prototypes (at the time of writing, no trans-specific safety apps have been deployed)	Trans legal support and support for incarcerated trans people, technologies to avoid police or report police harassment and violence	Transphobia, antitrans legislation, police state
Online identity	Trans online communities, trans-specific social platforms	Train designers and programmers on how to make systems more inclusive, develop more fluid information systems	Transphobia and trans exclusion in online systems, online harassment and abuse
Pressure to educate cisgender people about trans identities	Resource sites (e.g., Trans Language Primer)	Educate cisgender people about trans identities	Trans marginalization
Racial injustice	Resources specifically for trans people of color (e.g., Arm the Girls, U-Signal)	More resources specifically for trans people of color; educate white people about trans people of color's experiences, intersectionality, and racism	Racism, anti-Blackness, white supremacy, transmisogynoir
Violence	Safety app prototypes, self-defense kits (e.g., Trans Defense Fund LA), sites tracking trans violence (e.g., Remembering Our Dead)	Support for trans people facing violence, sexual assault, domestic violence, coerced sex work	Transphobia, violence
Miscellaneous challenges (e.g., lack of access to trans history, trans experiences being marginal to cisgender experiences)	Trans archives (e.g., Digital Transgender Archive), trans museums (e.g., Museum of Trans Hirstory & Art)	Educate people about trans history and experiences	Transphobia, marginalization, history erasure

"I want a world where everyone is capable of sitting down at a computer and making a game by herself," Anthropy (2012) writes. While it is exciting to think of a world where everyone has the ability to create their own technology, my thinking about trans technology creation diverges from Anthropy's vision in two fundamental ways. First, I do not think that everyone should need to have the skills to create technology; rather, I want a world where those with technological skills collaborate with those who may not have those skills but have big and important ideas that can help communities. Second, I do not think that people should always create technology in isolation; I want a world where people form teams to collaboratively make technology that can have real impact. One model is described by Bo Ruberg (2019) in their work on queer game designers: "a network of queer game-makers working individually or in small teams to make scrappy, impactful, and indeed revolutionary video games that relate directly to lived LGBTQ experiences." This is closer to what we could imagine for trans technology creation, because Ruberg's view includes both collaboration and impact— crucial considerations in an antitrans political climate.

I am not the first to argue for collaborative rather than individualist design approaches, and the ideas I have presented in this book could also apply beyond trans communities to other types of marginalized populations. Anthropologist Lucy Suchman (2007), in her feminist theorizing of design, critiques designers who create primarily based on their own experiences and consider those designs universal. Similarly, HCI scholar Daniela Rosner (2018) asserts that we should "decenter individualism" and instead design with communities. Rosner suggests that by "reimagin[ing] established design techniques" (such as individualist approaches and design that is separate from the communities it impacts), we can shift how we think about design and discover entirely new approaches. Rosner provides a set of tactics to move design processes from being individualist to community-based. These include building alliances to design with and for communities, foregrounding forgotten or silenced narratives, highlighting and addressing inequalities in design settings, and determining new ways to distribute content (Rosner 2018). Technology designers must understand users' relationships, identities, and use contexts in order to align technologies with social justice and ethics (Forlano and Halpern 2023). In the Design Justice Network and Sasha Costanza-Chock's (2020) design justice approach, creators should design to "sustain, heal, and empower our communities" by centering people whom a design will most impact and using collaborative, accessible, sustainable, community-led design processes. A trans technology design framework involves elements of design justice and human-centered design and at the same time prioritizes the elements of change and reconfiguration that are central to transing technology.

There is nothing inherently wrong with creating technology in isolation, and in this book I have shown many examples of important trans technologies created in isolation. I especially see the value of isolationist approaches when creating art and games, when the goal is often to draw from one's own experience and life stories to create something that resonates with audiences. Yet I have also highlighted important gaps between the challenges that trans people face in the world and the types of trans technologies that exist. These gaps signal that technology creation based primarily on individual tech creators' own needs is limited in what it can do for the trans community. There should be more synthesis and strategy between community needs and design goals—especially to ensure that multiply marginalized trans people's needs are also met, even when they do not have the time, resources, technical skills, and privilege to design technologies by themselves. Trans people and communities should be involved in trans technology design processes, so that technologies account for and design for users' needs.

In what follows, I outline several potential approaches that I see as ways forward. In chapter 4, I observed that many of the trans technologies that used human-centered and participatory approaches were never actually deployed. I offer a few suggestions to enable community-based technologies that meet trans people's needs to move toward deployment, so that their benefits can be experienced by larger groups of people. While these suggestions are described here in the context of trans technology, they could easily be broadened to apply to technology designed for other marginalized groups.

We need mechanisms to bridge the gaps between trans technologies that are needed, trans technologies that are designed, and trans technologies that are deployed. Some of these gaps relate to technical feasibility: the gap between what is needed socially and what is possible technically (Ackerman 2000). While gaps can sometimes be generative, such as in speculative or critical design when the gap between reality and an alternate reality that a design proposes open up space for discussion (Dunne and Raby 2013), vital needs and challenges remain. With technological advancements, trans technology's socio-technical gaps will narrow. Yet limitations related to trans tech creators' networks, resources, and capabilities will remain.

As I see it, the dilemma has three components: (1) Those who truly understand trans community needs often lack the expertise or desire to design and implement technology. (2) Technology designers or researchers who do understand and design for trans community needs often do not have the skills, interest, and resources to deploy and maintain the technology they design. (3) People with the technical skill and desire to build, deploy, and maintain trans technology often lack insight into community needs. As illustrated in figure C.1, the center of the Venn diagram—a person who understands trans community needs and values but also has the expertise, resources, and interest to design, build, and maintain a technology—is elusive. Thus, we need a combination of people from the three circles.

I suggest setting up several types of matching programs to help connect trans tech creators, trans communities, and people who can build, deploy, and maintain trans technologies. First, a match-making program could align promising designs with skilled trans developers who could build and deploy those technologies. In university settings, programs could connect student designers with developers and people (e.g., community organizers) capable of bringing designs to users. These approaches would work within capitalist or profit-driven frameworks, but they could also use nonprofit or grassroots setups that align better with many trans tech designers' political orientations. Another type of matching program could connect technology creators with trans community members, so that trans people could be involved in design processes. With community buy-in, this type of program could facilitate valuable connections between technology creators and community members. It could also ensure that community members are properly compensated for their involvement; programs matching technology designers and researchers with trans community members would need to understand and avoid the traditionally extractive and often harmful nature of research with trans populations (Minalga et al. 2022), such as by following Christina Harrington and colleagues' (2019) recommendations for more equitable design with marginalized communities.

Column B in table C.1 above provides some ideas for thinking about trans challenges that have not yet been addressed by technology but perhaps could be. A structured list like this, informed by community-based research, could be expanded by trans people and communities and used as a starting point for matching promising ideas with people who want to design and build trans technologies that can have real impact.

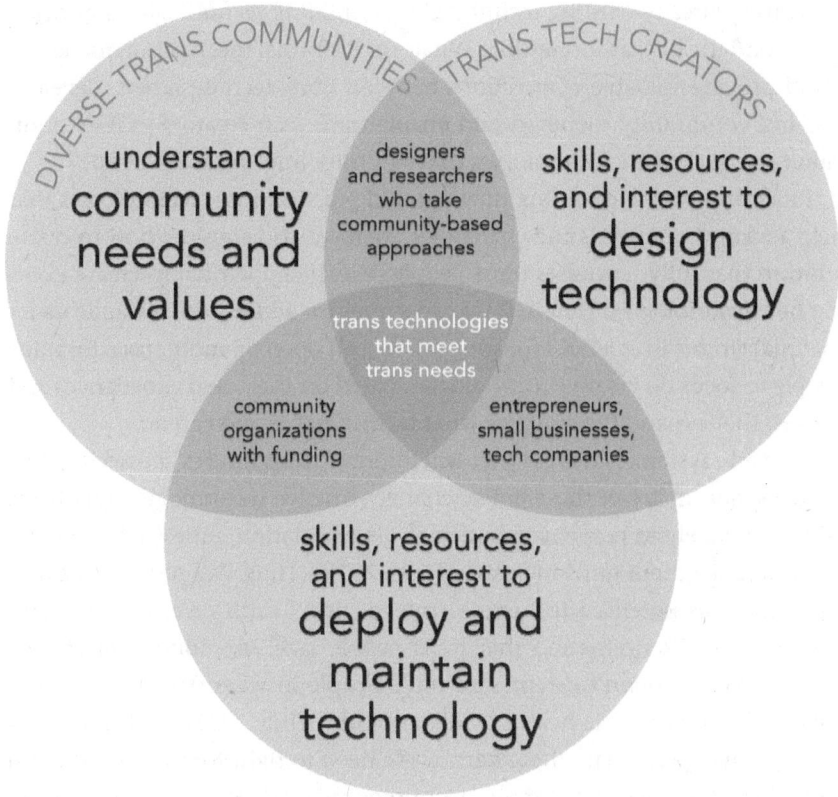

Figure C.1
Venn diagram showing the multiple types of people required to create trans technology that meets trans needs.

Matching programs could take many forms to enable coordination, idea-sharing, and knowledge exchange. Matching could be as simple as an online spreadsheet where designers, developers, funders, community members, and people with ideas could connect (with proper security measures and vetting mechanisms). A community-based organization could, with the necessary resources, take ownership of matching processes and even provide online and physical spaces for connection. A yearly event like a hackathon, workshop, or conference could also work as a matching mechanism and could include technological skill-sharing, training, talks from creators of successful trans technologies, and meetings with community members. Here, organizers would need to take steps to avoid typical hackathon traps like participants re-creating already-existing technologies or building technologies that never go beyond the hackathon setting. Whatever its formal mechanism, matching could provide valuable connections between trans tech designers, developers, and community members and enable trans tech creators to resist individualism and create technologies that can truly improve trans lives.

In addition to determining how to build practical trans technologies that help address trans needs and challenges, we must also consider how to create a future that fully harnesses trans people's creative potential to create exciting new technologies. That is, if we can somehow address the systemic issues that make trans lives a fight for survival, we can open up more space for trans people to focus on creative technologies, based on their own experiences and desires, that expand the realm of what technology is and can do.

To create systemic changes that will improve trans futures, we need policy changes, and many of these policy changes involve technology. Algorithms and AI are likely to perpetuate antitrans discrimination, unless we explicitly work to make them trans-inclusive (Hicks 2019). Thus, AI's pervasiveness in all sectors has potential to increase the existing health care, housing, and employment discrimination that trans people face. In addition, electronic medical records often misrepresent trans people in ways that can seriously negatively impact their health (Kirkland and Arthur 2021), and new technologies may perpetuate these harms. We need to fight for policies in these and other areas to ensure that new technological innovations will not further harm those who are already vulnerable to systemic injustice.

While trans technologies often exist apart from mainstream technologies, trans technologists may also impact positive social change by working to improve trans experiences in mainstream systems. I recently came face to face with this ambivalence when one of my most promising student mentees, who worked with me on the research for this book and on several other trans technology research and design projects, asked me for advice on next steps for her career. She wanted to create trans technology to improve health equity for trans people, especially trans people of color like herself. She was drawn to working at Epic, the health software company responsible for creating and maintaining the electronic medical records used in the majority of US hospitals and health care practices. My mentee asked me, Is it worth getting involved in the mainstream world of health technologies to try to make those technologies more inclusive for trans people? Or could she make more impact by staying outside of that world and creating her own trans technologies? It would be difficult for a young trans woman of color just starting her career to try to make meaningful changes in the massive, thorny systems at Epic. But the job would provide a steady paycheck, and she would have real potential to change the world in big ways. Working on her own "outsider" technologies would also enable her great potential to change the world, but it would bring its own challenges, like access to time and funding, potential burnout, and questions of sustainability. I could see my mentee achieving success on both career paths, but in terms of practical advice, I remained ambivalent about how to best advise her. Ultimately, she will make her own best choice, but the ambivalence will remain.

As table C.1 makes abundantly clear, many of the challenges that trans people and communities face are systemic: pervasive issues like transphobia, racism, poverty, exclusion, health disparities, and discrimination. We live in a hostile, antitrans climate. Technology cannot solve these problems; we need to engage in activism, advocacy, and resistance to work toward trans liberation. Often, trans people need community, safety, and care more than technological innovation. Yet in this book I have shown encouraging examples of trans technologies that can help with resistance and liberation and can bring trans communities together to work toward these collective goals. Especially when they are community-based and intersectional, trans technologies can be a hopeful way forward into the future we need and desire.

Acknowledgments

I sincerely thank everyone who supported me in big and small ways, directly and indirectly, while I wrote this book. Thanks to developmental editor Heath Sledge—I was fortunate to find someone who really gets my work. Her edits substantially improved the book's style and flow, and her encouraging comments were exactly what I needed to get over the finish line. Noah Springer at the MIT Press has been such a wonderful and supportive acquisitions editor to work with. I appreciate his guidance throughout this process. Bo Ruberg has helped substantially at so many different points throughout this process. Not only were they the first to invite me to seriously consider that I was someone who could write a book, but they also gave feedback on my book proposal, connected me with Noah, and provided mentorship throughout the writing process. Silvia Lindtner was ever available for questions, discussions, and encouragement. She brought me to her favorite writing spot on campus, forged the path as a prior book writer in our previously non-book-writing School, and organized my book manuscript workshop. I hope all aspiring book writers find a Heath, Noah, Bo, and Silvia.

In addition to Noah Springer, I want to thank Matt Valades, Anthony Zannino, Emma Martin, Debora Kuan, and Judith Bullent at the MIT Press, and Ruth Saavedra, Rupali Haldar, Rashmi Malhotra, and Nitesh Singh at Westchester Publishing Services, for their work in supporting this project. Thanks to Cathy Hannabach at Ideas on Fire for indexing work, and Isabella Nugent, Sarah Russo, Poppy Hatrick, and Margot Flanders at Page One Media and Noor Hindi and Jeffrey Smith at UMSI for publicity and marketing. Thanks to C.D. Rom for creating the cover art, and Kat Brewster for the type design.

This book would not exist without the trans tech creators I interviewed for this research. I learned so much from each of our conversations, and that collective wisdom formed this book. Getting to talk with so many brilliant people was such a gift.

My wonderful collaborators made this work possible but also made it enjoyable and less of an isolated process. Kai Nham, Hibby Thach, Aloe DeGuia, Ollie Downs, and Daniel Delmonaco all helped with conducting interviews and initial memoing. Aloe led transcription and transcript clean-up, along with Oliver Higgins. Kai conducted initial data analysis, and Hibby and Aloe contributed to subsequent analyses. Hibby, Avery Everhart, and Samuel Mayworm worked on separate data analyses on the trans tech creator interview dataset to inform other papers that we then collaborated on. Kai work on this project was supported by the University of Michigan School of Information (UMSI) Research Experience for Master's Students (REMS) Program, and Aloe's work was supported by the Riecker Undergraduate Research Fund and Center for the Education of Women+ at University of Michigan.

Other members of our trans tech research team worked on our participatory design sessions with trans communities: Phase 1 in 2019 included Dykee Gorrell, Denny Starks, and Zu Weigner. Phase 2 in 2023 included Kat Brewster, Aloe DeGuia, F. Ria Khan, Malaya Mañacop, Samuel Mayworm, and Denny Starks. Thanks to all of them for collaborating on this exciting work with me!

I especially want to thank the scholars who participated in my book manuscript workshop in October 2023: Sandy Stone, Cassius Adair, Mark Ackerman, Patricia Garcia, Anna Kirkland, Silvia Lindtner, and Chelsea Peterson-Salahuddin. Their comments and suggestions took my writing in so many important directions. Sandy, I fear the book may still not be as radical as you hoped it would be! Thanks also to Hibby Thach for taking notes throughout the day, and to UMSI's Carnegie Fund for Faculty Development for funding the workshop. I will never forget Mark's deadpan first assessment of the manuscript: "It's fine so far."

I am sincerely grateful to everyone who took the time to read parts of this book and give feedback that helped me move through the various iterations of this work. Thanks to the anonymous reviewers for valuable comments that enabled me to turn this from a draft into a book. I also received feedback on parts of the book or book proposal from Nazanin Andalibi, Katie Davis, Avery Everhart, Gillian Hayes, Anna Lauren Hoffmann, Senami Kojah, Megh Marathe, Mel Monier, Lisa Nakamura, Kai Nham, Sarita Schoenebeck, stef shuster, Anuba Singh, and Ben Zefeng Zhang. Big thanks to my dad, David

Haimson, for reading through the entire manuscript draft and giving me mountains of helpful suggestions. My apologies for all the split infinitives! Thanks to Lilly Nguyen for developmental editing and help with pulling out some of the book's most important threads. To Laura Portwood-Stacer, thank you for your support and feedback during the Book Proposal Accelerator program, which really helped me solidify the book's argument and understand how to approach the publishing process. Thanks also to the University of Michigan Institute for Research on Women and Gender (IRWG) for financially supporting me to attend the Book Proposal Accelerator. I also want to acknowledge Christina Dunbar-Hester and Bryce Renninger whose foundational trans technology work informed parts of the writing and analysis, and Tuck Woodstock for helping to connect me with some interviewees.

This work was funded in part by grant 2210841 from the National Science Foundation. I want to thank my co-PIs, Andrés Monroy-Hernandez, Rana Saber, and Tess Tanenbaum, as well as our community advisory board and advisory team members including Gaines Blasdel, Krystina Edwards, Vic Gipson, LaVelle Ridley, and Bo Ruberg. Big thanks to NSF program officers Andruid Kerne and Dan Cosley for supporting this work.

Thank you to members of Community Research on Identity and Technology (CRIT) Lab, past and present: Taika Augustaitis, Kat Brewster, Justin Buss, AJ Carter, Shanley Corvite, Aloe DeGuia, Daniel Delmonaco, Avery Everhart, Josh Guberman, Hayden Le, Shannon Li, Tianxiao (Sharol) Liu, F. Ria Khan, Senami Kojah, Francesca Lameiro, Samuel Mayworm, Mel Monier, Christian Paneda, Caoyang Shen, Denny Starks, Hibby Thach, Andrea Wegner, Zu Weinger, Brookelyn Wheeler, and Ben Zefeng Zhang. It is an honor to work with each of you!

To my colleagues at UMSI who have supported me in so many ways throughout the years, thank you: Mark Ackerman, Eytan Adar, Naz Andalibi, Robin Brewer, Ceren Budak, Matt Bui, Yan Chen, Tawanna Dillahunt, Nicole Ellison, Barb Ericson, Tom Finholt, Kristin Fontichiaro, Andrea Forte, Patricia Garcia, Eric Gilbert, Kishonna Gray, Ben Green, Mark Guzdial, Libby Hemphill, Julie Hui, Abbie Jacobs, Jesse Johnston, David Jurgens, Erin Krupka, Cliff Lampe, Silvia Lindtner, Gabi Marcu, Mustafa Naseem, Mark Newman, Steve Oney, Joyojeet Pal, Sun Young Park, Chelsea Peterson-Salahuddin, Ricky Punzalan, Paul Resnick, Daniel Romero, Christian Sandvig, Florian Schaub, Sarita Schoenebeck, Stephanie Teasley, Michaelanne Thomas, Andrea Thomer, Megan Threats, Kentaro Toyama, Tiffany Veinot, Beth Yakel, and Justine Zhang and staff members Stacy Callahan, Jacques Chestnut, Amy Eaton, Rebecca Epstein, Jocelyn Jacobs, Devon Keen, Noor Hindi, Becky O'Brien, James Park, Cathy Robinson, Nickie Rowsey, Heidi Skrzypek, Barb Smith, Todd Stuart, and Jocelyn Webber.

My collaborators, mentors and mentees, close colleagues, and academic friends outside of UMSI have also been a great source of inspiration and support: Gillian Hayes, Elena Agapie, Kendra Albert, Sanna Ali, Megan Ankerson, Mark Baldwin, Briar Sweetbriar Baron, Matt Bietz, TJ Billard, Jeremy Birnholtz, Rena Bivens, Lindsay Blackwell, Gaines Blasdel, Kayla Booth, LouAnne Boyd, Jed Brubaker, Amy Bruckman, Mary Byrnes, Scott Campbell, Tee Chuanromanee, Elizabeth Churchill, Avery Dame-Griff, Munmun De Choudhury, Michael Ann DeVito, Michael Dickard, Lynn Dombrowski, Daniel Epstein, Sheena Erete, Casey Fiesler, Claire Fitzsimmons, Kristi Gamarel, Tim Gorichanaz, Mary Gray, Mark Handel, Jean Hardy, Sen Hirano, Anna Lauren Hoffmann, Laura Horak, Megan Lane, Scott Larson, Calvin Liang, Jessa Lingel, Jules Madzia, Megh Marathe, Gloria Mark, Melissa Mazmanian, Sarah Murray, Lisa Nakamura, Jess Pater, Eugenia Rho, Kate Ringland, Morgan Scheuerman, Bryan Semaan, Nabeel Shakir, Ayman Shamma, Shakira Smith, Katta Spiel, John Tang, Cara Wallis, and Lauren Wilcox, thank you.

Finally, thank you to my friends and family, who have been here to listen to my excitement and worries about the book, over and over again, for years now, especially Amy Mishler. Mom, thank you for everything; I hope you are reading this from a beautiful home in Amsterdam. Dad, your house full of books no doubt set me along this path. Thank you always to Grandma Ruth, Corey, Felix, and Erika. To Charlie the cat (RIP), thank you for all of your excessive purring on the interview audio files. To Rufus Joon, you bring joy to all my days even when I am exhausted from writing and revising. And finally, to Naz Andalibi, thank you for your endless support, your reassurance, and your partnership, in life and along this wild book journey.

Appendix A: Technologies and Interviewees Included in This Study and Estimated Active Time Ranges

Technology	Interviewee(s) name or pseudonym	Active time range (estimated)
Aegis	Rosa Chapperri, Charlotte Danielle	2022–
Anna's Place	Anna-Jayne Metcalfe	2002–
Anonymized dating and social media platform	Anonymized product manager	2019–
Anonymized educational resource for trans young people	Mia (pseudonym)	2011–
Anonymized social media site	Delilah D'Lune (pseudonym)	2018–2020
Apple Face ID for new hybrid identities*	Saúl Baeza Argüello	2019–2021
Arm the Girls	Guerrilla Davis	2020–
Art (e.g. *Femme Maison-1*)	Myra Lilith Day	2008–
Art (e.g., *Probably Chelsea*)	Heather Dewey-Hagborg	2012–
Art (e.g., the Queer, Trans & Gender Variant Ancestors Project)	Edgar Fabián Frías	2010–
Art (e.g., *transeverythingism*)	Kaylee Koss	2005–
Art, performance, video, film (e.g., *Simple Identity, Public Genitals Project*)	Allucquére Rosanne "Sandy" Stone	1987–
Autonets (Local Autonomy Networks)	micha cárdenas	2011–2014
Bliss	Robbi Katherine Anthony (RKA)	2020–
Christella VoiceUp	Christella Antoni, Sam Brady	2018–
Creative Futures	Dylan Paré	2018–2018

Technology	Interviewee(s) name or pseudonym	Active time range (estimated)
Deadname Remover	Willow Hayward	2018–
Digital Transgender Archive	K.J. Rawson	2016–
Erin's Informed Consent HRT (Hormone Replacement Therapy) Map	Erin Reed	2019–
Euphoria (suite of apps including Solace, Bliss, Clarity, and Devotion)	Robbi Katherine Anthony (RKA)	2019–
Flux*	Manali Desai, Sona Rao, Jessie Zhou	2021–2021
Games (e.g., *GenderWrecked, Gay Monster Kiss Club*)	Ryan Rose Aceae	2018–
Games (e.g., *Secret Little Haven*)	Victoria Dominowski	2018–
Games (e.g., *TERF Defence*)	Lee Hulme	2021–
Games (e.g., *TRACES, Transgalactica*)	Jess Rowan Marcotte	2013–
Games (e.g., *If Found . . . , Curtain*)	Llaura McGee	2014–
Games (e.g., *Dysforgiveness, Animal Massage*)	Seanna Musgrave	2015–
Games (e.g., *Second Puberty, Dominique Pamplemousse*)	D. Squinkifer	2014–
Games (e.g., *I'm a Trans Man and I'm Here to Fuck, Logan: An Autobiographical Tabletop Game*)	Logan Timmins	2020–
Games (e.g., *The Girlfriend of My Girlfriend is My Friend, Wolves Inside Me*)	Sasha Winter (@stargazersasha)	2021–
Games and art (e.g., *Never Go to Work, Stealth Redux*)	Rani Baker	2015–
Games and art (e.g., *Becoming Dragon, Sin Sol*)	micha cárdenas	2009–
Games and art (e.g., *Ineffable Glossolalia, Sick Trans-Sex Gloria*)	Tabitha Nikolai	2017–
Games and art	Anonymous participant	2012–
Gender-affirming surgery	Dr. Mang Chen	2011–
Gender-affirming surgery	Dr. Geolani Dy	2019–
Gender-affirming surgery	Dr. Nabeel Shakir	2021–
Gender Affirming Surgery (GAS) app*	Malaya Mañacop	2021–2021
Gender Federation	GenderMeowster (they/them), Lee Hulme	2022–
Genderful talk show and podcast	GenderMeowster (they/them)	2021–
Gender Infinity Resource Locator	Justin Bantuelle	2016–
Gender Neutralize	Sophie Debs	2018–

Technology	Interviewee(s) name or pseudonym	Active time range (estimated)
Gender Reveal podcast	Tuck Woodstock	2017–
The Gender, Sex, and Sexual Orientation ontology (GSSO)	Clair Kronk	2019–
Gender Swap	Marte Roel	2014–
Hacking Biopolitics*	Avey	2022–2022
Healthy Trans	Gaines Blasdel	2018–
Homosaurus	Bri Watson, K.J. Rawson	1997–
Jailbreak the Binary	Dev (Github creator d3v-null)	2018–
LGBTrust*	Guilherme Colucci Pereira	2016–2017
Lynn Conway's website	Lynn Conway	2000–
Machine To Be Another	Marte Roel	2012–
Made This Way: Redefining Masculinity	Irem Harnak	2018–2018
Makeup support system for trans people*	Ash (pseudonym)	2020–2021
Mod Club/Club FTM	Keaton Kash	2021–
Museum of Trans Hirstory & Art (MoTHA)	Chris Vargas	2015–
N/A (trans media scholar; I interviewed Keegan because multiple other interviewees recommended I interview him, even though he was not technically a trans tech creator)	Cáel Keegan	N/A
NameBlock	LemmaEOF	2016–2022
NYC Trans Oral History Project	AJ Lewis	2014–
Open Source Gendercodes*	Rian Ciela Hammond	2015–
Patch Day	Juliya Smith	2020–
Plume	Dr. Jerrica Kirkley	2019–
Probably Chelsea	Heather Dewey-Hagborg	2017–
Project Spectra*	Alex Ahmed	2019–
PRYDE Voice and Speech Therapy App	Eryn Gitelis	2021–
QTBIPOC Design	Clarissa Diaz	2020–
Queer Code VR projects	Dylan Paré	2018–
Queer Digital History Project	Avery Dame-Griff	2017–
QueerDoc	Dr. Crystal Beal	2018–
QueerMed	Dr. Izzy Lowell	2017–
QueerViBE	Sam Martin	2018–2023

(*continued*)

Technology	Interviewee(s) name or pseudonym	Active time range (estimated)
Remembering Our Dead/Transgender Day of Remembrance website	Anna-Jayne Metcalfe	2018–
Remembering Our Dead/Transgender Day of Remembrance website	Gwendolyn Ann Smith	2014–2021
Royal Jelly*	Delilah D'Lune (pseudonym)	2021–
Safe Transgender Bathroom App	Karen	2021–2022
School Board Alerts*	Alison Stanton	2016–2016
ShotTraX	James Husband, anonymized cocreator	2019–
Solace	Robbi Katherine Anthony (RKA)	2019–2024
Spatial database of health care facilities*	Avery Everhart	2021–2022
Stealth Bros & Co.	Braxton Fleming	2017–
Stealth: Transmasculine Podcast	Kai McBride, Jackal	2021–
Tear It Up	Juniper Porter	2022–2022
TGRCNM Provider Directory	T. Michael Trimm	2019–
Through the Wardrobe	Rob Eagle	2018–
To Be Real*	Zoe Nolan	2016–2016
Top surgery nipple placement tool*	Gaines Blasdel	2020–2020
TRACE	Aydian Dowling	2022–
Trans Boxing	Nolan Hanson, Kerry Thomas	2017–
Transcapsule*	Tobey McKinley, F.J. Genus	2016–
Trans*Code Hackathon	Naomi Ceder	2015–
Trans Defense Fund LA	Nikki Nguyen	2020-
Trans Family Network	Jaylin Bowers, Laur Bereznai	2022–
TransFormaGear (pseudonym)	Leo (pseudonym)	2014–
Trans Formations Project	Alexander Petrovnia	2021–
Trans Fucking Rage Jam	Sasha Winter (@stargazersasha)	2022–2022
Transgender Community Forum	Gwendolyn Ann Smith	1993–2000
Transgender Map	Andrea James	1996–
Transgender Media Portal (https://www.transgendermediaportal.org/)	Laura Horak, Evie Ruddy	2017–
Transgender Usenet Archive	Avery Dame-Griff	2016–

Technology	Interviewee(s) name or pseudonym	Active time range (estimated)
Transguy Supply	Scout Rose	2018–
Trans in the South	Ivy Hill	2019–
Trans Language Primer	Greyson Simon	2018–
Trans Lifeline	Alice Barker, Yana Calou	2014–
Trans Metadata Collective	Bri Watson, K.J. Rawson	2021–
Transpedia	Clair Kronk	2020–2023
Trans Peer Network	Laur Bereznai, Alexander Petrovnia	2019–
Trans PhD Network	Avery Everhart	2017–
The Transphobia Project	Andrea James	2019–
Trans Reads	Anonymized creator	2019–
Trans Tape	Kai Jackson, Sarah Nelson	2018–
TransTech Social Enterprises	E.C. Pizarro III	2014–
The Trans Therapist Instagram account	Alo Johnston	2020–
The Transverse	Charlotte Danielle, Rosa Chapperri	2020–
Trans Women Connected	B.A. Laris	2019–
TranZap*	Taylor Chiang	2021–
Tretter Transgender Oral History Project	Myrl Beam	2015–
True Self	Wayne Temple	2019–
Tser	Derek Fung	2018–
U-Signal*	Denny Starks	2018–
Voluminous Arts	Gavilán Rayna Russom	2020–
VTube streaming with robot avatar	LemmaEOF	2021–
We Are All Made of Starstuff	Chitra Gopalakrishnan	2021–2021
We Are the Ones We've Been Waiting For	Guerrilla Davis	2019–
Zoom online trans support groups	Ryan Karnoski	2020–
Zoom online trans support groups	T. Michael Trimm	2020–

* Designates technologies that are (at the time of this writing) still prototypes or in development and not yet deployed, and those that were never deployed.

Appendix B: Lineage of the Term "Trans Technology"

Year	Source	Source description	Definition	Additional notes
2012	Plis and Blackwood 2012	An ethnographic study with a small sample of trans men in the Midwestern US	Trans technology includes "the information they gather so obsessively, the tools they use to construct their outward appearance, their methods of sexual practice, the medical resources they tap into to facilitate their existence in the space between male and female, and all of the practices that have brought them to their current identity."	Plis and Blackwood describe trans technologies that mostly fall under my "supplies" category in table I.1: "pissers, packers, binders, dildos, testosterone . . . help transmen to feel coherent as men—they are tools that cultivate confidence in gender presentation."
2013	Dunbar-Hester and Renninger 2013	An art show curated by Bryce J. Renninger and Christina Dunbar-Hester featuring trans tech creators and artists including Zach Blas, micha cárdenas, Zackary Drucker, and Sandy Stone	*Trans Technology* is an exhibit of technological art and artifacts that engage in trans, queer and feminist projects that help to *trans* (to use the word as a verb: spanning; interrogating; crossing; fusing) conceptions of the heterosexual matrix in technology."	Influences and inspirations: • Judith Butler's (1999) matrix of heterosexuality • Sandy Stone's (1995) book *The War of Desire and Technology at the Close of the Mechanical Age* • Zach Blas's (2012) concept "queer technology"
2019	Chen 2019	A book about "the cultural practices created by trans and gender-nonconforming artists and activists of color"	Chen discusses "the technologies and histories of racial and colonial gendering that have established binary gender/sex as one of the primary faultlines for securing and differentiating the national body of the white settler U.S. state and civil society" and the ways trans of color visual artifacts can be a way to resist and reconfigure cisgender dominance.	

| 2019 | Haimson et al. 2019a | A research study drawing from "interviews with Tumblr transition bloggers ($n = 20$), along with virtual ethnography, trans theory, and trans technological histories" | Technology that "allow[s] trans users the changeability, network separation, and identity realness, along with the queer aspects of multiplicity, fluidity, and ambiguity, needed for gender transition" | My theoretical definition in this book draws some elements from this definition. |
| 2020 | Haimson et al. 2020b | A research study drawing from "participatory design sessions (total $n = 21$ participants) to understand trans people's most pressing challenges and to involve this population in the design process" | Technology that "help[s] to address some of the challenges trans people and communities face" | This definition is similar to my practical definition in this book. |

References

Ackerman, Mark S. 2000. "The Intellectual Challenge of CSCW: The Gap Between Social Requirements and Technical Feasibility." *Human–Computer Interaction* 15 (2–3): 179–203. https://doi.org/10.1207/S15327051HCI1523_5.

Ahmed, Alex A., Levin Kim, and Anna L. Hoffmann. 2022. "'This App Can Help You Change Your Voice': Authenticity and Authority in Mobile Applications for Transgender Voice Training." *Convergence* 28 (5): 1283–1302. https://doi.org/10.1177/13548565221079459.

Ahmed, Alex A., Bryan Kok, Coranna Howard, and Klew Still. 2021. "Online Community-Based Design of Free and Open Source Software for Transgender Voice Training." *Proceedings of the ACM on Human-Computer Interaction* 4 (CSCW3): 258:1–258:27. https://doi.org/10.1145/3434167.

Ahmed, Sara. 2006. *Queer Phenomenology: Orientations, Objects, Others.* 1st ed. Durham: Duke University Press.

Ahmed, Sara. 2019. *What's the Use? On the Uses of Use.* Durham: Duke University Press.

Aizura, Aren, and Hil Malatino. 2019. "We Care a Lot: Theorizing Trans + Queer Affective Labor." In *Society for the Study of Affect.* https://affectsociety.com/.

Allen, Robert L. 1969. *Black Awakening in Capitalist America: An Analytic History.* New York: Doubleday.

Anthropy, Anna. 2012. *Rise of the Videogame Zinesters: How Freaks, Normals, Amateurs, Artists, Dreamers, Drop-Outs, Queers, Housewives, and People Like You Are Taking Back an Art Form.* New York: Seven Stories Press.

Anzaldúa, Gloria. 1981. *Borderlands/La Frontera: The New Mestiza.* 3rd ed. San Francisco: Aunt Lute Books.

Augustaitis, Laima, Leland A. Merrill, Kristi E. Gamarel, and Oliver L. Haimson. 2021. "Online Transgender Health Information Seeking: Facilitators, Barriers, and Future Directions." In *Proceedings of the 2021 CHI Conference on Human Factors in Computing*

Systems, 1–14. CHI '21. New York: Association for Computing Machinery. https://doi
.org/10.1145/3411764.3445091.

Awkward-Rich, Cameron. 2022. *The Terrible We: Thinking with Trans Maladjustment.*
Durham: Duke University Press.

Baeza Argüello, Saúl, Ron Wakkary, Kristina Andersen, and Oscar Tomico. 2021.
"Exploring the Potential of Apple Face ID as a Drag, Queer and Trans Technology
Design Tool." In *Designing Interactive Systems Conference 2021*, 1654–1667. DIS '21.
New York: Association for Computing Machinery. https://doi.org/10.1145/3461778
.3461999.

Baumer, Eric P. S., and M. Six Silberman. 2011. "When the Implication Is Not to Design
(Technology)." In *Proceedings of the SIGCHI Conference on Human Factors in Computing Systems*, 2271–2274. CHI '11. New York: Association for Computing Machinery.
https://doi.org/10.1145/1978942.1979275.

Beam, Myrl. 2018. *Gay, Inc.: The Nonprofitization of Queer Politics*. Minneapolis: University of Minnesota Press.

Beare, Zachary, and Melissa Stone. 2021. "By Queer People, For Queer People: FOLX,
Plume, and the Promise of Queer UX." In *The 39th ACM International Conference on
Design of Communication*, 20–25. Virtual Event USA: Association for Computing
Machinery. https://doi.org/10.1145/3472714.3473618.

Beauchamp, Toby. 2009. "Artful Concealment and Strategic Visibility: Transgender
Bodies and US State Surveillance after 9/11." *Surveillance & Society* 6 (4): 356–366.

Beirl, Diana, Anya Zeitlin, Jerald Chan, Kai Ip Alvin Loh, and Xiaodi Zhong. 2017.
"GotYourBack: An Internet of Toilets for the Trans* Community." In *Proceedings of the
2017 CHI Conference Extended Abstracts on Human Factors in Computing Systems*, 39–45.
Association for Computing Machinery. https://doi.org/10.1145/3027063.3049272.

Bellacasa, Puig de la. 2011. "Matters of Care in Technoscience: Assembling
Neglected Things." *Social Studies of Science* 41 (1): 85–106. https://doi.org/10.1177/0306
312710380301.

Bellacasa, Puig de la. 2017. *Matters of Care: Speculative Ethics in More Than Human
Worlds*. Minneapolis, MN: University of Minnesota Press. https://www.upress.umn
.edu/book-division/books/matters-of-care.

Benavente, Gabby, and Julian Gill-Peterson. 2019. "The Promise of Trans Critique:
Susan Stryker's Queer Theory." *GLQ: A Journal of Lesbian and Gay Studies* 25 (1): 23–28.
https://doi.org/10.1215/10642684-7275222.

Benjamin, Ruha. 2019. *Race After Technology: Abolitionist Tools for the New Jim Code*.
Cambridge: Polity Press.

Bennett, Cynthia L., Daniela K. Rosner, and Alex S. Taylor. 2020. "The Care Work of Access." In *Proceedings of the 2020 CHI Conference on Human Factors in Computing Systems*, 1–15. CHI '20. New York: Association for Computing Machinery. https://doi.org/10.1145/3313831.3376568.

Billard, Thomas J. 2023. "'Gender-Critical' Discourse as Disinformation: Unpacking TERF Strategies of Political Communication." *Women's Studies in Communication* 46 (2): 235–243. https://doi.org/10.1080/07491409.2023.2193545.

Billard, Thomas J., Avery R. Everhart, and Erique Zhang. 2022. "Whither Trans Studies? On Fields, Post-Disciplines, and the Need for an Applied Transgender Studies." *Bulletin of Applied Transgender Studies* 1 (1–2): 1–18. https://doi.org/10.57814/PE84-4348.

Bivens, Rena. 2017. "The Gender Binary Will Not Be Deprogrammed: Ten Years of Coding Gender on Facebook." *New Media & Society* 19 (6): 880–898. https://doi.org/10.1177/1461444815621527.

Bivens, Rena, and Oliver L. Haimson. 2016. "Baking Gender into Social Media Design: How Platforms Shape Categories for Users and Advertisers." *Social Media + Society* 2 (4): 2056305116672486. https://doi.org/10.1177/2056305116672486.

Blas, Zach. 2012. "Queer Technologies." Zach Blas. https://zachblas.info/works/queer-technologies/.

Blasdel, Gaines, Eugene Matthews, Oriana Cohen, and Rachel Bluebond-Langner. 2020. "Developing a Graphical Interface to Determine Patient-Defined Ideals in Gender Affirming Mastectomy." Presented at the 26th World Professional Association of Transgender Health Annual Conference.

Bolesnikov, Adrian, Karen Anne Cochrane, and Audrey Girouard. 2023. "Wearable Identities: Understanding Wearables' Potential for Supporting the Expression of Queer Identities." In *Proceedings of the 2023 CHI Conference on Human Factors in Computing Systems*, 1–19. CHI '23. New York: Association for Computing Machinery. https://doi.org/10.1145/3544548.3581327.

Bosch-Sijtsema, Petra, and Jan Bosch. 2015. "User Involvement throughout the Innovation Process in High-Tech Industries." *Journal of Product Innovation Management* 32 (5): 793–807. https://doi.org/10.1111/jpim.12233.

Branchik, Blaine J. 2002. "Out in the Market: A History of the Gay Market Segment in the United States." *Journal of Macromarketing* 22 (1): 86–97. https://doi.org/10.1177/027467022001008.

Braun, Virginia, and Victoria Clarke. 2021. *Thematic Analysis: A Practical Guide*. Thousand Oaks, CA: Sage.

Brody, Evan. 2023. "Branding Being True: Visibility Politics and Nike's Engagement with LGBTQ+ Communities." *Communication and Critical/Cultural Studies* 20 (4): 416–434. https://doi.org/10.1080/14791420.2023.2272834.

Broussard, Meredith. 2015. "The Secret Lives of Hackathon Junkies." *The Atlantic.* July 8, 2015. https://www.theatlantic.com/technology/archive/2015/07/the-secret -lives-of-hackathon-junkies/397895/.

Bruckman, Amy. 2022. *Should You Believe Wikipedia? Online Communities and the Construction of Knowledge.* Cambridge: Cambridge University Press.

Buehler, Erin, Stacy Branham, Abdullah Ali, Jeremy J. Chang, Megan Kelly Hofmann, Amy Hurst, and Shaun K. Kane. 2015. "Sharing Is Caring: Assistive Technology Designs on Thingiverse." In *Proceedings of the 33rd Annual ACM Conference on Human Factors in Computing Systems*, 525–534. CHI '15. New York: Association for Computing Machinery. https://doi.org/10.1145/2702123.2702525.

Butler, Judith. 1999. *Gender Trouble.* New York: Routledge.

Butler, Judith. 2018. "Solidarity/Susceptibility." *Social Text* 36 (4 (137)): 1–20. https://doi.org/10.1215/01642472-7145633.

cárdenas, micha. 2011. *The Transreal: Political Aesthetics of Crossing Realities.* New York: Atropos Press.

cárdenas, micha. 2022. *Poetic Operations: Trans of Color Art in Digital Media.* Durham: Duke University Press Books.

Care Collective, Andreas Chatzidakis, Jamie Hakim, Jo Litter, and Catherine Rottenberg. 2020. *The Care Manifesto: The Politics of Interdependence.* London: Verso Books.

Carthy, Shane, Kathryn Cormican, and Suzana Sampaio. 2021. "Knowing Me Knowing You: Understanding User Involvement in the Design Process." *Procedia Computer Science* 181 (January): 135–140. https://doi.org/10.1016/j.procs.2021.01.113.

Cavalcante, Andre. 2016. "'I Did It All Online:' Transgender Identity and the Management of Everyday Life." *Critical Studies in Media Communication* 33 (1): 109–122. https://doi.org/10.1080/15295036.2015.1129065.

Cavalcante, Andre. 2018. *Struggling for Ordinary: Media and Transgender Belonging in Everyday Life.* New York: NYU Press.

Cavalcante, Andre. 2019. "Tumbling into Queer Utopias and Vortexes: Experiences of LGBTQ Social Media Users on Tumblr." *Journal of Homosexuality* 66 (12): 1715–1735. https://doi.org/10.1080/00918369.2018.1511131.

Chapman, Allison, Alejandra Caraballo, and Erin Reed. 2023. "LGBTQ+ Legislative Tracking." Google Docs. 2023. https://docs.google.com/spreadsheets/d/1fTxHLjB a86GA7WCT-V6AbEMGRFPMJndnaVGoZZX4PMw/edit?usp=embed_facebook.

Chen, Jian Neo. 2019. *Trans Exploits: Trans of Color Cultures and Technologies in Movement*. Durham: Duke University Press.

Chiang, Taylor, and Gloria A. Bachmann. 2022. "TranZap: A Transgender Resource for Identifying Gender-Affirming Providers." *Sexual Medicine Reviews* 10 (4): 632–635. https://doi.org/10.1016/j.sxmr.2022.06.003.

Cho, Alexander. 2015. "Queer Reverb: Tumblr, Affect, Time." In *Networked Affect*, edited by Ken Hillis, Susanna Paasonen, and Michael Petit, 43–58. Cambridge, MA: MIT Press.

Chokly, Kit, Jay Cooper, Oliver Debney, and Laura Horak. 2020. *Transgender Media Portal Usability Test Report 2020*. Transgender Media Portal. https://hcommons.org /deposits/item/hc:30641/.

Chong, Toby, Nolwenn Maudet, Katsuki Harima, and Takeo Igarashi. 2021. "Exploring a Makeup Support System for Transgender Passing Based on Automatic Gender Recognition." In *Proceedings of the 2021 CHI Conference on Human Factors in Computing Systems*, 1–13. CHI '21. New York: Association for Computing Machinery. https://doi .org/10.1145/3411764.3445364.

Chuanromanee, Tee, and Ronald Metoyer. 2021. "Transgender People's Technology Needs to Support Health and Transition." In *Proceedings of the 2021 CHI Conference on Human Factors in Computing Systems*, 1–13. CHI '21. New York: Association for Computing Machinery. https://doi.org/10.1145/3411764.3445276.

Chuanromanee, Tee, and Ronald Metoyer. 2022. "Designing the Trans Experience: Technology and Common Gender Transition Narratives." In *Designing Interactive Systems Conference*, 1–3. DIS '22 Companion. New York: Association for Computing Machinery. https://doi.org/10.1145/3532107.3532871.

Chuanromanee, Tee, and Ronald Metoyer. 2023. "Understanding Gender Transition Tracking Habits and Technology." In *Proceedings of the 2023 CHI Conference on Human Factors in Computing Systems*, 1–16. Hamburg, Germany: Association for Computing Machinery. https://doi.org/10.1145/3544548.3581554.

Cifor, Marika, and K. J. Rawson. 2022. "Mediating Queer and Trans Pasts: The Homosaurus as Queer Information Activism." *Information, Communication & Society* 26 (11): 2168–2165. https://doi.org/10.1080/1369118X.2022.2072753.

Cohen, Cathy J. 1997. "Punks, Bulldaggers, and Welfare Queens: The Radical Potential of Queer Politics?" *GLQ: A Journal of Lesbian and Gay Studies* 3 (4): 437–465.

Combahee River Collective. 1983. "The Combahee River Collective Statement." In *Home Girls: A Black Feminist Anthology*, edited by Barbara Smith, 264–274, New Brunswick: Rutgers University Press.

Corbin, Juliet, and Anselm Strauss. 2008. *Basics of Qualitative Research: Techniques and Procedures for Developing Grounded Theory*. Thousand Oaks, CA: Sage.

Costanza-Chock, Sasha. 2020. *Design Justice: Community-Led Practices to Build the Worlds We Need*. Cambridge, MA: MIT Press.

Crenshaw, Kimberlé. 1991. "Mapping the Margins: Intersectionality, Identity Politics, and Violence against Women of Color." *Stanford Law Review* 43 (6): 1241–199. https://doi.org/10.2307/1229039.

Currah, Paisley, and Tara Mulqueen. 2011. "Securitizing Gender: Identity, Biometrics, and Transgender Bodies at the Airport." *Social Research* 78 (2): 557–582.

Cushing, Amber L. 2023. "PIM as a Caring: Using Ethics of Care to Explore Personal Information Management as a Caring Process." *Journal of the Association for Information Science and Technology* 74 (11): 1282–1292. https://doi.org/10.1002/asi.24824.

Dame-Griff, Avery. 2023. *The Two Revolutions: A History of the Transgender Internet*. New York: NYU Press.

Davis, Dominic-Madori. 2022. "Trans Founders to VCs: 'Cut Me a Check.'" *TechCrunch* (blog). August 31, 2022. https://techcrunch.com/2022/08/31/trans-founders-to-vcs-cut-me-a-check/.

Dawson, Lindsey, and Jennifer Kates. 2024. "The Proliferation of State Actions Limiting Youth Access to Gender Affirming Care." *KFF* (blog). January 31, 2024. https://www.kff.org/policy-watch/the-proliferation-of-state-actions-limiting-youth-access-to-gender-affirming-care/.

Delmonaco, Daniel, and Oliver L. Haimson. 2023. "'Nothing That I Was Specifically Looking for': LGBTQ + Youth and Intentional Sexual Health Information Seeking." *Journal of LGBT Youth* 20 (4): 818–835. https://doi.org/10.1080/19361653.2022.2077883.

DeVito, Michael Ann. 2022. "How Transfeminine TikTok Creators Navigate the Algorithmic Trap of Visibility Via Folk Theorization." *Proceedings of the ACM on Human-Computer Interaction* 6 (CSCW2): 380: 1–31. https://doi.org/10.1145/3555105.

DeVito, Michael Ann, Ashley Marie Walker, and Julia R. Fernandez. 2021. "Values (Mis) Alignment: Exploring Tensions Between Platform and LGBTQ+ Community Design Values." *Proceedings of the ACM on Human-Computer Interaction* 5 (CSCW1): 88:1–27. https://doi.org/10.1145/3449162.

Dourish, Paul. 2001. *Where the Action Is: The Foundations of Embodied Interaction*. Cambridge, MA: MIT Press.

Dowshen, Nadia, and Elle Lett. 2022. "Telehealth for Gender-Affirming Care: Challenges and Opportunities." *Transgender Health* 7 (2): 111–112. https://doi.org/10.1089/trgh.2021.0206.

Drucker, Peter. 2015. *Warped: Gay Normality and Queer Anti-Capitalism*. Leiden: Brill.

Dua, Tanya. 2021. "Trans and Non-Binary Representation Is Going Mainstream in Advertising, with Brands like e.l.f. Beauty, Mastercard, and Starbucks on Board." Business Insider. June 30, 2021. https://www.businessinsider.com/trans-and-non-binary -representation-is-going-mainstream-in-advertising-2021-6.

Duffy, Mignon. 2011. *Making Care Count: A Century of Gender, Race, and Paid Care Work*. New Brunswick: Rutgers University Press.

Duggan, Lisa, and José Esteban Muñoz. 2009. "Hope and Hopelessness: A Dialogue." *Women & Performance: A Journal of Feminist Theory* 19 (2): 275–283. https://doi.org/10 .1080/07407700903064946.

Dunbar-Hester, Christina. 2019. *Hacking Diversity: The Politics of Inclusion in Open Technology Cultures*. Princeton, NJ: Princeton University Press.

Dunbar-Hester, Christina, and Bryce Renninger. 2013. "Trans Technology: Circuits of Culture, Self, Belonging." Institute for Women and Art, Rutgers, The State University of New Jersey. http://dx.doi.org/10.17613/vzzt-kx06.

Dunne, Anthony, and Fiona Raby. 2013. *Speculative Everything: Design, Fiction, and Social Dreaming*. Cambridge, MA: MIT Press.

Durkin, Erin. 2019. "New Gillette Ad Shows Father Helping Transgender Son to Shave." *The Guardian*, May 28, 2019, sec. World news. https://www.theguardian.com /world/2019/may/28/gillette-ad-shaving-transgender-son-samson-bonkeabanut -brown.

Editors, The. 2023. "For Them Acquires Autostraddle: An Explainer." *Autostraddle* (blog). August 23, 2023. https://www.autostraddle.com/for-them-acquires-autostraddle -an-explainer/.

Emirbayer, Mustafa, and Ann Mische. 1998. "What Is Agency?" *American Journal of Sociology* 103 (4): 962–1023. https://doi.org/10.1086/231294.

Erete, Sheena, Aarti Israni, and Tawanna Dillahunt. 2018. "An Intersectional Approach to Designing in the Margins." *Interactions* 25 (3): 66–69. https://doi.org/10.1145 /3194349.

Erete, Sheena, Yolanda Rankin, and Jakita Thomas. 2023. "A Method to the Madness: Applying an Intersectional Analysis of Structural Oppression and Power in HCI and Design." *ACM Transactions on Computer-Human Interaction* 30 (2): 24:1–45. https://doi .org/10.1145/3507695.

Everhart, Avery R., Laura Ferguson, and John P. Wilson. 2023. "Measuring Geographic Access to Transgender Hormone Therapy in Texas: A Three-Step Floating Catchment Area Analysis." *Spatial and Spatio-Temporal Epidemiology* 45 (June): 100585. https://doi .org/10.1016/j.sste.2023.100585.

Everhart, Avery R., Kristi E. Gamarel, and Oliver L. Haimson. 2024. "Technology for Transgender Healthcare: Access, Precarity & Community Care." *Social Science & Medicine*, 345 (March 2024):116713. https://doi.org/10.1016/j.socscimed.2024.116713

Feuston, Jessica L., Michael Ann DeVito, Morgan Klaus Scheuerman, Katy Weathington, Marianna Benitez, Bianca Z. Perez, Lucy Sondheim, and Jed R. Brubaker. 2022. "'Do You Ladies Relate?': Experiences of Gender Diverse People in Online Eating Disorder Communities." *Proceedings of the ACM on Human-Computer Interaction* 6 (CSCW2): 420:1–32. https://doi.org/10.1145/3555145.

Fisher, Bernice, and Jean Tronto. 2003. "Toward a Feminist Theory of Caring." In *Family: Critical Concepts in Sociology. Volume II: Family and Gender Issues*, edited by David Cheal, 29–54. London: Routledge.

Forlano, Laura E., and Megan K. Halpern. 2023. "Speculative Histories, Just Futures: From Counterfactual Artifacts to Counterfactual Actions." *ACM Transactions on Computer-Human Interaction* 30 (2): 22:1–37. https://doi.org/10.1145/3577212.

Fouché, Rayvon. 2006. "Say It Loud, I'm Black and I'm Proud: African Americans, American Artifactual Culture, and Black Vernacular Technological Creativity." *American Quarterly* 58 (3): 639–61. https://doi.org/10.1353/aq.2006.0059.

Gatehouse, Cally, Matthew Wood, Jo Briggs, James Pickles, and Shaun Lawson. 2018. "Troubling Vulnerability: Designing with LGBT Young People's Ambivalence Towards Hate Crime Reporting." In *Proceedings of the 2018 CHI Conference on Human Factors in Computing Systems*, 109:1–109:13. CHI '18. New York: Association for Computing Machinery. https://doi.org/10.1145/3173574.3173683.

Gentleman, Rye. 2021. "Trans/Materiality: Digital Media and the Production of Bodies." PhD dissertation, University of Minnesota. https://conservancy.umn.edu/bitstream/handle/11299/226651/Gentleman_umn_0130E_22922.pdf?sequence=1.

Gibbons, Sarah. 2016. "Design Thinking 101." Nielsen Norman Group. July 31, 2016. https://www.nngroup.com/articles/design-thinking/.

Gill-Peterson, Julian. 2014. "The Technical Capacities of the Body: Assembling Race, Technology, and Transgender." *TSQ: Transgender Studies Quarterly* 1 (3): 402–418. https://doi.org/10.1215/23289252-2685660.

GLAAD. 2023. "Social Media Safety Index 2023." GLAAD. https://assets.glaad.org/m/7adb1180448da194/original/Social-Media-Safety-Index-2023.pdf.

Gleeson, Jules Joanne, and Elle O'Rourke. 2021. *Transgender Marxism*. London: Pluto Press.

Goodman, J. David, and Edgar Sandoval. 2024. "Anti-Trans Policies Draw Scrutiny After 16-Year-Old's Death in Oklahoma." *The New York Times*, February 21, 2024, sec. U.S. https://www.nytimes.com/2024/02/21/us/oklahoma-transgender-law-teen-dead.html.

Gossett, Reina. 2013. "On Untorelli's 'New' Book." March 13, 2013. https://www .tumblr.com/thespiritwas/45275076521/on-untorellis-new-book.

Gossett, Reina, Eric A. Stanley, and Johanna Burton, eds. 2017. *Trap Door: Trans Cultural Production and the Politics of Visibility*. Cambridge, MA: MIT Press.

Gray, Kishonna L. 2020. *Intersectional Tech: Black Users in Digital Gaming*. Baton Rough: Louisiana State University Press.

Gray, Mary L. 2009a. "Negotiating Identities/Queering Desires: Coming Out Online and the Remediation of the Coming-Out Story." *Journal of Computer-Mediated Communication* 14 (4): 1162–1189. https://doi.org/10.1111/j.1083-6101.2009.01485.x.

Gray, Mary L. 2009b. *Out in the Country: Youth, Media, and Queer Visibility in Rural America*. New York: NYU Press.

Greene, Joss. 2021. "Labor of Love: The Formalization of Care in Transgender Kinship Organizations." *Organization* 28 (6): 930–948. https://doi.org/10.1177/1350508 421995763.

Haimson, Oliver L. 2018. "Social Media as Social Transition Machinery." *Proceedings of the ACM Human-Computer Interaction* 2 (CSCW): 63:1–27. https://doi.org/10.1145 /3274332.

Haimson, Oliver L., Jed R. Brubaker, Lynn Dombrowski, and Gillian R. Hayes. 2015. "Disclosure, Stress, and Support During Gender Transition on Facebook." In *Proceedings of the 18th ACM Conference on Computer Supported Cooperative Work & Social Computing*, 1176–1190. CSCW '15. New York: Association for Computing Machinery. https://doi.org/10.1145/2675133.2675152.

Haimson, Oliver L., Justin Buss, Zu Weinger, Denny L. Starks, Dykee Gorrell, and Briar Sweetbriar Baron. 2020a. "Trans Time: Safety, Privacy, and Content Warnings on a Transgender-Specific Social Media Site." *Proceedings of the ACM on Human-Computer Interaction* 4 (CSCW2): 124:1–27. https://doi.org/10.1145/3415195.

Haimson, Oliver L., Avery Dame-Griff, Elias Capello, and Zahari Richter. 2019a. "Tumblr Was a Trans Technology: The Meaning, Importance, History, and Future of Trans Technologies." *Feminist Media Studies* 21 (3): 345–361. https://doi.org/10.1080 /14680777.2019.1678505.

Haimson, Oliver L., Daniel Delmonaco, Peipei Nie, and Andrea Wegner. 2021. "Disproportionate Removals and Differing Content Moderation Experiences for Conservative, Transgender, and Black Social Media Users: Marginalization and Moderation Gray Areas." *Proceedings of the ACM on Human-Computer Interaction* 5 (CSCW2): 466:1–35. https://doi.org/10.1145/3479610.

Haimson, Oliver L., Dykee Gorrell, Denny L. Starks, and Zu Weinger. 2020b. "Designing Trans Technology: Defining Challenges and Envisioning Community-Centered Solutions." In *Proceedings of the 2020 CHI Conference on Human Factors in Computing*

Systems, 1–13. CHI '20. Honolulu: Association for Computing Machinery. https://doi .org/10.1145/3313831.3376669.

Haimson, Oliver L., and Anna Lauren Hoffmann. 2016. "Constructing and Enforcing 'Authentic' Identity Online: Facebook, Real Names, and Non-Normative Identities." *First Monday* 21 (6).

Haimson, Oliver L., Kai Nham, Hibby Thach, and Aloe DeGuia. 2023. "How Transgender People and Communities Were Involved in Trans Technology Design Processes." In *Proceedings of the 2023 CHI Conference on Human Factors in Computing Systems*, 1–16. CHI '23. New York: Association for Computing Machinery. https://doi.org/10.1145 /3544548.3580972.

Haimson, Oliver L., Bryan Semaan, Brianna Dym, Joey Chiao-Yin Hsiao, Daniel Herron, and Wendy Moncur. 2019b. "Life Transitions and Social Technologies: Research and Design for Times of Life Change." In *Conference Companion Publication of the 2019 on Computer Supported Cooperative Work and Social Computing*, 480–486. CSCW '19. Austin, TX: Association for Computing Machinery. https://doi.org/10.1145/3311957.3359431.

Halberstam, J. Jack. 2005. *In a Queer Time and Place*. New York: NYU Press.

Halberstam, Jack. 2016. "Trans*—Gender Transitivity and New Configurations of Body, History, Memory and Kinship." *Parallax* 22 (3): 366–375. https://doi.org/10.1080 /13534645.2016.1201925.

Halberstam, Judith. 1991. "Automating Gender: Postmodern Feminism in the Age of the Intelligent Machine." *Feminist Studies* 17 (3): 439. https://doi.org/10.2307/3178281.

Halley, Janet E. 2006. *Split Decisions: How and Why to Take a Break from Feminism*. Princeton, NJ: Princeton University Press.

Hamidi, Foad, Morgan Klaus Scheuerman, and Stacy M. Branham. 2018. "Gender Recognition or Gender Reductionism? The Social Implications of Embedded Gender Recognition Systems." In *Proceedings of the 2018 CHI Conference on Human Factors in Computing Systems*, 8:1–13. CHI '18. New York: Association for Computing Machinery. https://doi.org/10.1145/3173574.3173582.

Hardy, Jean, Caitlin Geier, Stefani Vargas, Riley Doll, and Amy Lyn Howard. 2022. "LGBTQ Futures and Participatory Design: Investigating Visibility, Community, and the Future of Future Workshops." *Proceedings of the ACM on Human-Computer Interaction* 6 (CSCW2): 525:1–25. https://doi.org/10.1145/3555638.

Harrington, Christina, Sheena Erete, and Anne Marie Piper. 2019a. "Deconstructing Community-Based Collaborative Design: Towards More Equitable Participatory Design Engagements." *Proceedings of the ACM on Human-Computer Interaction* 3 (CSCW): 216:1– 25. https://doi.org/10.1145/3359318.

Harrington, Christina N., Katya Borgos-Rodriguez, and Anne Marie Piper. 2019b. "Engaging Low-Income African American Older Adults in Health Discussions through

Community-Based Design Workshops." In *Proceedings of the 2019 CHI Conference on Human Factors in Computing Systems*, 1–15. CHI '19. Glasgow: Association for Computing Machinery. https://doi.org/10.1145/3290605.3300823.

Hemmings, Clare. 2018. *Considering Emma Goldman: Feminist Political Ambivalence and the Imaginative Archive*. Durham: Duke University Press.

Hicks, Mar. 2019. "Hacking the Cis-Tem: Transgender Citizens and the Early Digital State." *IEEE Annals of the History of Computing* 41 (1): 20–33. https://doi.org/10.1109/MAHC.2019.2897667.

Hines, Sally. 2019. "The Feminist Frontier: On Trans and Feminism." *Journal of Gender Studies* 28 (2): 145–157. https://doi.org/10.1080/09589236.2017.1411791.

Hoffmann, Anna Lauren, and Anne Jonas. 2017. "Recasting Justice for Internet and Online Industry Research Ethics." In *Internet Research Ethics for the Social Age: New Challenges, Cases, and Contexts*, edited by Michael Zimmer and Katharina Kinder-Kurlanda, 3–19. Lausanne: Peter Lang Publishing.

Holpuch, Amanda. 2023. "Behind the Backlash Against Bud Light's Transgender Influencer." *The New York Times*, April 28, 2023, sec. Business. https://www.nytimes.com/article/bud-light-boycott.html.

Human Rights Watch. 2023. "#OUTLAWED: 'The Love That Dare Not Speak Its Name.'" 2023. https://features.hrw.org/features/features/lgbt_laws.

Huppatz, D. J. 2015. "Revisiting Herbert Simon's 'Science of Design.'" *Design Issues* 31 (2): 29–40. https://doi.org/10.1162/DESI_a_00320.

Hussain, Suhauna. 2021. "Uber Blocks Transgender Drivers from Signing Up: 'They Didn't Believe Me.'" *Los Angeles Times*, December 10, 2021. https://www.latimes.com/business/technology/story/2021-12-10/uber-transgender-drivers-blocked-accounts-rejected-ids.

IDEO. 2015. *The Field Guide to Human-Centered Design: Design Kit*. San Francisco: IDEO.

INCITE! Women of Color Against Violence. 2017. *The Revolution Will Not Be Funded: Beyond the Non-Profit Industrial Complex*. Rpt. ed. Durham: Duke University Press.

Jackson, Sarah J., Moya Bailey, and Brooke Foucault Welles. 2020. *#HashtagActivism: Networks of Race and Gender Justice*. Cambridge, MA: MIT Press.

James, Sandy E., Jody L. Herman, Laura E. Durso, and Rodrigo Heng-Lehtinen. 2024. "Early Insights: A Report of the 2022 U.S. Transgender Survey." Washington, DC: National Center for Transgender Equality.

James, Sandy E., Jody L. Herman, Susan Rankin, Mara Keisling, Lisa Mottet, and Ma'ayan Anafi. 2016. "The Report of the 2015 U.S. Transgender Survey." Washington, DC: National Center for Transgender Equality.

Keegan, Cáel M. 2018. "Getting Disciplined: What's Trans* About Queer Studies Now?" *Journal of Homosexuality* 67 (3): 384–387. https://doi.org/10.1080/00918369.2018.1530885.

Keegan, Cáel M., and Laura Horak. 2022. "Introduction to In Focus: Transing Cinema and Media Studies." *Journal of Cinema and Media Studies* 61 (2): 164–168.

Keeling, Kara. 2014. "Queer OS." *Cinema Journal* 53 (2): 152–157. https://doi.org/10.1353/cj.2014.0004.

Kelley, Robin D. G. 2017. "What Did Cedric Robinson Mean by Racial Capitalism?" *Boston Review*, January 12, 2017. https://www.bostonreview.net/articles/robin-d-g-kelley-introduction-race-capitalism-justice/.

Kendall, Lori. 1998. "Meaning and Identity in 'Cyberspace': The Performance of Gender, Class, and Race Online." *Symbolic Interaction* 21 (2): 129–153. https://doi.org/10.1525/si.1998.21.2.129.

Kirkland, Anna, and F. Thurnau Arthur. 2021. "Dropdown Rights: Categorizing Transgender Discrimination in Healthcare Technologies." *Social Science & Medicine*, September, 114348. https://doi.org/10.1016/j.socscimed.2021.114348.

Kivel, Paul. 2017. "Social Service or Social Change?" In *The Revolution Will Not Be Funded: Beyond the Non-Profit Industrial Complex*, by INCITE! Women of Color Against Violence, Rpt. ed. Edited by INCITE! Women of Color Against Violence. 129–150, Durham: Duke University Press Books.

Krell, Elías Cosenza. 2017. "Is Transmisogyny Killing Trans Women of Color? Black Trans Feminisms and the Exigencies of White Femininity." *TSQ: Transgender Studies Quarterly* 4 (2): 226–242. https://doi.org/10.1215/23289252-3815033.

Laine, Madie. 2023. "TransGPT." Notion. 2023. https://madielaine.notion.site/TransGPT-7aefa2fcd9f14c7a93f7c83b56c9ed09.

Landström, Catharina. 2007. "Queering Feminist Technology Studies." *Feminist Theory* 8 (1): 7–26. https://doi.org/10.1177/1464700107074193.

LaRochelle, Lucas. 2020. "Queering the Map: On Designing Digital Queer Space." In *Queer Sites in Global Contexts*, edited by Regner Ramos and Sharif Mowlabocus, 133–147. London: Routledge.

Lawson, Clive. 2010. "Technology and the Extension of Human Capabilities." *Journal for the Theory of Social Behaviour* 40 (2): 207–223. https://doi.org/10.1111/j.1468-5914.2009.00428.x.

Leach, Darcy. 2013. "Prefigurative Politics." In *The Wiley-Blackwell Encyclopedia of Social and Political Movements*. https://doi.org/10.1002/9780470674871.wbespm167.

Leveque, Sophia Cecelia. 2017. *Trans / Active: A Biography of Gwendolyn Ann Smith*. Winston Salem, NC: Library Partners Press.

Liang, Calvin A., Katie Albertson, Florence Williams, David Inwards-Breland, Sean A. Munson, Julie A. Kientz, and Kym Ahrens. 2020. "Designing an Online Sex Education Resource for Gender-Diverse Youth." In *Proceedings of the Interaction Design and Children Conference*, 108–120. IDC '20. London: Association for Computing Machinery. https://doi.org/10.1145/3392063.3394404.

Light, Ann. 2011. "HCI as Heterodoxy: Technologies of Identity and the Queering of Interaction with Computers." *Interacting with Computers* 23 (5): 430–438. https://doi.org/10.1016/j.intcom.2011.02.002.

Lima, Gabriely de, Lucas Lopes, Natã Raulino, Caio Nunes, Inga Saboia, and A. J. M. Leite, Jr. 2023. "TRANSforming Design Through Emotion: An Application to Support Brazilian Transgender Student Women." *Interacting with Computers*, 35 (2): 53–54. https://doi.org/10.1093/iwc/iwac038.

Lindtner, Silvia M. 2020. *Prototype Nation*. Princeton, NJ: Princeton University Press.

Lingel, Jessa. 2017. *Digital Countercultures and the Struggle for Community*. 1st ed. Cambridge, MA: MIT Press.

Liu, Songyin. 2023. "Performative Authenticity: Chinese Transgender People's Digital Gender Practices." PhD dissertation, London School of Economics.

Mackenzie, Lars Z. 2017. "The Afterlife of Data Identity, Surveillance, and Capitalism in Trans Credit Reporting." *TSQ: Transgender Studies Quarterly* 4 (1): 45–60. https://doi.org/10.1215/23289252-3711529.

Malabou, Catherine. 2011. *Changing Difference*. Cambridge: Polity Press.

Malatino, Hil. 2017. "Biohacking Gender: Cyborgs, Coloniality, and the Pharmacopornographic Era." *Angelaki Journal of the Theoretical Humanities* 22 (2): 179–190. https://doi.org/10.4324/9781003099130-20.

Malatino, Hil. 2020. *Trans Care*. Minneapolis, MN: University of Minnesota Press.

Malatino, Hil. 2022. *Side Affects: On Being Trans and Feeling Bad*. Minneapolis, MN: University of Minnesota Press.

Massa, Paula, Dulce Aurélia de Souza Ferraz, Laio Magno, Ana Paula Silva, Marília Greco, Inês Dourado, and Alexandre Grangeiro. 2023. "A Transgender Chatbot (Amanda Selfie) to Create Pre-Exposure Prophylaxis Demand Among Adolescents in Brazil: Assessment of Acceptability, Functionality, Usability, and Results." *Journal of Medical Internet Research* 25 (1): e41881. https://doi.org/10.2196/41881.

Maxwell, Joseph A. 2012. *Qualitative Research Design: An Interactive Approach*. Thousand Oaks, CA: Sage Publications.

McIlwain, Charlton D. 2019. *Black Software: The Internet & Racial Justice, from the AfroNet to Black Lives Matter*. Oxford: Oxford University Press.

McKinney, Cait. 2020. *Information Activism: A Queer History of Lesbian Media Technologies*. Annotated ed. Durham: Duke University Press.

McLuhan, Marshall. 1964. "The Medium Is the Message." In *Understanding Media: The Extensions of Man*. Cambridge, MA: MIT Press.

Meyersohn, Nathaniel. 2023. "Target Is Being Held Hostage by an Anti-LGBTQ Campaign." *CNN*. May 25, 2023. https://www.cnn.com/2023/05/25/business/target-lgbtq -merchandise-pressure-trans/index.html.

Minalga, Brian, Cecilia Chung, J. D. Davids, Aleks Martin, Nicole Lynn Perry, and Alic Shook. 2022. "Research on Transgender People Must Benefit Transgender People." *The Lancet* 399 (10325): 628. https://doi.org/10.1016/S0140-6736(21)02806-3.

Monea, Alexander. 2023. *The Digital Closet: How the Internet Became Straight*. Cambridge, MA: MIT Press.

Monteil, Abby. 2024. "Fire Completely Destroyed this Georgia Gender Clinic. Authorities Say It Was Arson." Them. January 29, 2024. https://www.them.us/story/fire-georgia -gender-clinic-queer-med-arson.

Morse, Brad, Andrey Soares, Kate Ytell, Kristen DeSanto, Marvyn Allen, Brooke Dorsey Holliman, Rita S. Lee, Bethany M. Kwan, and Lisa M. Schilling. 2023. "Co-Design of the Transgender Health Information Resource: Web-Based Participatory Design." *Journal of Participatory Medicine* 15 (1): e38078. https://doi.org/10.2196/38078.

Muñoz, José Esteban. 2009. *Cruising Utopia: The Then and There of Queer Futurity*. New York: NYU Press.

Muñoz, José Esteban. 2013. *Disidentifications: Queers of Color and the Performance of Politics*. Minneapolis, MN: University of Minnesota Press.

Nadasen, Premilla. 2023. *Care: The Highest Stage of Capitalism*. Chicago: Haymarket Books.

Nakamura, Lisa. 2002. *Cybertypes: Race, Ethnicity, and Identity on the Internet*. London: Routledge.

Nakamura, Lisa. 2014. "Indigenous Circuits: Navajo Women and the Racialization of Early Electronic Manufacture." *American Quarterly* 66 (4): 919–941. https://doi.org/10 .1353/aq.2014.0070.

Namaste, Viviane. 2000. *Invisible Lives: The Erasure of Transsexual and Transgendered People*. Chicago: University of Chicago Press.

Nelson, Sandra L. 2020. "Computers Can't Get Wet: Queer Slippage and Play in the Rhetoric of Computational Structure." PhD dissertation, University of Pittsburgh.

Neustaedter, Carman, and Phoebe Sengers. 2012. "Autobiographical Design in HCI Research: Designing and Learning through Use-It-Yourself." In *Proceedings of the*

Designing Interactive Systems Conference, 514–523. DIS '12. New York: Association for Computing Machinery. https://doi.org/10.1145/2317956.2318034.

Nielsen, Jakob. 1993. *Usability Engineering*. San Francisco: Morgan Kaufmann.

Noble, Safiya Umoja. 2018. *Algorithms of Oppression*. New York: NYU Press.

Norman, Donald A. 2005. "Human-Centered Design Considered Harmful." *Interactions* 12 (4): 14–19. https://doi.org/10.1145/1070960.1070976.

Norman, Donald A., and Stephen W. Draper. 1986. *User Centered System Design: New Perspectives on Human-Computer Interaction*. Mahwah, NJ: Lawrence Erlbaum Associates.

Ogbonnaya-Ogburu, Ihudiya Finda, Angela D. R. Smith, Alexandra To, and Kentaro Toyama. 2020. "Critical Race Theory for HCI." In *Proceedings of the 2020 CHI Conference on Human Factors in Computing Systems*, 1–16. CHI '20. New York: Association for Computing Machinery. https://doi.org/10.1145/3313831.3376392.

Oung, Katherine. 2023. "Just Made a Queer Memory? Drop a Pin." *The New York Times*, June 25, 2023, sec. Style. https://www.nytimes.com/2023/06/25/style/queering-the-map-lucas-larochelle.html.

Overskride, Raina. 2021. "Taking Pride Back from the Corporations." *People's World* (blog). June 25, 2021. https://www.peoplesworld.org/article/taking-pride-back-from-the-corporations/.

Oyesiku, Linda O. 2021. "A Plea for Making Brown Bandages Stick." *Pediatric Dermatology* 38 (S2): 152–154. https://doi.org/10.1111/pde.14414.

Ozcelik, Derya, Javier Quevedo-Fernandez, Jos Thalen, and Jacques Terken. 2011. "Engaging Users in the Early Phases of the Design Process: Attitudes, Concerns and Challenges from Industrial Practice." In *Proceedings of the 2011 Conference on Designing Pleasurable Products and Interfaces*, 1–8. DPPI '11. New York: Association for Computing Machinery. https://doi.org/10.1145/2347504.2347519.

Paré, Dylan. 2022. "Extending 'Othered' Bodies into Learning Environments: Queer Reorientations, Virtual Reality, and Learning about Gender and Sexuality." In *Proceedings of International Conference of the Learning Sciences*, 9.

Paré, Dylan, and Scout Windsor, dirs. 2018. *Creative Futures*. https://queercode.org/projects/creative-futures/.

Park, Joo Young, Nadia Campo Woytuk, Deepika Yadav, Xuni Huang, Rebeca Blanco Cardozo, Marianela Ciolfi Felice, Airi Lampinen, and Madeline Balaam. 2023. "Ambivalences in Digital Contraception: Designing for Mixed Feelings and Oscillating Relations." In *Proceedings of the 2023 ACM Designing Interactive Systems Conference*, 416–430. DIS '23. New York: Association for Computing Machinery. https://doi.org/10.1145/3563657.3596062.

Pearce, Ruth. 2018. *Understanding Trans Health: Discourse, Power and Possibility*. Bristol: Policy Press.

Pereira, Guilherme C., and M. Cecilia C. Baranauskas. 2017. "Supporting People on Fighting Lesbian, Gay, Bisexual, and Transgender (LGBT) Prejudice: A Critical Codesign Process." In *Proceedings of the XVI Brazilian Symposium on Human Factors in Computing Systems*, 46:1–10. IHC '17. New York: Association for Computing Machinery. https://doi.org/10.1145/3160504.3160522.

Pereira, Guilherme C., and M. Cecilia C. Baranauskas. 2018. "Codesigning Emancipatory Systems: A Study on Mobile Applications and Lesbian, Gay, Bisexual, and Transgender (LGBT) Issues." *SBC Journal on Interactive Systems* 9 (3): 13.

Piepzna-Samarasinha, Leah Lakshmi. 2018. *Care Work: Dreaming Disability Justice*. Vancouver: Arsenal Pulp Press.

Plett, Casey. 2023. *On Community*. Windsor: Biblioasis.

Plis, Ryan, and Evelyn Blackwood. 2012. "Trans Technologies and Identities in the United States." In *Technologies of Sexuality, Identity and Sexual Health*, edited by Lenore Manderson, 185–204. London: Routledge.

Pow, Whit. 2018. "Reaching Toward Home: Software Interface as Queer Orientation in the Video Game *Curtain*." *The Velvet Light Trap* 81 (March): 43–56. https://doi.org/10.7560/VLT8105.

Prosser, Jay. 1998. *Second Skins: The Body Narratives of Transsexuality*. New York: Columbia University Press.

Rawson, K.J. 2014a. "Transgender Worldmaking in Cyberspace: Historical Activism on the Internet." *QED: A Journal in GLBTQ Worldmaking* 1 (2): 38–60. https://doi.org/10.14321/qed.1.2.0038.

Rawson, K.J. 2014b. "Archive." *TSQ: Transgender Studies Quarterly* 1 (1–2): 19–21. https://doi.org/10.1215/23289252-2399470.

Reed, Erin. 2023. "June Anti-Trans Legislative Risk Map." Erin in the Morning. May 20, 2023. https://www.erininthemorning.com/p/june-anti-trans-legislative-risk.

Rêgo, Beatriz Brito do, Caique Yan Conceição de Amorim, Suyane Miranda Sodré, Filipe Adeodato Garrido, and Ecivaldo de Souza Matos. 2022. "Investigation on Equity and Otherness in the Interaction Design Process: A Systematic Mapping." *International Journal of Human–Computer Interaction* 39 (20): 4126–4138. https://doi.org/10.1080/10447318.2022.2109251.

Remembering Our Dead. 2024. "Remembering Our Dead—Statistics." Remembering Our Dead. 2024. https://tdor.translivesmatter.info/pages/stats.

Rhodes, P. J. 1994. "Race-of-Interviewer Effects: A Brief Comment." *Sociology* 28 (2): 547–558.

Ridley, LaVelle. 2019. "Imagining Otherly." *TSQ: Transgender Studies Quarterly* 6 (4): 481–490. https://doi.org/10.1215/23289252-7771653.

Riggs, Alexandra Teixeira. 2024. "Queer Archival Design in Tangible Embodied Interactive Experiences." In *Proceedings of the Eighteenth International Conference on Tangible, Embedded, and Embodied Interaction*, 1–6. TEI '24. New York: Association for Computing Machinery. https://doi.org/10.1145/3623509.3634896.

Ritter, Frank E., Gordon D. Baxter, and Elizabeth F. Churchill. 2014. *Foundations for Designing User-Centered Systems*. London: Springer. https://doi.org/10.1007/978-1-4471 -5134-0.

Robinson, Cedric J. 2005. *Black Marxism: The Making of the Black Radical Tradition*. Durham: University of North Carolina Press.

Roque Ramírez, Horacio N. 2011. "Gay Latino Cultural Citizenship: Predicaments of Identity and Visibility in San Francisco in the 1990s." In *Gay Latino Studies: A Critical Reader*, edited by Michael Hames-García and Ernesto Javier Martínez, 175–197. Durham: Duke University Press.Rosner, Daniela K. 2018. *Critical Fabulations: Reworking the Methods and Margins of Design*. Cambridge, MA: MIT Press.

Ruberg, Bo. 2015. "No Fun: The Queer Potential of Video Games That Annoy, Anger, Disappoint, Sadden, and Hurt." *QED: A Journal in GLBTQ Worldmaking* 2 (2): 108–124. https://doi.org/10.14321/qed.2.2.0108.

Ruberg, Bo. 2019. *Video Games Have Always Been Queer*. New York: NYU Press.

Ruberg, Bo. 2020. *The Queer Games Avant-Garde: How LGBTQ Game Makers Are Reimagining the Medium of Video Games*. Durham: Duke University Press.

Ruberg, Bo. 2022. "Trans Game Studies." *JCMS: Journal of Cinema and Media Studies* 61 (2): 200–205. https://doi.org/10.1353/cj.2022.0006.

Ruberg, Bo, and Adrienne Shaw. 2017. *Queer Game Studies*. Minneapolis, MN: University of Minnesota Press.

Ruddy, Evie, and Laura Horak. 2021. "Orienting Toward Social Justice: Trans, Anti-Racist, Anti-Colonial, Feminist, Queer, and Crip Approaches to Ethical Practices in the Digital Humanities." In *Canadian Society for Digital Humanities Online Conference*.

Rude, Mey. 2019. "Trace Lysette Is Latest Trans Woman Banned by Tinder." *Out Magazine*. September 19, 2019. https://www.out.com/transgender/2019/9/19/trace-lysette -latest-trans-woman-be-banned-tinder.

Rude, Mey. 2022. "Target Now Sells Chest Binders & Packing Underwear, Thanks to TomboyX." *Out Magazine*. May 11, 2022. https://www.out.com/pride/2022/5/11/target -2022-lgbtq-pride-collection-trans-gender-nonconforming-tomboyx-binders-packing -briefs.

Sanabria, Emilia. 2016. *Plastic Bodies: Sex Hormones and Menstrual Suppression in Brazil.* Durham: Duke University Press.

Scheuerman, Morgan Klaus, Stacy M. Branham, and Foad Hamidi. 2018. "Safe Spaces and Safe Places: Unpacking Technology-Mediated Experiences of Safety and Harm with Transgender People." *Proceeding of the ACM on Human-Computer Interaction* 2 (CSCW): 155:1–27. https://doi.org/10.1145/3274424.

Sedgwick, Eve Kosofsky. 1990. *Epistemology of the Closet.* Berkeley: University of California Press.

Sender, Katherine, and Adrienne Shaw. 2017. *Queer Technologies: Affordances, Affect, Ambivalence.* Oxford: Taylor & Francis.

Shakir, Nabeel A., and Lee C. Zhao. 2021. "Robotic-Assisted Genitourinary Reconstruction: Current State and Future Directions." *Therapeutic Advances in Urology* 13 (January): 17562872211037111. https://doi.org/10.1177/17562872211037111.

Shapiro, Eve. 2015. *Gender Circuits: Bodies and Identities in a Technological Age.* London: Routledge.

Sharp, Helen, Jennifer Preece, and Yvonne Rogers. 2019. *Interaction Design: Beyond Human-Computer Interaction.* 5th ed. Indianapolis, IN: Wiley.

Shelton, Jama, Kel Kroehle, Emilie K. Clark, Kristie Seelman, and S. J. Dodd. 2021. "Digital Technologies and the Violent Surveillance of Nonbinary Gender." *Journal of Gender-Based Violence*, 5 (3): 517–529. https://doi.org/10.1332/239868021X16153783053180.

shuster, stef m. 2021. *Trans Medicine: The Emergence and Practice of Treating Gender.* New York: NYU Press.

Simonsen, Jesper, and Toni Robertson, eds. 2013. *Routledge International Handbook of Participatory Design.* 1st ed. London: Routledge.

Skeen, Simone J., and Demetria Cain. 2022. "mHealth for Transgender and Gender-Expansive Youth: An Update on COVID, Venture Capital, and the Cultural in/Congruence of Revenue-Driven Sustainability Models." *mHealth* 8 (July 20). https://doi.org/10.21037/mhealth-22-10.

Skeen, Simone J., Demetria Cain, Kristi E. Gamarel, Lisa Hightow-Weidman, and Cathy J. Reback. 2021. "mHealth for Transgender and Gender-Expansive Youth: Harnessing Gender-Affirmative Cross-Disciplinary Innovations to Advance HIV Prevention and Care Interventions." *mHealth* 7 (April 20): 37. https://doi.org/10.21037/mhealth-20-60.

Snorton, C. Riley. 2017. *Black on Both Sides.* Minneapolis, MN: University of Minnesota Press.

Spade, Dean. 2015. *Normal Life: Administrative Violence, Critical Trans Politics, and the Limits of Law.* Durham: Duke University Press.

Spade, Dean. 2020. *Mutual Aid: Building Solidarity During this Crisis (and the Next).* London: Verso Books.

Spillers, Hortense J. 1987. "Mama's Baby, Papa's Maybe: An American Grammar Book." *Diacritics* 17 (2): 65–81. https://doi.org/10.2307/464747.

Starks, Denny L., Tawanna Dillahunt, and Oliver L. Haimson. 2019. "Designing Technology to Support Safety for Transgender Women & Non-Binary People of Color." In *Companion Publication of the 2019 Designing Interactive Systems Conference*, 289–294. DIS '19 Companion. New York: Association for Computing Machinery. https://doi.org /10.1145/3301019.3323898.

Steele, Catherine Knight. 2021. *Digital Black Feminism.* New York: NYU Press.

Steinmetz, Katy. 2014. "The Transgender Tipping Point." TIME.com, June 2014. http:// time.com/135480/transgender-tipping-point/.

Stelarc. 1991. "Prosthetics, Robotics and Remote Existence: Postevolutionary Strategies." *Leonardo* 24 (5): 591–595. https://doi.org/10.2307/1575667.

Stone, Allucquère Rosanne. 1995. *The War of Desire and Technology at the Close of the Mechanical Age.* Cambridge, MA: MIT Press.

Stone, Allucquère Rosanne (Sandy). 1991. "The Empire Strikes Back: A Posttranssexual Manifesto." http://sandystone.com/empire-strikes-back.pdf.

Strohmayer, Angelika, Jenn Clamen, and Mary Laing. 2019. "Technologies for Social Justice: Lessons from Sex Workers on the Front Lines." In *Proceedings of the 2019 CHI Conference on Human Factors in Computing Systems*, 1–14. New York: Association for Computing Machinery. https://doi.org/10.1145/3290605.3300882.

Stryker, Susan. 1994. "My Words to Victor Frankenstein Above the Village of Chamounix: Performing Transgender Rage." *GLQ: A Journal of Lesbian and Gay Studies* 1 (3): 237–254. https://doi.org/10.1215/10642684-1-3-237.

Stryker, Susan, Paisley Currah, and Lisa Jean Moore. 2008. "Introduction: Trans-, Trans, or Transgender?" *Women's Studies Quarterly* 36 (3–4): 11–22.

Suchman, Lucy A. 2007. *Human-Machine Reconfigurations: Plans and Situated Actions.* Cambridge: Cambridge University Press.

Tao, Summer. 2023. "The Untapped Potential of AI for Gender-Affirming Art." *TransLash Media* (blog). October 4, 2023. https://translash.org/the-untapped-potential-of-ai -for-gender-affirming-art/.

TGEU. 2023. "Trans Murder Monitoring 2023 Global Update." *TvT* (blog). November 13, 2023. https://tgeu.org/trans-murder-monitoring-2023/.

To, Alexandra, Hillary Carey, Geoff Kaufman, and Jessica Hammer. 2021. "Reducing Uncertainty and Offering Comfort: Designing Technology for Coping with

Interpersonal Racism." In *Proceedings of the 2021 CHI Conference on Human Factors in Computing Systems*, 1–17. CHI '21. New York: Association for Computing Machinery. https://doi.org/10.1145/3411764.3445590.

To, Alexandra, Angela D. R. Smith, Dilruba Showkat, Adinawa Adjagbodjou, and Christina Harrington. 2023. "Flourishing in the Everyday: Moving Beyond Damage-Centered Design in HCI for BIPOC Communities." In *Proceedings of the 2023 ACM Designing Interactive Systems Conference*, 917–33. DIS '23. New York: Association for Computing Machinery. https://doi.org/10.1145/3563657.3596057.

Toombs, Austin, Laura Devendorf, Patrick Shih, Elizabeth Kaziunas, David Nemer, Helena Mentis, and Laura Forlano. 2018. "Sociotechnical Systems of Care." In *Companion of the 2018 ACM Conference on Computer Supported Cooperative Work and Social Computing*, 479–485. CSCW '18. New York: Association for Computing Machinery. https://doi.org/10.1145/3272973.3273010.

Toombs, Austin L., Shaowen Bardzell, and Jeffrey Bardzell. 2015. "The Proper Care and Feeding of Hackerspaces: Care Ethics and Cultures of Making." In *Proceedings of the 33rd Annual ACM Conference on Human Factors in Computing Systems*, 629–638. CHI '15. New York: Association for Computing Machinery. https://doi.org/10.1145/2702123 .2702522.

W3C Web Accessibility Initiative. 2022. "Making the Web Accessible." Web Accessibility Initiative (WAI). 2022. https://www.w3.org/WAI/.

Wade, Peter, and Patrick Reis. 2023. "CPAC Speaker Calls for Transgender People to Be 'Eradicated.'" *Rolling Stone*, March 6, 2023. https://www.rollingstone.com/politics /politics-news/cpac-speaker-transgender-people-eradicated-1234690924/.

Warner, Michael. 2000. *The Trouble with Normal: Sex, Politics, and the Ethics of Queer Life*. Cambridge, MA: Harvard University Press.

Weber, Harri. 2023. "Queer Social App Lex Gets a New CEO and $5.6M to Grow." *TechCrunch* (blog). October 2, 2023. https://techcrunch.com/2023/10/02/queer-social -app-lex-gets-a-new-ceo-and-5-6m-to-grow/.

Weidinger, Laura, Jonathan Uesato, Maribeth Rauh, Conor Griffin, Po-Sen Huang, John Mellor, Amelia Glaese, et al. 2022. "Taxonomy of Risks Posed by Language Models." In *Proceedings of the 2022 ACM Conference on Fairness, Accountability, and Transparency*, 214–229. FAccT '22. New York: Association for Computing Machinery. https://doi.org /10.1145/3531146.3533088.

Wong, Horas T. H., Sujith Kumar Prankumar, Jialiang Cui, Christopher Tumwine, Isaac Yeboah Addo, Wansang Kan, and Muhammad Naveed Noor. 2022. "Information and Communication Technology-Based Health Interventions for Transgender People: A Scoping Review." *PLOS Global Public Health* 2 (9): e0001054. https://doi.org/10.1371 /journal.pgph.0001054.

Yurman, Paulina. 2017. "Designing for Ambivalence: Mothers, Transitional Objects and Smartphones." In *Proceedings of the 2017 CHI Conference Extended Abstracts on Human Factors in Computing Systems*, 344–348. Denver: Association for Computing Machinery. https://doi.org/10.1145/3027063.3027120.

Zimmerman, John, Jodi Forlizzi, and Shelley Evenson. 2007. "Research Through Design as a Method for Interaction Design Research in HCI." In *Proceedings of the SIGCHI Conference on Human Factors in Computing Systems*, 493–502. CHI '07. New York: Association for Computing Machinery. https://doi.org/10.1145/1240624.1240704.

Zuboff, Shoshana. 2019. *The Age of Surveillance Capitalism: The Fight for a Human Future at the New Frontier of Power*. New York: PublicAffairs.

Index